In Search of Ancient Ireland

In Search of Ancient Ireland

✳

THE ORIGINS OF THE IRISH,
FROM NEOLITHIC TIMES TO THE
COMING OF THE ENGLISH

by

Carmel McCaffrey
and
Leo Eaton

𝒩𝒜

NEW AMSTERDAM BOOKS

Ivan R. Dee, Publisher • Chicago • 2002

Library of Congress Cataloging-in-Publication Data:
McCaffrey, Carmel.
    In search of ancient Ireland : the origins of the Irish from neolithic times to the coming of the English / by Carmel McCaffrey & Leo Eaton.
        p. cm.
    Includes bibliographical references and index.
    ISBN 1-56663-525-X (pbk.)
    1. Ireland—History—To 1172. 2. Ireland—History—English Conquest, 1166–1186. 3. Ireland—Civilization. I. Eaton, Leo. II. Title.

DA930 .M39 2002
941.501—dc21   2002025528

For Andrew and Ciara,

Jeri and Alexander

Contents

Acknowledgments

THIS BOOK could never have been written without the support and encouragement of many Irish scholars, archaeologists, and historians, especially our core advisory team from the television series that accompanied it. We'd especially like to thank Donnchadh Ó Corráin at the National University of Ireland in Cork, Barry Raftery at the National University of Ireland in Dublin, John Waddell at the National University of Ireland in Galway, and Patrick Wallace, director of the National Museum of Ireland. Each of these four men guided and counseled us through initial research and more than a year of television production, as well as commenting on completed chapters and correcting errors.

In addition, we'd like to thank Michael Baillie, Edel Bhreathnach, Mary Cahill, Paurigeen Clancy, Abbot Christopher Dillon, Charles Doherty, Thomas Charles Edwards, Father Frank Fahey, Joe Fenwick, Jim Fitzpatrick, Peter Harbison, Maire Herbert, Elva Johnston, Fergus Kelly, Patricia Kelly, Conor Newman, William O'Brien, Mícheál Ó Colláin, Simon and Maria O'Dwyer, Raghnall Ó Floinn, Richard Kemp, Tim O'Neill, Dagmar Ó Riain-Raedel, Helen Roche, Richard Warner, Sir David Wilson, and Michael Wood. All of these scholars generously shared their time and expertise and added immeasurably to our knowledge of ancient Ireland and the wider world in which it existed, and all are quoted in this book.

Because book and television series are so closely linked, we'd also like to thank those whose work on the series provided the solid foundation on which the book was written: our executive producers Bill Grant, from WNET in New York, James Mitchell, from Little Bird Television in Dublin, and Andrew Singer, from Café Productions, Ltd. in London. We'd like to thank our wonderful and tireless producer Leslie McKimm and her assistant Aisling Ahmed, our location researcher Christine Thornton, our associate producers Wendy Wolf and Niamh Barrett, and our production manager Katherine O'Connor. Gary Griffin brought Ireland alive in pictures while Petr Cikhart captured its sounds, and Barbara Ballow edited sound and vision together with her usual brilliance, helped by a majestic musical score from Mícheál Ó Súilleabháin. We'd like to thank Sandy Herberer from PBS in Washington, Tammy Robinson from WNET in New York, and Clare Duignan and Kevin Dawson from RTE in Dublin, all of whose confidence in the overall project allowed it to come into existence. And we'd like to add an additional thank you to Wendy Wolf who, on both book and television series, organized us, bullied us, and kept us working over the three long years it took to bring this project to completion.

Finally we'd like to thank our families, who put up with our long absences with loving patience, always encouraging us to make both television series and book the best they could possibly be. To Andrew and Ciara, Jeri and Alexander, we want you to know that we couldn't have done this without you.

C. M. and L. E.

Westminster, Maryland
April 2002

Preface

THIS BOOK is about Ireland before the twelfth century A.D.—when an Anglo-Norman invasion first attempted to bring the island under the rule of the English monarchy—and it is about how this ancient past continues to affect how Ireland sees itself today.

As many as fifty million Americans now claim direct Irish descent, with almost as many more Irish "descendants" scattered elsewhere around the world. Irish pubs are crowded with Irish and would-be Irish in Russia, Australia, Japan, even in the Congo. St. Patrick's Day has become a worldwide celebration while Celtic music, art, spirituality, and mythology are growth industries of the late twentieth and early twenty-first centuries. Epic fantasies like J. R. R. Tolkien's *Lord of the Rings* draw their inspiration directly from Celtic Irish sources; indeed the words "Celtic" and "Irish" have become so interwoven that most people today assume they are one and the same.

All this has meant that interest in Ireland and her ancient history has flourished in recent years, even if what many people believe to be true comes more from the imagination of poets and storytellers than the rigorous scholarship of historians and archaeologists.

We wrote this book, and the television series that accompanies it (produced for PBS and RTE, Ireland's national TV network) because Irish prehistory is undergoing massive re-evaluation in light of recent discoveries. Ireland has yielded up more of her secrets in the past few years than she has in the past century. Research for the book and series took place together, as much out in the field as in the archives. It is not essential to "walk the ground" in order to write history, but when one has an opportunity to do so, the past comes alive in a completely different way.

To stand on the summit of the remote monastery island of Skelligmichael and see the Atlantic waves crashing against its sheer mountain cliffs is to understand in a visceral way how seventh-century monks created a different kind of Christianity, seeking isolated hermitages in the middle of the ocean that took them as far afield as Iceland and perhaps all the way to America. To venture deep in the heart of a five-thousand-year-old passage tomb is to marvel at the ingenuity, organization, and architectural skill of Irish Neolithic farmers who raised such ancestral temples a thousand years before the first pyramids were built in Egypt.

To explain the history of Ireland, we chose also to give a sense of "place," for in Ireland, history and landscape are inseparable. Every mountain and valley has its story, just as every major event over the past five thousand years is anchored in a particular place. We visited monasteries and ring forts, climbed mountains and delved deep into sacred caves, and we were accompanied on this journey through the historical landscape by many of Ireland's best-known scholars, historians, and archaeologists. For months on end we tramped the ancient sites with historian Donnchadh Ó Corráin and archaeologists Pat Wallace, Barry Raftery, and John Waddell. They and many others explained and interpreted Ireland's ancient past in the places where history actually happened, generously sharing with us their knowledge and love of Ireland. Their scholarship and insights appear frequently in these pages.

Many times in the past five thousand years this small island has stood at the heart of European culture. In the middle of the eighth century B.C. it may have been the wealthiest place in Europe, its gold ornaments and beautiful bronze musical instruments unequalled anywhere north of Egypt. Because Ireland was never absorbed into the Roman Empire, it retained into the second millennium A.D. unique cultural traditions stretching back perhaps to the Bronze Age, if not earlier. When Christianity arrived in the fifth century A.D., a strong spiritual presence was already on the island. Yet there was no conflict between the newly arrived religion and the pagan past, instead there was an extraordinary convergence of the two which developed into a unique Christian church whose influence would eventually spread throughout Europe. After the fall of Rome, Ireland kept scholarship alive for Europe and ultimately carried civilization back to the new barbarian kingdoms rising among the ruins. By the tenth century A.D., European kingdoms did not think themselves well served unless they had Irish philosophers and theologians advising their courts.

Ireland has always been a place where myth and reality existed side-by-side, but the latest research is now making clear the distinction between them. This book is full of new information, some of it at odds with what many Irish descendants believe about their ancestral home. Interestingly, most of what we think of as Irish is rooted in the nineteenth century. It was then that Ireland began reinventing itself as a nation and culture separate from the "occupying English." Poets and writers of the Celtic Revival reached back to old Irish legends and stories to provide a cultural foundation for their newly emerging national identity. The term "Celtic" was little used prior to this time, so Ireland's view of itself as a Celtic nation is a modern invention. But this reaching back into an ancient past has always been at the heart of the Irish character. Past and present, myth and reality are inexorably mixed. Nothing is forgotten, and the past continues to color the present. Stories sometimes take on a life of their own. When Irish rebels rose up on Easter Monday of 1916 to proclaim a republic, they invoked the name and spirit of Cú Chulainn, Ireland's mythological hero who stood single-handed against the armies of Queen Mebd of Connaught when she invaded the province of Ulster. This is the central story of *The Táin*, Ireland's greatest literary epic and one of many pre-Christian stories that have defined Ireland's view of itself and its people.

Are the stories a memory of a half-forgotten past committed to writing centuries later, or are they just invention? The further back in time we go, the less certain we are of answers. Ireland's ancient past is still full of many mysteries (like how Ireland developed a Celtic culture and language when there is little archaeological evidence of any Celts in Ireland). But because of a cascade of new archaeological discoveries and new techniques for interpreting them, the truth about this past is coming into sharper focus.

Ancient history is most often concerned with the great empires of the world. Much more has been written about the Greeks, the Romans, the Egyptians, or the Chinese, to name just a few. But the vast majority of our ancestors never lived in great empires. Whether in Europe, Africa, Asia, or the Americas, they lived in tribal warrior cultures like those of Bronze and Iron Age Ireland. So this book is not only a history of a people who have had a tremendous impact on the world for many thousands of years, it is also a glimpse into the way most people lived for much of human history. Above all, however, it is a search for the roots of a people now called Irish.

In Search of Ancient Ireland

Ireland,
9000 B.C.–A.D. 1167

*Atlantic
Ocean*

Iona

*Rathlin
Island*

Grianan of
Aileach

Glen Colmcille

**Northern
Uí Néill**

Bangor

Inishmurray
*Killala
Bay*

Emain Macha
Armagh

Rath
Croghan

Lough Crew

Kells
Newgrange

Croagh Patrick

**Southern
Uí Néill**

Tara

Clontarf

Clonmacnoise

Dublin

River Shannon

Kildare

*Aran
Islands*

**Thomond
(Dál Cais)**

Glendalough

Kincora

Limerick

*Lough
Gur*

Ferns

Cashel
(Eóganacht)

Wexford

*Inisfallen
Ross Island*

*Lough
Leane*

Skelligmichael

N

0   50 mi

0   50 km

Note: All of the items on this map
were not extant at the same time.

[1]

The First Irish

❋

THE HELICOPTER flew in low across open countryside, less than a hundred feet above the ground. The side door had been removed earlier in the day so the archaeologist could take photographs. The slipstream heavily buffeted him as he held his camera nervously in the backseat, leaning out to study the farmland slipping away below his feet. Barry Raftery, professor of archaeology at University College, Dublin, was riding a helicopter for the first time in his life, searching for eskers, the long gravel ridges left behind by the last Ice Age. The ridges show up best from the air, like great snakes slithering across the midlands of Ireland. They were the superhighways of Ireland throughout Irish prehistory, the best way to cross a forested land if you could not travel by boat on the rivers and lakes. "You'd get lost pretty fast among the trees," Barry said, "but gravel ridges were almost free of vegetation cover so they made good route-ways. You could see where you were going. You didn't get lost if you were on an esker."

Unfortunately Barry was lost. For thousands of years the Irish navigated their way cross-country along the eskers, but such ancient route-ways do not appear on modern maps. He remembered seeing one from a train window between Dublin and Galway, so the pilot was flying west along the railroad track, watching for the quarries that are often sited on these vast gravel deposits formed by Ice Age glaciers a hundred thousand years ago.

"Is that a gravel truck?" Barry's voice was hopeful, anxious for

3

the search to succeed so he could return safely to ground level. Archaeologists are happier with feet planted firmly on the ground where their evidence is usually found, but the opportunity to see and photograph eskers from the air was enough to overcome Barry's initial apprehension. The pilot swung the jet-ranger around to hover briefly over a heavily loaded truck before following the road back the way the truck had come. Within seconds a quarry came in sight, an ugly scar of gray and white gravel slicing deep into the soft green of an Irish hillside. Barry had found his esker, a narrow ridge rising thirty feet above the surrounding countryside and snaking away for nearly a mile before losing itself in a distant pine forest. In the quarry, diggers sliced into the hillside while trucks belched diesel fumes as they roared off to deliver gravel to building sites across the country.

The pilot brought the helicopter in to land on the top of the ridge, and Barry unbuckled his harness and stepped thankfully to the ground. It was like standing on the back of a great snake; one St. Patrick might have missed in his mythical expulsion of all the snakes from Ireland. The ridge may have been part of the famous *Slí Asail*, or Way of the Donkey, whose name survived into Christian times. "Everyone used these eskers," Barry said. "Kings, poets, warriors, priests. Imagine chariots, carts, wagons bringing people and goods, cattle being driven, family groups on their way to a solstice celebration at one of the great royal sites, like Tara in the east or Cruachan in the west."

The eskers were first used as roadways back in the Stone Age, when Ireland's early farmers raised great burial mounds as memorials to their ancestral gods, but Barry was speaking of a later time, around 200 B.C. during the Iron Age. He is one of Ireland's leading archaeologists, steeped in ancient Ireland before he could walk since his father was an archaeologist as well. Barry specializes in the Iron Age, those nine hundred years between the sixth century B.C. and the coming of Christianity to Ireland in the fifth century A.D., but he loves all periods of Irish prehistory, right back to the very beginning.

The prehistory of any country is what happened before the advent of writing. Literacy did not develop in Ireland until the coming of Christianity in the fifth century A.D. As people first arrived at least eight thousand years earlier, there are millennia that are known only through myth, legend, and the archaeological evidence left in the ground.

The gravel eskers are woven into the fabric of Irish history. Formed when great glaciers scoured the bedrock of Ireland during the last Ice Age, they are only now succumbing to the industrial boom of twenty-first century Ireland, their gravel part of new concrete and steel buildings rising in every modern Irish city. They were still roadways in early Christian times when monastic scribes first wrote Ireland's history and invented fantastic stories about their country's pre-Christian Celtic past. They felt the feet of Neolithic farmers who five thousand years earlier were clearing forests to plant their crops and raise their cattle. Ten thousand years ago they were crossed by wolf and bear when the land stood empty, awaiting the first hunter-gatherer immigrants to cross from Britain. For Barry Raftery, an archaeologist who has spent his life investigating the past, the eskers symbolize the continuity of Irish history; with every age and every generation shaped and rooted in the landscape where they lived.

PEOPLE FIRST ARRIVE IN IRELAND

In the beginning there was a lot of ice. Until the last Ice Age ended around twelve thousand years ago, there is no evidence of human occupation in Ireland, although early humans were present as far north as southeastern England half a million years ago. The last Ice Age put Ireland in the freezer around 115,000 B.C. As the weather turned colder, ice caps formed around the high mountain peaks of Donegal and Antrim in the north, Wicklow in the east, and perhaps Cork and Kerry in the south. During the next few thousand years, glaciers moved out from these mountain ice caps to meet and join other glaciers from Scotland and Iceland, inching south until Ireland, like much of northern Europe, was locked in a thick prison of ice.

Elsewhere in Europe, beyond the range of the glaciers, people used fire to keep warm, pressed their handprints on rock to create the first cave-paintings, and developed new tools and weapons for the hunt. But in Ireland, cold winds howled across empty snowfields and ice sheets thousands of feet thick ground the country's bedrock into the gravel later left behind as eskers.

No Ice Age is continuous. There were periods of warmth when the glaciers retreated for a while. So much water was locked up in the ice that sea levels were as much as forty feet lower than today. Land bridges linked Ireland with Britain, Britain with Europe, and Russia with Alaska. Across the Atlantic, a temporary warming permitted the first people to walk into America from Asia before the cold returned in 30,000 B.C. and ice again blocked the way south. But by 14,000 B.C. the last Ice Age was near its end, glaciers were in retreat, and the Bering land bridge from Asia to America was permanently open. The ancestors of today's Native Americans crossed around 12,000 B.C. and spread south to reach the farthest tip of South America within two thousand years. Ireland too had ice-free areas during the Ice Age, south of a line that runs from Waterford in the east to the Dingle peninsula in the west. People could have lived there, although no trace has ever been found. But from 10,000 B.C., Ireland was open for settlement.

Archaeologists like the past to fit into neat categories so the Stone Age, which refers to a pre-metal age when people used stone to make tools and weapons, is divided into three periods. The Paleolithic period—or Old Stone Age—is irrelevant to Irish history since it falls during the Ice Age when Ireland was uninhabited. The Mesolithic period—or Middle Stone Age—began in Ireland after 10,000 B.C., when people first arrived in the country and ended around 4500 B.C. with the coming of the first farmers. The Neolithic period—or New Stone Age—covers the time of these first farmers until a new metal technology arrived in Ireland around 2400 B.C. at the start of the Bronze Age. Such divisions are useful to archaeologists but mean nothing to people living at the time. Stone tools were used long after 2400 B.C., and bronze was being smelted and forged into Christian times. So we should not imagine a tribal chief, having just purchased an iron sword from a traveling smith, shaking his wife awake one morning with the news, "Guess what, dear? We're in the Iron Age."

The first people to arrive in Ireland found a land covered in forests of pine, oak, elm, and hazel. Bogs had already begun to form, covering only a small fraction of the 14 percent of Ireland they covered in the twentieth century. The first arrivals were already sophisticated hunters with a superb technology for producing weapons and tools out of chipped flint. They used bows and arrows, knew how to make nets and set fish traps, and were as intelligent in their own way as people are today. We can imagine these first immigrants walking through the wooded countryside in small family groups around 9000 B.C., leaving southwest Scotland to enter Ireland north of Belfast, up by Ballycastle in County Antrim. Much of the archaeological evidence from the Mesolithic period is in the northeast, where Ireland and Scotland are less than fifteen miles apart and where there are rich beds of flint, the necessary raw material for making stone knives and axe-heads.

Scholars argue about whether Ireland and Britain were still joined by a land bridge at this time. As the ice began melting, sea levels began to rise. The land bridge could have been cut much earlier, in which case the first Irish might have come by boat. We have no way of knowing. It is a popular misconception that Ireland has been subject to many different invasions throughout its history, each in their turn sweeping ashore to seize the land. The Fir Bolg, the Túatha Dé Danann, the Sons of Míl—better known as the Celts—have all left their mark on Ireland's mythology. But archaeology shows no indication of large-scale movements of people into Ireland from overseas; immigrants trickled in over hundreds or thousands of years. It was the same in Mesolithic times; the first immigrants arrived family by family. The population of Mesolithic Ireland was not likely more than a few thousand people, living in small family tribes, since a hunting and gathering lifestyle does not encourage large populations.

LIVING OFF THE LAND

In the 1970s archaeologist Peter Woodman excavated a Mesolithic site at Mount Sandel, in County Derry, which has been carbon-dated to around 7000 B.C. This was a rare find, the first clear evidence of how people lived at the dawn of Irish prehistory. Finding evidence of Mesolithic occupation is often a matter of luck. Most sites have been plowed under, covered by water as sea levels continued to rise, or have simply vanished without a trace. Not much is left after nine thousand years, although two hundred sites have been found, the majority in the northeast of Ireland. They are all near water, either along the coast or beside inland lakes and rivers. Hunter-gatherers in early Ireland lived in round huts made of tree branches and animal skins, easy to assemble and light enough to carry when people moved from place to place. They were like the tepees of Native Americans or the yurts of Mongolian herdsmen today, all nomadic peoples.

Although the Mount Sandel site has been dated to 7000 B.C., people may have been living in Ireland thousands of years earlier. The excavated area at Mount Sandel covers more than eight hundred square yards and shows frequent use over many centuries. These are the first Irish people whose life we can describe. What they left behind provides tantalizing clues to how they lived. There was charcoal from hearths, and signs of ten circular huts, each about twenty feet in diameter. There was even an industrial area where flints were worked into axe-heads and other tools. And there were fragments of burned bones, shells, and nuts. Mount Sandel was probably a base camp for a small family group of no more than ten people. Organic remains found on site give us a snapshot of their life. They ate a lot of fish, mostly salmon and eel, along with pig, hare, and wild birds; there is no sign of deer bones, so perhaps Ireland's red deer were not around at the time. They collected hazelnuts, an excellent source of protein, while water lily and wild pear seeds show that fruit and vegetables were also a part of their diet. In Ireland a wide range of food was available, so it was probably a comfortable and healthy life, staying near the coast in spring, moving inland along the rivers and lakes to take advantage of the summer migrations of salmon and eel. Fall and winter could be spent on higher ground, collecting hazelnuts and butchering young pigs to supplement their diet. Other European peoples had domesticated dogs by this time, and fragments of dog or wolf bones were found at Mount Sandel. It is possible the ancestor of today's Irish wolfhound loped along the forest trails beside these first hunter-gatherers, ears pricked and nose down as it followed a trail of tasty wild pig.

Burned stones found near the camp are reminiscent of the *fulacht fiadh,* or burned mounds of the Bronze Age more than six thousand years later, where stones were heated in a fire before being raked into a stone or wood-lined pit full of water. More than 4,500 have been found across the country; they are Ireland's most common prehistoric monuments. Bronze Age *fulacht fiadh* have been tested many times; fire-heated stones bring the water to the boil and keep it boiling with the addition of fresh stones for hours at a time—long enough to cook an entire wild boar. There are no pits like this at Mount Sandel, but fire-burned stones suggest a similar style of cooking. Hot stones could have been placed inside leather containers to heat liquids and make a form of soup or gruel.

If Mount Sandel started off as a winter camp, so many different foods have been found there that it was certainly occupied at other times of the year. An extended family band of twenty-five, including children, is considered the ideal size for a hunter-gatherer tribe; any larger and they exhaust the resources in their immediate territory; any smaller and their breeding group is too small to survive for many generations. If only ten people lived at Mount Sandel, the site may have been part of a larger community with other sites in the area. Hunters and food-gatherers may have traveled among smaller temporary camps set up at different times of the year to take advantage of seasonal changes in the food supply.

Elsewhere in the world in 7000 B.C., Jericho and other small farming communities in the Middle East and Pakistan were beginning to develop into the world's first towns. Jericho's first houses were circular, like the simple skin and branch huts at Mount Sandel, reproducing in mud-brick the shapes of the tents used by their earlier nomadic hunting ancestors. Jericho and other new communities were growing up around the cultivation of cereal crops like wheat and barley and the raising of domestic animals. It would be another two thousand years before this farming revolution reached Ireland. In the meantime, much was happening.

WHEN THE WORLD WAS DROWNED

If land bridges existed between Ireland and Britain at the beginning of the Mesolithic period, they were cut before 6000 B.C. when the warming melted the last of the glaciers and the ocean reached levels perhaps twenty-five feet higher than today, a sea rise of possibly seventy feet since the Ice Age. The waters would slowly recede to present levels as polar ice caps grew larger, but 6000 B.C. was an age of inundation. In places the land rose too. Like a sponge pressed flat by a heavy rock, Ireland had been compressed under the weight of ice for nearly a hundred thousand years. Once weight is removed, a sponge will gradually expand; Ireland was rising, in places as much as fifteen feet. Two opposite reactions, sea rise and land lift, changed and twisted Ireland's coast, drowning some areas while lifting others clear of the advancing waves.

By 6000 B.C. any land bridge was cut between Britain and Europe. Isolated for the first time, populations were beginning to develop individual characteristics, depending on the climate and geography where they lived. In Ireland, archaeology shows that Mesolithic societies developed differently from similar communities in Britain. Through most of prehistory, up to the time of the Roman Empire, the Irish shared a measure of common character and culture with people across the entire western seaboard of Europe. But for a long period of time during the Mesolithic Age, archaeologists believe there was little or no interaction between people on either side of the Irish Sea. Perhaps sea rise and coastal flooding made the shoreline too dangerous. Perhaps sailing was a skill either forgotten or not yet learned by these hunter-gatherers who lived on lands around a storm-tossed Irish Sea.

While sea levels were reaching these record levels, farming towns further south began to develop on the fertile flood plains of the Tigris and Euphrates rivers in present-day Iraq. Within two thousand years these communities were absorbed into Sumer, which went on to develop the world's earliest urban civilization and the world's first written language. The Sumerian epic of Gilgamesh includes the story of a great flood which drowns most of mankind. The Hebrews adopted this Sumerian legend when they collected together the stories that became the Book of Genesis. Oral story-telling traditions can span thousands of years, so the Christian Bible probably records the memory of an event eight thousand years ago, when fertile lands around the world were inundated by the sea and the islands of Britain and Ireland far to the north were finally cut off from the great continental landmass of Europe.

CORACLES AND CURRACHS— THE FIRST IRISH BOATS

People may have been using boats in one form or another since at least the last Ice Age. If the land bridge between Ireland and Scotland was cut before the beginning of the Mesolithic period, then the first Irish certainly arrived by boat. One of the earliest known

Simon O'Dwyer carefully navigates the coracle he built himself.
(*Leo Eaton*)

forms is the coracle. They were still being used on Irish rivers into the twentieth century, and their use goes back to Neolithic times, probably earlier. The coracle is a simple framework of light branches, lashed together and covered with animal skins. It looks like a large bowl, an upside-down version of the huts used by Ireland's Mesolithic inhabitants. We can never know how human innovations first occurred, but coracles resemble Mesolithic huts so much so that it is tempting to imagine an early hunter sheltering one day from the gale-force winds so common in Ireland. He might have watched in amazement as his hut was picked up, overturned, and sent spinning out over a lake to land upside-down, bobbing gently on the water. "Hmmm!" our imaginary hunter might have said, "That gives me an idea." And so the coracle was born.

The Irish also used dugout canoes, but the hide-covered coracle and its oceangoing cousin, the currach, were plying the rivers, lakes, and seaways around the Irish coast from earliest times. Simon O'Dwyer is a traditional Irish musician who has studied and re-created musical instruments from Irish prehistory, including bird-bone flutes that may have been played by these Mesolithic hunter-gatherers. He has also built his own coracle in traditional style with a cowhide lashed around a light framework of willow branches. Coracles are difficult to navigate until you get the hang of them, as Simon quickly discovered the first time he launched it on a lake in Connemara and took the single paddle to move it away from the dock. Coracles are circular and buoyant as corks, so one wrongly applied paddle stroke sends them spinning like a top. Eventually he got the hang of it, sitting in the middle and leaning forward so that the coracle tipped like a lopsided teacup. To go forward, one must paddle from the front, pushing the water back under the hull. Handled correctly, coracles are fast and dependable little craft, difficult to sink but easy to capsize if you make a mistake.

Their oceangoing big brother, the currach, is longer and thinner, shaped like a real boat rather than a floating teacup, with bows raised to cut through breaking seas. In the early twentieth century, forty-foot currachs were still being used on the Aran Islands off Ireland's west coast. Some fishermen still prefer them to wooden-planked boats, and smaller versions are raced each year during Sports Day on Inismor, Aran's largest island. Canvas has replaced animal skins while tar takes the place of animal fat to keep them waterproof, but a Stone Age fisherman would feel right at home in a modern currach. Such boats probably brought the first farmers to Ireland around 4500 B.C.

THE COMING OF THE FIRST FARMERS

Ireland had no sheep or cattle in Mesolithic times. No ancestral wheat or barley grew wild on Irish hillsides. Everything needed for a farming existence had to be carried by boat. The first Neolithic farmers may have been new immigrants, spreading northward from Europe into Britain and across to Ireland, seeking new opportunities in an emptier land, but perhaps agricultural knowledge was brought back by Mesolithic traders or fishermen from Ireland who traveled overseas and caught a glimpse of the future in communities in Britain or Europe where cattle were raised and cereal crops harvested. All the great innovations of prehistoric Ireland—farming, building great stone burial tombs, bronze and iron technology—arrived gradually over many generations, carried either by new arrivals or by native Irish who had sailed to other lands and were returning home, eager to show friends and relations what they had learned in foreign parts. Irish people have always had a tendency to wander abroad, a characteristic well documented over the past two thousand years. Why should they have been any different in Mesolithic or Neolithic times?

It is misleading to think of such huge changes in society in respect to more recent examples, such as America's pioneer farmers moving west to displace Native American hunter-gatherers from their land. This involved much greater numbers of people. With Ireland's Mesolithic population no more than a few thousand, huge areas of the country would have been uninhabited. Although farming would eventually take over as the dominant Irish lifestyle, farmers and hunter-gatherers could have lived side-by-side for a long period of time. So cattle first brought across the sea in skin-covered boats became the original breeding stock for herds that grew into the primary measure of wealth in Ireland for the next six thousand years.

THE COWMOBILE

The Dingle peninsula is in the far southwest of Ireland. It juts out into the Atlantic like a great finger, its spine of mountains ending in the same Mount Brendan where an ice cap formed during the last Ice Age. The peninsula has an ancient magic, especially outside the tourist months when fog rolls down from the hills and the walls of ancient ring forts and beehive huts loom out of the mist like ghosts from the Otherworld. There are legends that the Dingle peninsula is where the Celts, or Sons of Míl, first came ashore with their iron swords to defeat the magical Túatha Dé Danann and force them into the Otherworld, where they became the Celtic gods. Myth and history go hand in hand in Dingle. At the far end of the peninsula, a Mesolithic campsite was excavated at Ferriter's Cove and dated to around 4500 B.C., a time just before farm animals first arrived in Ireland.

One day in early fall, archaeologist Mícheál Ó Colláin traveled down to "the Kingdom," as the peninsula is called, to meet a friend. Bobby Goodwinn is a farmer in his late seventies who owns one of the Magharee islands off Tralee Bay, known as the Seven Hogs. Bobby's island has a few acres of flat treeless pastureland where he raised his family in a stone house, the only house on the island. With his wife dead and his children grown, he now lives on the mainland. The house is still there, let to summer tourists, though there is no electricity and just a hand-pumped well. At the far end of the island are the ruins of an ancient Irish monastery, its dry-stone walls slowly being washed away by winter storms. Christian monks in the seventh and eighth centuries A.D. sought out these remote places, calling their self-imposed exile the White Martyrdom. Bobby still keeps cattle on the island, letting them roam free all year until it is time to market them on the mainland.

A generation ago it was common to see farmers on outlying islands load their cattle into small boats—often traditional skin-covered currachs—to bring them to market. If distances were not too great, they would even swim them over. Cattle are good swimmers but their heads drop down when they get tired so they drown easily. Bobby has created his own unique animal transport, which Mícheál Ó Colláin calls a cowmobile. It is a wooden pen large enough to hold two cows. The platform, about 12 feet long and 5 feet wide, was built on top of empty oil barrels. Mícheál had come to help Bobby bring one of his heifers back from the island.

We set out in pouring rain from the little fishing port of Fahamore, towing the cowmobile with Bobby's fishing boat. A fifteen-minute journey later, he anchored the fishing boat in the bay while we poled the cowmobile onto the beach. Catching the cow was more difficult but eventually Bobby had it running across the sand, lashing out with its back legs and twisting around to stop him getting a rope over its head. "This is the modern-day version of what must have happened six thousand years ago," Mícheál explained. "Those first cattle and sheep all had to be brought across by boat. Of course the boats weren't so good, and the ropes weren't so strong."

Bobby looked up from where he was heaving the cow's hindquarters up onto the cowmobile. "All they had was stronger men," he panted. Of course the first farmers did not bring full-grown animals. Calves and lambs would have been laid on a bed of straw at the bottom of the currach with their feet tied with grass rope to stop them kicking a hole in the side of the boat during the ocean crossing. "The first evidence we have of cattle in Ireland is around 4500 B.C.," Mícheál said. "They'd have been headland hopping, island hopping, never out of sight of land. And they had to cross the sea on a calm day." Hopefully their crossings were easier than ours. As we towed the cowmobile out from the shelter of the island, the wind and sea picked up and the raft tossed and plunged like a spirited horse, with the cow bellowing mournfully the whole way over.

BUILDING SOIL FROM SAND AND SEAWEED

Ireland's first farmers probably came from Britain, crossing the Irish Sea, carrying the animals and seed crops needed to establish a farming economy. On a clear day you can see Ireland from the coast of Scotland and Wales, the shortest crossing is just eleven miles. Today it is difficult to imagine a world in which nation and nationality have no meaning. Loyalty would be to family alone, and a single extended family might have roots on both sides of a body of water. Through most of prehistory, the Irish Sea was a link, not a division, between Ireland and the neighboring island of Britain, as were the shorter sea-routes between the Irish mainland and its many offshore islands. Professor John Waddell, head of the department of archaeology at the National University of Ireland, Galway, took us out to Inis Meain—the middle and least spoiled of the Aran islands that guard the entrance to Galway Bay off Ireland's west coast—in a one-hundred-year-old Galway hooker. This fifty-foot sailing ship had bright red sails and an oak hull stained black with sea-spray and age. Such hookers once carried all the cargo up and down Ireland's west coast.

The present slips away in a sailing ship when the only sounds come from wind, waves, the creak of rigging, and the soft Gaelic language the skipper spoke with his son who held the tiller. John Waddell sat at the bow, looking out to where the island slowly drew closer. "Water was the principal means of communication around Ireland throughout ancient times," he said. "Cross-country travel was much more difficult than going by sea. Thousands of years ago the seas around Ireland would have been full of boats; fishermen, traders, even families going backwards and forwards. Communities on one side of the water often had closer family ties with people on the other side than they did with people inland."

Inis Meain is two hours sailing out into Galway Bay with a

good wind, although modern ferries make the trip in less than an hour. The Aran Islands are made up of great slabs of limestone, cracked through with fissures that run northeast across the islands. There are few trees and rock is everywhere, peeping up from beneath thin soil, broken up for the dry-stone walls that ring every tiny field, or built into two-thousand-year-old stone forts like Dún Aengus and Dún Connor that dominate the Aran landscape. On the Irish mainland, where soil was good, Neolithic farmers just cleared areas of forest to plant their crops and pasture their animals. On Aran they had to make the soil itself. Hundreds of generations of islanders have carried sand and seaweed from the shoreline, spreading it out on the limestone bedrock to rot into soil before the fields could produce crops.

John Waddell had come to meet Dara Beag O'Flaherty, who still gathers seaweed from the beach to dig into his fields, as islanders have done as long as people have lived on Inis Meain. Like most on the island, Dara prefers to speak Gaelic. He cut handfuls of kelp left behind by the retreating tide and packed them into baskets hung over the saddle of his donkey. The beach was full of kelp harvesters, most with donkeys and handcarts, although one man used a big tractor and trailer. Much of this seaweed is edible and can be baked into the laver bread that was once a staple of the island diet. Rich in nitrates, it also makes excellent fertilizer. That is how Dara used it, digging it into his fields that lay in the shadow of the Dún Connor fort. "What you're seeing is timeless," John said later as he watched Dara forking the seaweed into the neatly turned rows where he would soon plant his potatoes. "Neolithic farmers on Aran probably built their fields up just the same, using the seaweed and sand to form cultivation ridges for their wheat and barley." Dara did not care that his actions had such ancient roots, but he knew the seaweed helped him grow the best potatoes on the island.

TOMBS FOR TRIBAL LEADERS, TEMPLES FOR ANCESTRAL GODS

For a millennium after 4000 B.C., the weather in the Northern Hemisphere was warm and moist, temperatures several degrees higher than they are today; in other words perfect farming weather.

The dolman at the Lough of Doon in County Donegal is the remains of a five-thousand-year-old Neolithic portal tomb. (*Leo Eaton*)

In the Fertile Crescent, the world's first cities were developing new urban ways of life made possible by the food surpluses farming provided. In Northern Europe, Neolithic farmers were raising great stone tombs for their dead. The most spectacular of these are passage tombs, covered by mounds of earth or stone up to forty feet high and often built on hilltops to emphasize their size. Similar tombs are found in Spain, France, Britain, and Ireland, suggesting that Ireland shared its culture and a related language with much of Northern Europe at this time. More than fifteen hundred mega-lithic—the word means "made of big stones"—tombs survive in Ire-land from the Neolithic Age, the majority built between 4000 and 2000 B.C.

Building such massive tombs required strong local leadership and a ready supply of workers able to spend months away from crops and herds. Populations were much bigger than in Mesolithic times, and farming was providing food surpluses in Ireland. Four different types of megalithic tombs have been found, although why a community chose to build in one style rather than another is any-one's guess. Simplest are the portal tombs commonly known as dol-mans. Thousands of years of erosion often leave nothing but the portal or gateway stones and a huge capstone, rearing up like the prow of a ship in front to slope down and rest on smaller slabs of stone at the back. The most famous of these is Poulnabrone, in County Clare.

Next come the court tombs, so called because there is an open circular or semicircular courtlike area sometimes entered through a narrow gateway that stands in front of the tomb entrance. It is im-possible to tell how these courts were used; even the biggest could only hold a few dozen people. Maybe priests and tribal leaders went into the court for important religious ceremonies while the rest of the people waited outside. Or if they were simply family temples, they may have been just big enough for the family to assemble. Today visitors only see fallen slabs of stone, but court and portal tombs, like all megalithic tombs, were originally covered by cairns of rock or mounds of earth.

Wedge tombs are the most recent of all and were still being built in the Bronze Age after 2000 B.C. The burial chambers are wedge-shaped passages, which narrow and lose height from front to back, and are covered with a low mound. These barrows can be up to thirty feet long; anyone who has read J.R.R. Tolkein's epic fan-tasy *Lord of the Rings* will remember Frodo's terror at being trapped underground in such a place in the company of the dreaded barrow-wites. Legends must have grown up around the megalithic tombs within a few generations of their construction. Later people thought them the work of giants, magical entrances to the Other-world where gods and spirits lived. The most impressive of all these Irish tombs are the passage tombs, whose great hilltop mounds often tower over the surrounding countryside. Even by today's standards, they are magnificent architectural achievements. Built more than a thousand years before the first pyramids rose in Egypt, they clearly show the sophistication and skill of the Neolithic Irish.

NEWGRANGE

The Boyne Valley northwest of Dublin contains sixty passage tombs built in three distinct groups. The greatest of these, the most famous passage tomb in Ireland, is Newgrange, a great mound of stone almost three hundred feet across and thirty-five feet high. Unlike court, portal, and wedge tombs, which appear on their own, passage tombs often appear in clusters in cemeteries, smaller tombs gathered around the largest mound in the center like children around a family patriarch. Newgrange is such a patriarch, built between 3300 and 2900 B.C. The tomb entrance has been open since the seventeenth century, but only a small part has been properly excavated. The Irish Heritage Service recently restored the tomb, facing the front with sparkling white quartz. Most days in summer the roads to Newgrange are choked with tourist buses, attracted to Ireland's best known Stone Age monument like bees to honey. The newly faced white tomb wall is a dazzling display as it reflects the morning sun. It seems almost modern, a gleaming mound bordered by carparks, a visitor's center, and neat gravel paths that package tourists into carefully controlled groups. Entry is restricted as the Heritage Service is increasingly worried about the damage tourism is doing to the five-thousand-year-old monument. Once inside, a passage runs seventy feet back into the heart of the mound to end in a cruciform burial chamber with a high vaulted roof. Newgrange is the only Neolithic tomb found so far with a light well above the main passage that frames the first rays of the sun on the winter solstice so they shine directly through to the back of the tomb. But for all its size and import, there is little sense of mystery in daytime. Like Stonehenge in Britain, too much bureaucratic regulation and too many visitors have leached it of its ancient power. But at dawn or dusk, with mist rising from the grass and no one around, it is still possible to understand the hold this tomb, and others like it, have had on human imagination for thousands of years.

Not all of Ireland's great passage tombs have given up their mystery to an excess of package tours and camera-clicking tourists. At Carrowkeel and Carrowmore, in County Sligo in the west, and Lough Crew, north of Dublin in County Meath, the tombs stand open to wind and weather, and sheep graze across the high hillsides where the mounds were raised five thousand years ago to look down on surrounding tribal lands. The Carrowmore cemetery is dominated by the huge mound called Knocknarea that sits on top of a high ridge of hills that overlook the Sligo coast. Locally it is called Medb's tomb or Medb's pap as it resembles a human breast. Medb was a Celtic earth goddess and the legendary queen of Connaught who sent her armies against Cú Chulainn, hero of Ireland's most famous ancient saga, *The Táin*. Previous generations believed Medb herself was buried inside, but Neolithic tombs were built thousands of years before the time of Celtic legends. Knocknarea has yet to be excavated, but archaeologists believe it could contain a passage tomb at least as big as the one in Newgrange.

THE HILL OF THE WITCHES

The Lough Crew tombs are just outside Oldcastle, in County Meath. We arrived with archaeologist Barry Raftery an hour before dawn, racing the light in the hope of reaching one of the hilltops before sunrise. Of course we got hopelessly lost in the maze of small lanes that wander haphazardly around the base of the hills on which the tombs were built. At last we stopped at a cottage with a light showing in the kitchen window. The old farmer who answered the door showed little surprise; people get up early in these parts. He simply shrugged on his coat and boots and told us to park our car in his yard. "I'll take you up myself," he said. "You'll never find your way in the dark." His name was Mick Tobin, and he told us proudly he was eighty-two on his last birthday and had been climbing the Lough Crew hills all his life. Looking like a figure out of Irish legend with his battered hat, flapping raincoat, crooked walking stick, and bowed legs, he led us on a merry chase as we panted along behind him, climbing almost a mile up a hillside slippery with morning dew to emerge where great Neolithic mounds lay in black silhouette against the lightening sky.

The wind had picked up, moaning around the collapsed stones of some of the smaller tombs. About thirty tombs remain, spread out over three hilltops, although there had been double that number. The site is known locally as Sliabh na Caillighe, or the Hill of the Witches, and Mick told us the local legend. "She was a hag and a fairy queen," he said. "She came flying by with her apron full of stones, dropping them on the three hills to make these cairns. She was about to go to another hill and leaped off—it's called the hag's hop—when she fell and broke her neck. Now she's said to be buried in a heap of stones at the back of Patrickstown hill."

Most of the older locals still swear the hills are haunted, and there is no shortage of stories about mysterious fires seen flickering around the tombs on solstice nights. Mick Tobin swears he saw a banshee there one night in 1939, but she was not crying; only when a banshee cries is someone about to die. Every new generation builds on existing folklore. Mick showed us a flat rock in the side of the largest mound. "This was the witch's chair," he said, rapping it firmly with his stick. "She was the mistress of all Ireland, and she'd sit here, smoking her pipe, and make laws for all the people. Everyone had to do exactly what she said. If they didn't, she'd cast a spell on them and turn them into anything she liked."

The sun rose as Mick finished his story, flooding the hilltop with light. The big tomb beside us was positioned to catch the sun, although without the precision of Newgrange. Yet at sunrise on a cold February morning, with sunlight flooding into the entrance of the tomb and a cold wind moaning around the fallen stones, it is easy to see why pre-Christian people believed they were magic entryways to the Otherworld. Barry Raftery remarked that Mick's folklore held echoes of ancient reality. The tombs were much more than simple burial mounds. Probably sacred to the earth goddess, they were also places of assembly where tribal laws were given and disputes judged.

"The importance of the site is the hilltop location," Barry said. "These were ceremonial places, central places within the tribal landscape, symbolizing the importance and continuity of the tribe. If you look around, you see a wide expanse of countryside. That means the dead up here could look down and watch over the living.

More important, the living could look up to the dead. I imagine at different times of the year the people assembled here to celebrate the importance and unity of the tribe."

The biggest tomb on the hilltop is sealed by a heavy iron gate fastened with an ancient padlock. Barry had the key, usually kept by a farmer down the hill, and we went inside, stooping to enter the narrow passage. It is nowhere near as big as Newgrange but has much more atmosphere. The passage leads back twenty feet to open into the main burial chamber that has a vaulted ceiling twelve feet high in the center. Three chambers open off the end in the shape of a crucifix, each with a stone basin that once held cremated human remains. In each of these chambers, and along the passage itself, are slabs of stone worked with exquisite circles and whirls, as fresh today as when they were carved five thousand years ago. Most passage tombs have been found to contain just a small amount of burned bone. Perhaps like Egypt's pyramids, they were built for chosen leaders or priests of great spiritual importance, ancestral gods with power to protect the tribe and its land for all time. It is an interesting coincidence that the intricately carved spirals and circles of the artwork look like the artwork now called "Celtic," even though it would be another thousand years before Celtic people migrated west into Europe.

It was quiet inside the tomb, the light slanting in through the narrow entrance and barely reaching the burial chamber at the back. Sitting on a carved rock at the very center of the mound, it was possible to imagine what the people were like who had built such a place. They would not be so different from us, probably worried about the weather and crops, looking forward to the next celebration, concerned that their kids were running wild. We know they were small farmers, living in scattered communities that held no more than two or three houses. Neolithic Ireland was not particularly warlike, so there were no defensive walls. The houses were wood with thatched roofs, not built for permanence but presumably comfortable and dry. Such houses would disintegrate and vanish within fifty years if they did not burn down first; fire must have been a constant hazard. As Barry observed, "The houses of the living didn't need to be permanent, only the houses of the dead."

Tomb building calls for sophisticated organization and a de-

gree of specialization in human activity. People had to be gathered
together under strong leadership over a wide area. There would be
architects to design the tombs so that they did not collapse under
the weight of the covering mound, and stone carvers to split and
shape the great stone boulders. Astronomers had to calculate the
solar calendar so tomb entrances could be precisely aligned with
the rising or setting sun on solstice days. Masons were needed to
build the corbelled dry-stone tomb walls that curved inward until
capped by a single slab. Engineers must have devised ramps and
pulleys to transport and position heavy stone slabs. Artists were
probably called in from far away to carve the intricate spirals, circles, triangles, lozenges, and zigzags that decorate the tombs, some
positioned so only the gods could see them. There would be musicians to keep up the spirits of the workers, cooks to feed them,
healers to dress the cuts, bruises, and broken bones that occur on
any construction site. No doubt the priests fussed busily around,
supervising everything to be sure the work was completed according to the will of the gods. It is not surprising that later people
thought the mound builders were gods. It would be thousands of
years before the Irish could build such spectacular structures
again. Only with the coming of Christianity in the first millennium
A.D. were the ancient gods demonized and diminished, the great
tombs becoming no more than homes for witches and fairies, banshees and leprechauns, Irish for "creatures with a little body." It is
easy to discount the old tales, but few local people will go near the
tombs at night. "The hills are haunted," Mick Tobin said firmly.
"Fairy folk, ghosts, banshees; believe what you want. They're here
just the same."

It was mid-morning before we were ready to leave Lough
Crew, the winter sun blinding after the dark stillness of the tomb.
The iron gate sealing the entrance squealed in rusty protest as
Barry closed and locked it behind us. It was installed to stop vandals damaging the tomb, but earlier peoples would have thought it
had a different purpose. Many English and Irish fairytales tell how
fairy folk cannot pass cold iron; so perhaps the iron bars serve to
keep Otherworld forces in, not people out. The same belief is behind hanging a horseshoe on the front door to stop fairies and dev-
ils coming in the house to do small acts of mischief like souring

milk or giving the baby colic. Such legends may be distant echoes of the great changes in store for all the people around the Irish Sea when the arrival of metal brought the Stone Age to an end and began Ireland's first industrial revolution.

[2]

The Age of Bronze

LOUGH LEANE is one of Ireland's popular tourist spots as well as being the most beautiful of all the "lakes of Killarney" in County Kerry. Here Billy O'Brien, an archaeologist at the National University of Ireland, Galway, discovered the place where the Bronze Age began in Ireland. Ross Island is a tree-covered spit of land jutting out into the lake. It is an idyllic spot if one ignores the clouds of midges, tiny biting insects that gather in their thousands to feast on any uncovered flesh not liberally doused in insect repellant.

Billy stood on a beach made up of the rocky spoil of thousands of years of mining and looked out across mirror-still water reflecting the mountain peaks that ring the lake; Torc Mountain and Purple Mountain and the great spine of MacGillycuddy's Reeks that stride west to where cloud-capped Carrantuohill—Ireland's highest mountain—gleams white with snow late in the spring. Hillsides were thick with pine trees and rhododendrons; valleys were filled with ancient trees from one of Ireland's last old-growth forests. Safe from logging inside the Killarney National Park, oak and ash trees crowded to the water's edge as though eager to show how Ireland looked at the beginning of the Bronze Age when forests still covered most of the land. Ross Island is a timeless place, miraculously unspoiled by the thousands of tourists who swarm at a nearby fourteenth-century castle built across the narrow neck of land connecting the island to the Killarney shore. For centuries Ross Castle was the stronghold of the O'Donoghue clan until it fell in 1652 to an English army sent by dictator Oliver Cromwell to prevent Ireland from helping the defeated royalists regain power.

Billy O'Brien had come looking for a much older history. Although archaeologists like to divide up the ancient past into neat categories, these are just arbitrary names for a more complex and messy process. People are people, whenever they live. Some are conservative, clinging to old ideas and habits long past their "sell by" date, while others embrace new customs and fashions with alacrity. The Irish were never a homogenous people. Any time during the third or second millennium B.C., they may have been made up of a number of different societies speaking a number of different languages. When the Bronze Age came to Ireland, it came in fits and starts, adopted wholeheartedly in some areas while bypassing others completely. The use of tools allows human beings to reshape their environment. Metals allowed them to do it faster and more effectively, so the development of metal technology was a great watershed in human history. The pace of change was faster afterward, an acceleration in human knowledge leading onward across centuries and civilizations to the present day.

When Billy O'Brien started digging at Ross Island ten years ago as part of a multi-year university project, he expected to find plenty of evidence from the early Bronze Age. The limestone of the area is veined with metallic ore, one of the richest sources of copper anywhere in Ireland. For forty-five hundred years it has been a center of metallurgy for all the lands around the Irish Sea. Axeheads and daggers made from Ross Island copper in the centuries after 2400 B.C. were used across Ireland and even into Britain. Mining first stopped sometime after 1800 B.C., probably because the shallow Bronze Age pits were flooded by a rise in lake level. But Ross Island miners were back in business in early Christian times—between the seventh and ninth centuries A.D.—when island metal was the raw material for many of Ireland's most beautiful monastic treasures. The fame of the area was so great that in A.D. 829 a Welsh monk called Nennius—writing one of the first histories of Britain—described its mineral wealth as one of the wonders of the known world: "There is a lake called Lough Lein. Four circles are around it. In the first circle, it is surrounded by tin, in the second by lead, in the third by iron, and in the fourth by copper."

During the eighteenth and nineteenth centuries, mining continued on a grand scale. More than five hundred people worked at Ross Island, and four thousand tons of copper ore were shipped across the Irish Sea between 1804 and 1810 for smelting in England. Billy O'Brien found the roof of a Bronze Age mine damaged when miners blasted through it in the nineteenth century. Records from the time describe finding "chambers of rudely vaulted form, worked by kindling large fires on the limestone." Mining was finally abandoned in 1829, again because of flooding from the lake. The buildings were demolished, the mine workings filled, and the whole area reforested. When Billy began excavating in 1992, he hoped to learn more about Bronze Age mining techniques, but what he discovered was even better than he hoped. Ross Island was the first place copper was mined in Ireland, the place the Irish Bronze Age began.

THE COMING OF BRONZE TO NORTHERN EUROPE

Around 4500 B.C., farmers living in the Balkans and Anatolia—in modern Turkey—learned to extract metal from rocks that contained copper ore. Like most world-changing discoveries, it probably happened by chance, perhaps as a result of a potter trying to make a hotter furnace to fire his clay. However it happened, early metalsmiths found out that when copper-bearing rock was crushed and heated above two thousand degrees, molten metal puddled out and collected in droplets at the bottom of the fire. It must have seemed a god-given gift, tears from the sun god himself; from earliest times religion and metal work have been closely related. People soon discovered copper was good for things other than decoration. They learned that adding tin to molten copper produced an alloy harder and longer lasting than copper alone. Bronze, this alloy of copper and tin, became the most important ingredient for tools and weapons until the coming of iron thousands of years later. So the Bronze Age spread along the trade routes, arriving in Spain as early as 3500 B.C. and moving north through Europe. Sometime around 2400 B.C. it reached the islands around the Irish Sea.

THE BEAKER FOLK

Who were the people who brought this new bronze technology to Ireland? Were they sea-borne traders and traveling smiths looking for new markets, or new settlers arriving from Spain or Britain, or were they native Irish who had traveled overseas and learned new skills to carry home? Scholars pose the same question about every major change in Irish culture, from the arrival of farming practices to the adoption of a Celtic language. Does each change suggest the arrival of large numbers of new settlers from outside Ireland, or is it simply the result of centuries of to-and-fro contact along ocean trade routes that linked Ireland to Britain, France, and Spain? We might imagine archaeologists digging in the ruins of Moscow, Paris, or Rome thousands of years in the future who knew nothing about our time. They would find evidence of Russian, French, or Italian cultures, but they would also find such quantities of cola cans, American movie posters, and a thousand other artifacts that they might suppose Europe had been overrun by hordes of Americans who imposed their rule at the end of the twentieth century. On one level these future archaeologists would be right; American culture did dominate, even though local populations retained their own languages and political control. Substitute Americans in the twenty-first century A.D. for Beaker folk in the third millennium B.C. and you get the picture.

As the Neolithic period gave way to the early Bronze Age, a distinctive style of pottery—known as Beaker—appeared across Europe. Beaker pots were better fired than earlier ceramics, with thin sides and beautiful decoration. Many were bell-shaped with elegant "S" curved sides, a major advance in ceramic technology. Beaker pots and distinctive copper knives, daggers, and wrist guards—to protect the arm from a bowstring's recoil—have been found in burials from the Mediterranean to Poland and in many parts of Ireland. Europe may have shared a common culture for many centuries.

Earlier scholars suggested that a migration of Beaker warrior aristocrats—out of their homelands in either Spain or the Rhine valley of Germany—eventually took over much of the rest of Europe. No one today accepts such invasion theories, but the spread of metalworking across Western Europe is clearly linked to the spread of Beaker pottery. Europe was going through a great cultural and technological transition. Along with better ceramics and new skills in working metal, religious practices were changing. Stone circles appeared for the first time. And these changes arrived in southern Ireland around 2400 B.C., centered on the rich copper deposits of Ross Island.

IRELAND'S FIRST COPPER MINE

Once away from the lake, midges swarmed around us as if they had not tasted blood since 1829, the year the miners left. "We put up with this every summer during the excavations," Billy O'Brien said as he led the way along a narrow path that skirted a deep pool filled with what looked like green milk. There are many of these at Ross island, flooded mineshafts where the water takes on the color of the minerals in the rock. They are a perfect breeding ground for midges. "Insect repellant was the most expensive part of the dig." Billy swatted at them ineffectively with his hat. "What do they live on when they can't find archaeologists?"

Billy was a passionate and intense guide, proud of the work his team had done over several summers of excavation in the 1990s, darting ahead to point out each new object of interest: a rock-face flecked with brown and blue veins of metal, a flooded ditch where nineteenth-century blasting exposed the earlier Bronze Age mine. "Look at these colors," he enthused. "The first prospectors wouldn't have just landed from France or Spain and gone wandering off through the Irish countryside looking for copper. There had to be local knowledge. People living in the Killarney area would have told them about the bright green, blue, and golden colors in the rock."

The colored streaks of ore are as obvious today as when early prospectors first saw them, thousands of tons of copper ore close enough to the surface to be accessible to Bronze Age miners whose shafts could not go deeper than fifty feet. Between 2400 and 1800 B.C. this one mine supplied most of the copper in circulation across Ireland and into mainland Britain. "We can match the chemistry of copper ore from here with metal from early Bronze Age tools," Billy explained. "Think of the exchange networks in place for this metal to be traded as far north as Donegal."

He was off again, clambering over a chain-link fence and vanishing into a low cave mouth that opened out of the side of a lime-stone cliff. This was his prize exhibit at Ross Island, the earliest mine, hardly changed from when miners walked away four thousand years earlier. Inside the cave, Billy was flat on his stomach, wriggling over a tumble of fallen rock to where the roof curved down to meet the floor, showing the smooth concave surface of a fire-worked mine. "We carbon-dated wood and charcoal to between 2400 and 2200," he explained. "The miners lit fires against the rock face and then pounded the fire-weakened rock with stone hammers to break it away. They did this day and night for decades, maybe centuries, and ended up carving out a cave that goes back thirty feet into the cliff."

Beneath us more extensive Bronze Age mine workings had been flooded by the lake. Ross Island is honeycombed with pits and tunnels, sealed off ever since people were drowned exploring the flooded shafts with scuba gear.

It was cool in the mine, and the killer midges remained safely outside. To reach the back, one must wriggle forward on one's stomach, the roof sloping down less than a foot above head height. Once there, it is possible to touch a rock surface polished smooth by centuries of stone hammers. The work was probably seasonal, done by farmers who came to Ross Island at quiet times in the agricultural year, perhaps after the harvest was in. Billy had found shards of Beaker pottery in a nearby work camp. It is not difficult to imagine them coming across the lake in big dugout canoes like the fifty-two-foot monster on display at the National Museum of Ireland in Dublin. They would scramble ashore, unloading tools and food before walking back past the mine-workings to repair any damage at the camp since the previous year. Charcoal burners would set up their fires as charcoal was a vital ingredient in the smelting process; woodsmen with stone axes would spread out through the forest to cut the trees. The site was probably active day and night. Wood cut and dried over the previous summer would be stacked in piles against the cliff face. Fires would be lit and left to burn overnight, flames casting lurid red reflections across the dark waters of the lake. In the gray dawn as fires burned low, miners would have coughed their way through the smoke to the mine-face with leather buckets filled with water to pour over the heated rock. The sounds would be distinct, the hiss of steam as white clouds swirled up into the sky, a sharp crack of exploding limestone, and then the ceaseless chip, chip, chip of stone hammers breaking away the fire-weakened rock face, accompanying the songs of workers as they dragged great wicker baskets of ore out into the sunshine to be sorted at the work camp nearby.

Sitting in the mine four thousand years on, Billy O'Brien brought the ancient scene alive. Archaeologists are traditionally cautious with facts, hesitant to make claims that cannot be proven—a huge problem in Irish prehistory where so little is known—but beneath the professional caution, most archaeologists are also dreamers, their imaginations captured by the eras in which they spend so much of their lives.

HOW TO MAKE AN AXE-HEAD

As we left the mine and walked back along the lakeshore, Billy picked up a large round stone from the beach. "Look!" he said. "This is an original stone hammer. The miners chose suitable rocks from nearby rivers and either added handles or just held them in their hands. You're looking at a multi-purpose rock-smashing tool."

This ancient tool was casually tossed aside by a Bronze Age miner to lie unnoticed on the beach for more than four thousand years. During his excavations, Billy found other tools, including cattle shoulder bones that miners used as scoops during the mining process. Nothing was wasted; today's meal became tomorrow's shovel.

Billy picked up more rocks that showed traces of copper ore. "I'm doing just what they did," he said, piling his collection onto a large flat boulder and pulverizing it with the stone hammer. "While the fires were burning at the rock face, the miners in the work camp would be organized in small teams working on anvil-like slabs of rock. They'd take the ore extracted the previous day and use hammers to break it up as finely as possible. Slowly they'd build up a concentrate, throwing away the spoil—the useless rock—and crushing what was left into an ore-rich powder. This was what went into the smelters to be turned into pure copper."

Early miners made furnaces by lighting charcoal fires in pits dug in the ground. They would sprinkle in alternate layers of charcoal and powdered copper ore and then use bellows to raise the temperature above two thousand degrees. Droplets of ore were then collected from the bottom of the fire and remelted in crucibles to create ingots of copper. This final stage of operations at Ross Island was hardly mass-production. Billy's research suggests that similar mines at Mount Gabriel in County Cork produced less than fifty pounds of metal in any one year. If the output of Ross Island was comparable there was only enough metal to make fifty axe-heads.

Casting the axe-heads, daggers, and halberds—pointed dagger-like blades attached to long shafts—took place away from the mine at homesteads in the Killarney area. At the end of every mining season, workers carried copper ingots back across the lake when they returned to their fields and herds. Casting required as much skill as mining and smelting. Archaeologists have found open-faced molds chipped out of stone into which molten copper was poured, perhaps mixed with tin that came across the sea from the Cornish coast of Britain. Such tools would be crude and require a lot of cold hammering to produce a hard cutting edge, but the molds could be used a number of times. Closed clay molds would be more efficient, but there is no evidence this sort of casting was done so early in the Irish Bronze Age.

"It was a complex technology," Billy said, "and it required a huge amount of effort. Why go to all this trouble? We know they weren't looking for more efficient tools; stone axes were perfectly good for chopping down trees. It was all about the prestige value of the metal itself. Today we don't think of copper as having great value, but at the beginning of the Bronze Age it was like gold." And the smith, a master craftsman with the skills necessary to mine, refine, smelt, and cast these copper tools, would be among the elite of Bronze Age society, gifted with sacred knowledge from the gods themselves. Most ancient cultures include the "smith of the gods" in their religious pantheon.

STONE CIRCLES

Even people who know nothing about the European Bronze Age have heard of stone circles; Stonehenge in Britain, prehistoric stone circles in France and the Orkney Islands off Scotland, and

An early Bronze Age stone circle in County Kerry from around 2000
B.C.—a temple for a religion based on the sun and probably the religious
center for copper miners from Ross Island. (*Leo Eaton*)

Irish circles with eloquent names like the Piper's Stones and the
Petrified Dancers, all reflecting a belief by later generations that
these were places of magic and enchantment. There are hundreds
of Irish stone circles—big and small—built over a two-thousand-
year period between the end of the Neolithic and the start of the
Iron Age around 500 B.C. Billy O'Brien led us to a small circle he
thinks was linked directly to the miners of Ross Island. Three miles
from the mine, we arrived in a grassy open space in the middle of a
wood. In the center was a ring with seven stones, none more than
three feet high. These were not graceful standing stones like those

of Stonehenge, just squat boulders poking out of the grass and surrounded by an enclosing bank less than fifty feet across with a circular inside ditch overgrown with bracken and blackthorns.

In forts built for war, defensive ditches are always on the outside to stop enemies getting in. At religious sites, ditches are placed
inside the banks to stop supernatural powers within the circle getting out. A hundred yards outside the circle two standing stones,
each as tall as a man, were set as portals of a ritual gateway through
which worshippers passed to approach the temple. It was a rustic,
hidden spot, and the farmer who owned the land wanted to keep it
that way. Billy said he often chased off modern pagans who tried to
celebrate solstice nights among the ancient stones.

Most stone circles are too crude to be solar observatories, as is
claimed for sophisticated temples such as Stonehenge, but they
still symbolize the movements of the sun. "Of course communities
concerned with death and fertility are going to include the movements of the sun into the monuments they build," Billy said.
"These were the temples of a solar religion."

More than 120 of these stone circles exist in the southwest of
Ireland, spread across the landscape of Cork and Kerry. It has been
suggested that each community had its own sacred circle, just as
communities today have local churches. Was this where the miners
of Ross Island worshipped? Billy likes to think so. "One of our
problems in understanding early mining in Killarney is we've never
discovered where the Beaker people lived," he said. "The best we
can do is find their sacred sites. Chronologically this is from the
same period, 2400–2000 B.C. It's so close to Ross island, it's got to
be the same community."

EVERYDAY LIFE IN
EARLY-BRONZE-AGE IRELAND

While archaeologists have not found the permanent home sites of
Killarney's Beaker folk, a number of houses from the early Bronze
Age have been found in other parts of the country. They give clues
to how people lived, coming together for major religious festivals
and community projects but otherwise living apart in single-family
farmsteads spread throughout the countryside. Houses were
thatched with walls of wickerwork or wood—occasionally stone—

while fields were fenced with dry-stone walls. Deforestation, as woods were cut and cleared for new fields and pasture, probably accelerated the spread of bogs that began to cover earlier fields where crops had once been grown back in the Neolithic Age. The climate was getting wetter as the Bronze Age continued.

Along with growing wheat and barley, Bronze Age farmers raised cattle, pigs, and—to a lesser extent—sheep and goats. Cattle were the most important, as Pat Wallace, director of the National Museum of Ireland, made clear. "In every century since the Stone Age," he insisted, "raising cattle is the key to understanding Ireland. Irish history, Irish archaeology, the great Irish sagas, Irish culture; everything is about cattle." Anyone who has seen the small farming crofts in the west of Ireland would find the ancient landscape quite familiar, although cows would have been smaller and shaggier. Today visitors invited into a remote croft will be offered a cup of tea or a pint of beer, back then it would have been a mug of strong mead, an alcoholic drink made from fermented honey. Mead residue has been found in Beaker pots of the period.

There is little evidence of weapons in the early Bronze Age, so it was probably a quite peaceful time. The country was caught up in huge social changes taking place across Europe at the end of the third millennium B.C., brought about by the increasing availability of metal. Archaeologist John Waddell put things in perspective. "Previously ancestral lineage and family connections decided your place in society. But that's started to change," he explained. "Prestigious material goods have become more important in defining your status."

It is not so different from Ireland today in the era of the "Celtic Tiger," when people are more likely to be judged by what they own and how much they earn than who they are. Instead of a new BMW or Mercedes, the Bronze Age aristocrat strutted around carrying a ceremonial copper axe, new Beaker bowls, and wearing a hammered half-moon of gold—called a lunula—around his neck. People in areas that did not have these prestige goods had to make deals with people who did, and so long-distance trade was well developed. It was a status-conscious time and getting more so as the Bronze Age continued.

Some artifacts from this period have been buried with their owners—presumably aristocrats of high status—but many more seem to have been deliberately placed as offerings in pools or watery ground. The best metal weapons, tools, and jewelry must have been created and displayed for sacred rather than everyday use, ultimately given to water gods and goddesses whose goodwill—as the climate got worse—would have been all important.

THE BURIAL EVIDENCE

At the start of the second millennium B.C., Egypt, Sumer, and the Indus Valley were major urban centers in the ancient world. Within a few centuries, scribes in Egypt and Babylon would be writing descriptions of the people and their society. But writing did not come to Ireland for another 2,500 years, so what little is known about the Irish at this time comes from things that are dug up, especially from graves.

People living in early Bronze Age Ireland seem to have practiced a bewildering array of different burial customs. In some parts of the country they were still building megalithic wedge tombs—a continuation of Neolithic practices—while newer fashions associated with the Beaker folk had the dead crouching in their graves, accompanied by Beaker bowls. Big cemeteries were located next door to cremation grounds where dozens of sets of ashes were set in individual pottery vessels. Other grave mounds combined burned and unburned bodies side-by-side. Sometimes burials were all male, other times both sexes were equally represented. Children are seldom found as they were not yet considered full members of society. These burials are a potpourri of different customs, rituals, and religious beliefs. The population of Ireland at the beginning of the second millennium B.C. must have been made up of people from different societies, speaking different languages, and following different customs. Sea routes seem to have linked the southwest—today's Kerry and Cork counties—with Spain and the Atlantic coast of France. The northwest—counties Donegal, Derry, and Antrim—had links with Scotland while the rich east coast farmlands of counties Meath and Wicklow were within sailing range of Wales and Cornwall. Such different peoples and tribes were linked by well-organized exchange routes along which bronze tools, weapons, and gold moved efficiently around the country.

No one has found rich gold deposits—like Ross Island copper—in Ireland. What little existed in the early Bronze Age came from the Wicklow hills. It was hammered and beaten until paper thin before being crafted into crescent-shaped lunulae earrings and ornaments—sun discs, some with the shape of a cross inscribed into the metal—that may have been fastened to cloaks of wool or leather. Decoration on the lunulae can be stunningly beautiful, with triangles, lozenges, and zigzags delicately carved into the thin gold, echoing the designs on Beaker pots. Unlike bronze, gold is seldom found in graves, it is more likely to be left in bogs or hidden close to prominent landmarks like great standing stones. In the National Museum of Ireland there is a beautiful lunula found in a bog in County Monaghan, still inside its original oak box, just like a modern Tiffany necklace in its presentation case. While bronze represented aristocratic status as well as religious ritual, gold may have been reserved for the gods alone, adorning priest kings whose job was to mediate between the tribe and the Otherworld, where the gods lived.

Confidence in priestly mediators must have been in short supply in the twelfth century B.C. as the quality of Bronze Age life in Ireland deteriorated very quickly. Initially thought to be part of a more gradual deterioration, there is increasing evidence that a single environmental event in 1159 B.C. brought disruption and chaos to Ireland and the rest of the ancient world; the greatest climate catastrophe humanity had faced in thousands of years.

A WORLDWIDE CLIMATE CATASTROPHE

Amazingly, evidence for such a huge event has been discovered only recently, the clues revealed in three-thousand-year-old tree rings. Professor Michael Baillie of Queen's University, Belfast, is one of the scholars who have been investigating this ancient disaster. He is a dendrochronologist, a scientist who studies tree rings. In the middle of a cow pasture in County Armagh, Northern Ireland, he looked more like a lumberjack than a scientist as he used a chain saw to attack an eight-foot high pile of blackened oak stumps. Cows looked on in mild surprise as he cut off several thin wedges of wood and handed them down to the graduate students who had driven out with him from Belfast. "It's pure luck these trees survived," Michael said. "If the farmer hadn't kept them as a windbreak for his cattle, they'd have been cut up and burned long ago." The trees from which he was slicing samples were thousands of years old, oaks that had died and been swallowed up by the bog to emerge only recently as land was drained and peat cut for fuel. At the beginning of the twentieth century, bogs covered 14 percent of the Irish landscape. Weapons, cauldrons, canoes, gold, even complete mummified bodies of sacrificial victims have been found perfectly preserved in Ireland's peat bogs. Chemical properties in the peat stop anything from rotting, so bogs are the "bank vaults" of Irish history, protecting whatever is put in them. A bog-cutter recently described finding a slab of butter, still edible after more than a hundred years.

Back in his university lab, Michael Baillie rummaged through cardboard boxes that contained dozens of bog oak samples, a tiny portion of the 10,000 slices that have been dried, polished, and carefully stacked away as an archive of precisely 7,480 years of Irish environmental records. "These trees preserve information in a way nothing else does," he said. "You're looking at the response of a living organism to what was happening in its environment." Michael put a slice under the microscope, cut from a tree growing on the north side of Lough Neagh—in today's County Antrim—during the mid-twelfth century B.C.

"Each ring represents a year's growth," he explained, "so look at the cellulose vessels in the wood. Eleven sixty B.C. was a perfectly normal year and the tree goes dormant around October. It wakes up again around May 1159 and starts growing but that's it; there's no summer growth in 1159, 1158, and 1157. For eighteen years this tree only stays alive by putting on spring vessels." He looked up from the microscope. "It's like intruding into the private life of a corpse."

The mark of the catastrophe was obvious once Michael told us what to look for, wide healthy rings up to a certain point, then tightly crushed rings with wood cells bunched together so close it was hard to tell where one year ended and the next began. He said they had cross-referenced dozens of samples from many different locations. All tell the same story, as do tree samples from elsewhere in Europe: beginning in 1159 B.C. there was a disaster of biblical proportions.

Calculating such accurate dates is the drudgery of dendro-

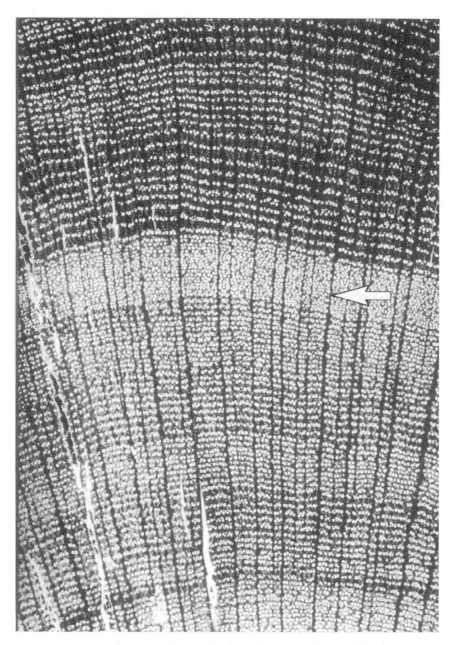

A cross section of a bog oak sample found at Garry Bog in Northern Ireland. The arrow points to the band of eighteen narrow rings from 1159 to 1141 B.C., when a warrior aristocracy first developed in Ireland. (*Michael Baillie*)

chronology, a scientific study less than a century old. Trees live a long time, and those whose dates are known can be matched ring for ring with older trees from the same region, gradually building a chronology back through time. Each time late rings from a previously undated tree match early rings from a tree whose dates are known, the horizon moves further back into the past. It is painstaking work, cross-referencing hundreds of thousands of measurements. Michael unrolled a fat scroll of graph paper on a light-box in his laboratory, a timeline of Irish history running backward from the present to before the first Neolithic farmers arrived in Ireland, then stopped with his finger on a dip between 1159 and 1141 B.C. It looked like graphs more often seen when the bottom falls out of the stock market. "These are the worst growth conditions the trees have seen in more than eight hundred years," he said. "Eighteen years is a horrendously long time. Imagine what eighteen years of failed harvests would do to any civilization. It would pretty much wipe out any agricultural group."

Across the world, Bronze Age civilizations faced similar disaster. The date suggested for the fall of Homeric Troy, the collapse of Mycenae, and the beginning of the Greek Dark Ages is close to 1159 B.C. In the same period the Hittite Empire of Anatolia ended in rebellion and economic chaos while Babylonian poems, inscribed on clay tablets, speak of abandonment by the gods. Egypt was almost overrun by an invasion of sea peoples, nations were on the move, and in distant China terrible events heralded the fall of the mighty Shang dynasty. All these events took place in the mid-twelfth century B.C. Since dendrochronology can pinpoint environmental change within a few months, it is not unreasonable to assume that the root cause of all these worldwide disasters—of which Ireland's troubles were just a small part—struck sometime during the summer of 1159 B.C.

It has been suggested that disaster may have been caused by massive volcanic eruptions throwing up so much dust into the atmosphere that the sun was dimmed for almost two decades. During the cold war, scientists predicted a similar "nuclear winter" effect in the aftermath of nuclear war. It is known that Mount Hekla in Iceland erupted on a massive scale in the mid-twelfth century. But could a massive volcanic eruption create such a worldwide effect? Michael Baillie has a different explanation. "A number of astrophysicists think our planet has had several nasty brushes with cometary debris in the last few thousand years," he said. "Showers of broken up comets entering the atmosphere would cause effects similar to a major volcanic eruption."

Whether from volcanic or cometary strike, a dust-veil shrouding the sun for years would cause serious planetary cooling, but Michael thinks something else was going on to compound the disaster. Tree rings from bog oaks at lower elevations show greater damage than trees higher up. The dust cloud could have caused toxic chemicals to rain down and concentrate in the groundwater. Trees growing in bogs would show more serious effects than trees at higher elevations. Whatever the cause, people did not like the conditions any more than the trees did.

While some scholars think stories of catastrophe and collapse overdramatize what happened in Ireland during the twelfth century B.C., there is no question that society was facing serious problems. There is evidence of more weapon production and a warrior aristocracy gaining power. Hill settlements were fortified for the first time and as Barry Raftery explained: "You don't go to the trouble of building massive hill forts unless you've got a very good reason."

HAUGHEY'S FORT AND THE KING'S STABLES

Hill forts are hilltop settlement sites protected by fortified banks and ditches. A number were first occupied around the time of the climate disaster, including Haughey's Fort in County Armagh, Northern Ireland, less than two miles from Navan Fort—Emain Macha in the Celtic legends—royal site of the Iron Age kings of Ulster. Today Haughey's Fort is an unassuming hill in the center of farmland. In the twelfth century B.C. it was a prominent landmark surrounded by a series of high banks and deep ditches. Excavated postholes suggest the banks were topped with a wooden stockade. Along with the usual archaeological finds of pottery, copper, and even a tiny bit of gold are bones of cattle, pigs, and dogs that are unusually large for the period. Measurements from dog skulls suggest animals more than two feet tall, the size of Labradors or German shepherds today. They are the largest dogs ever found in prehistoric Ireland. John Waddell suggests that those who lived at Haughey's Fort were either selectively breeding their animals for size or were important and powerful enough to be offered gifts of the finest cattle, pigs, and dogs in the region. Carbon dating places Haughey's Fort between 1250 and 900 B.C. but a piece of wood found in one of the ditches was still growing in 1161 B.C. Has dendrochronology again provided a clear date for the fort's construction? Was the tree cut down and built into a defensive wall around a warlord's home in the unsettled years immediately following the 1159–1141 B.C. climate disaster?

Just a short walk away from Haughey's Fort is a grass-choked pool surrounded by a low earth bank. It is called the King's Stables, but the name comes from more recent folklore. Richard Warner, keeper of antiquities at the Ulster Museum in Belfast, took us there on a rainy day as water dripped from overhanging trees and the ground squelched underfoot when we walked to the water's edge. It was appropriate weather for discussing the aftermath of a climate disaster.

"Think about what's happened," Richard said. "Everything's colder and wetter and the corn's not ripening. People are starving; refugees are moving into areas where food's still available. There's fighting everywhere. In such times, people want strong leaders to give them protection. That's how warrior aristocracies begin. Whoever was in charge here built Haughey's Fort as a defense against human enemies, and built this artificial pool in defense against angry gods. The gods who've been causing all this trouble are the gods of the underworld, living in the streams and pools, and it's through the water that they have to be reached and appeased. We found part of the skull of a man who was executed and thrown in, also bones of red deer and dogs. We think bronze swords were thrown in, maybe gold as well."

Anyone who has thrown a coin into a fountain is following a ritual of appeasement that may have begun in the twelfth century B.C. during this catastrophic weather change. While stone circles suggest that the sun still dominated religious belief, water gods and goddesses now assumed a new importance that they would retain into Christian times. Celtic legends in Ireland and Wales about the Lady of the Lake, medieval fairy tales of enchanted underwater castles, even the continuing Catholic practice of pilgrimage to holy wells, come from a time when the powers of water had to be appeased.

"Society's now more warlike," Richard explained. "It always happens during times of stress. People become more warlike; people become more religious." For archaeologists and historians, this period in Irish prehistory is a bonanza because there is so much more to find, more weapons, more things in general. Periods of warfare and trouble usually encourage spurts of technological growth. Ireland recovered and blossomed into a new age of prosperity, but it was a different world; warriors were the new ruling elite, weapons, military might, and ostentatious display the measure of a man's importance.

THE COOKING PIT

It is said you cannot walk a hundred yards through Ireland's countryside without tripping over some kind of ancient monument, but no monuments are more common than the *fulacht fiadh*. More than 4,500 of them are known, 2,000 in County Cork alone, with probably thousands more to find. *Fulacht fiadh* are mounds of burned stone and rock usually found beside a stone or wood-lined pit, close to a lake or dug in boggy ground where the pit naturally fills with water. Stones baked in the fire and raked into the pit will bring 100 gallons of water to the boil in half an hour. A freshly heated rock added from time to time keeps the water boiling for hours; long enough to cook an entire wild boar—favorite meat of warriors—or a whole sheep.

Sagas describe such open-air cooking places being used on hunting trips by heroic warriors of the Fianna and their legendary leader Fionn Mac Cumhaill. The Fianna were a mythical band of warriors sworn to serve the high-king and keep the peace between the warring under-kings of Ireland, much as the Knights of the Round Table served King Arthur in Britain. Until recently it was thought the sagas gave an accurate picture of pre-Christian Celtic Ireland, so it was also taken for granted that the *fulacht fiadh* were cooking sites from the Celtic Iron Age. In reality they are much older—from between 1800 and 800 B.C.—and may not have been used for cooking at all. Producing such large quantities of hot water, they could have been used for washing and dying cloth, or softening animal hides as part of leather manufacture. It has even been suggested that they may have been ritual bathing or sweat houses, covered by a temporary hut of animal skins like Native American sweat lodges. So much of Bronze Age Ireland was bound up with ritual that the *fulacht fiadh* probably served some ceremonial purpose, even if only cooking ritual feasts in honor of a god.

This ancient world is now too distant to be recaptured with any certainty but it is not only scholars and scientists who are fascinated with their country's past. Traditional musician Simon O'Dwyer is founder and leader of a musical group called Bronze Age Horns. He and his colleagues have tried to recreate the music of the Bronze Age by playing instruments identical in every way to those used 3,000 years ago. More than 120 bronze horns have been found in bogs around Ireland, cast sometime after 1000 B.C. For 15 years, Simon has studied these ancient instruments, taught himself how to play them, and commissioned exact replicas to be cast in bronze. Now he and his fellow enthusiasts came to Craggaunowen, in County Clare, to play their authentic Bronze Age instruments in a Bronze Age setting.

In 1973 a philanthropic Irish family with a passion for ancient history restored a ruined Norman castle and created a living history park among the lakes and unspoiled forest that surround it. Here they constructed a crannóg—a prehistoric lake homestead built on an artificial island—and a fully operating *fulacht fiadh*. Simon had arranged to stay there overnight, sleeping in one of the huts and playing music around the fire. But first came the feast.

Simon and his friends had taken a large slab of mutton and wrapped it carefully in straw woven together into a long rope. This straw rope was wound around and around the meat until the bundle was more than twice its original size. The fire had already been burning for several hours, alternate layers of wood and rock, and the pit was full of murky water that had seeped in through the planked wood frame from the nearby lake. One of the musicians started raking the hot stones into the water, along with a lot of ash from the fire. The rocks hissed and bubbled as they sank, and the water soon acquired an unappetizing scum of white ash. It was easy to see why wrapping the meat was so essential. Soon steam was rising from the water, and in a surprisingly short time—no more than twenty minutes—the water in the pit was boiling. Simon carefully lowered the wrapped meat into it. Experiments in ancient living seldom run smoothly. First the straw-wrapped package refused to sink,

A twenty-first-century Irish musician plays an exact replica of a Bronze Age horn from around 800 B.C., which was found buried in a peat bog. (*Leo Eaton*)

bobbing around in the scummy water until Simon set a large rock on it and it sank under the surface with a sinister bubbling. Keeping the water boiling was easy; a new stone every five or ten minutes did the trick, but after a couple of hours bedraggled straw began floating to the surface. The meat wrapping was obviously not up to Bronze Age standards.

Bronze Age diners used flesh-hooks—long pronged bronze hooks—to pick their boiled meat out of pits or the bronze cauldrons found ritually buried in bogs. Simon and his friends improvised with a garden fork, spearing the bleached slab of meat and bringing it to the surface. Surprisingly it was quite good, if bland, once the outside had been cut away. Sagas tell of battles over the "warrior's portion," the choicest cut of the meat. We were happy just to taste it before returning to the crannóg to listen to Simon's Bronze Age horns.

MUSIC IN A BRONZE-AGE HOMESTEAD

Craggaunowen is really a reproduction of an early Christian cran-nóg, but these lake dwellings were in use for thousands of years, from the late Bronze Age to the fifteenth century A.D. Crannógs were made by driving wooden piles into the lake bottom and then building up an artificial island with layers of brushwood, turf, stones, and any other material at hand until it stood above the water's surface. Crannógs were single-family homesteads, so there were usually no more than two huts built on such an artificial is-land. These huts could be round or square with thatched roofs overhanging walls made of wood or wickerwork and plastered with clay. Craggaunowen has two such huts and a small lean-to shed like those where potters or bronze smiths would have worked. Evidence of bronze casting has been found at crannóg sites; metalworking was a cottage industry throughout the Bronze Age. Unlike Crag-gaunowen, which is linked to the shore by a narrow planked bridge, true crannógs could be reached only by boat or causeway. Later Iron Age crannógs show defensive stockades. While these have not been found from the Bronze Age, warlike times would certainly call for some form of defensive palisade. Building a crannóg was a lot of work, and these were high-status homesteads, belonging to local nobility.

On their first night in Craggaunowen, Simon O'Dwyer and his friends settled down around a fire inside one of the huts. Mud and thatch make excellent insulation, and it quickly grew hot, the smoke hanging in a dense cloud just above their heads as it filtered slowly out through the thatch. In earlier times this is where meat and other perishable food was hung and smoked for the winter. They soon retreated outside to sit around a campfire where they played music from a different age. Simon's horns are exact replicas of the 3,000-year-old instruments found in the bog, cast in the same way, in two-piece clay molds with a clay core. Once cast, the two sides are welded together. They look like long cow horns, which were probably models for the original molds. Many of the 120 dis-covered horns can be blown from the end like a modern horn, but others are blown through an opening in the side. Scholars had diffi-culty explaining how these horns were played until musicians like

Simon O'Dwyer got involved. It took an Australian *didgeridoo* player to add the final piece to the puzzle, pointing out that the same circular breathing and tone control used to play a *didgeridoo* would also coax a range of different notes from the ancient instruments.

"They're not particularly loud so we know they weren't war instruments," Simon said. "You wouldn't want to march at the head of an army playing one of these. But they give a great mood feeling, so we think they were used for religious purposes." He and three other horn players sat around the fire while Simon's wife Maria accompanied them on the bodhran, a small Irish drum. The sound was atonal but compelling, moaning and booming across the crannóg between the huts and the palisade wall. Shadows from the fire danced and flickered on the posts of the stockade. Beyond the crannóg was nothing but darkness, just as it would have been in the Bronze Age.

Such times make one wonder about the people who lived in these homesteads so long ago. For all their sophistication, their intelligence, their skill in metals and ceramics, they viewed their world in a very different way. Magic was real, curses worked and could kill. The Otherworld—that unseen world of gods and spirits—existed just outside the circle of firelight. By today's standards they were ruled by superstition, but they also understood the arbitrary forces of nature that ruled their lives. Ritual was everything, to bring the sun and the rain, to encourage fertility and new life, to dispel disease and misfortune. Craftsmen who made the most beautiful weapons, cauldrons, and jewelry were making them as much for ceremonial display as for everyday use. And the greatest achievement of these late Bronze Age craftsmen was in gold.

THE AGE OF GOLD

"This is the real Eldorado period. Ireland may have been the richest place in all of Northern Europe during the late Bronze Age." Back in Dublin, Pat Wallace was showing off the National Museum of Ireland's gold collection, one of the best in the world, a treasure trove of solid gold collars, gold hair ornaments, necklaces, sunflower pins, and heavy cloak fasteners shaped like old-fashioned telephone receivers. "If you were a king wearing one of those, you'd look like a chest of drawers," Pat said. It was a dazzling display. More gold made between 1000 and 800 B.C. has been found in Ireland than anywhere else in Europe, but where it was mined is still a mystery. Ireland's only known source of native gold is in the Wicklow hills, but it could not have produced enough to make even a fraction of the jewelry in circulation at the time. So unless there is a rich Irish gold mine still waiting to be discovered, it probably arrived as gold ingots from somewhere in Central Europe. The Irish might live in thatched houses rather than great cities like those in Egypt and China but the skill of Irish goldsmiths and bronzesmiths was equal to the world's best. A huge range of merchandise—buckets, cauldrons, swords, shields, spears, and a bewildering array of ornamental gold—was commissioned by the warrior aristocracy who controlled the trade routes and processes of exchange. John Waddell suggested that "Ireland in 800 B.C. was made up of lots of small chiefdoms linked one to another, and with similar communities in Western Britain, by an extensive system of alliances." It was a world preoccupied with ritual, status, and ostentatious displays of wealth.

THE ROYAL SITES

By the late Bronze Age several of the ceremonial sites in use since Neolithic times were taking on greater regional importance, ritual centers for growing tribal federations. Ireland's numerous small chiefdoms may already have begun coming together into the sort of regional kingdoms monastic records tell us existed much later in the seventh and eighth centuries A.D. So-called royal centers, like Tara in the east, site of the legendary high-kingship of Ireland, Emain Macha in the north, and Rathcroghan in the west, were among the most important. Rather than centers of secular power, these were religious and ritual centers for an entire area, much as modern cathedrals are centers for dioceses containing many different parishes. Historian and Gaelic language scholar Edel Bhreathnach likes to call Tara and the other royal sites "cathedrals of a certain society in Ireland." Throughout prehistory, religion and leadership were inseparable. "For thousands of years," Edel said, "these sites were associated with important ceremonies like the inauguration of a king, the administration of justice, and the making of laws. In a land with no towns, they were places for a scattered people to get together for fairs, races, and markets. But everything was secondary to their overall purpose; they were where you came to worship your gods."

Today nothing remains of these sites but grass-covered mounds and great ditches where sheep and cattle graze. Here too, like the stone circle at Ross Island, the ditches lie inside circular earth banks. The builders enclosed the sites to contain the magic and power of the Otherworld forces in the center.

It is impossible to know if these sites were as important in the late Bronze Age as they later became, but archaeologists have found a continuity of ceremonial monuments, concentrations of wooden circles and henges built in the same style and the same places for hundreds of years. Archaeologist Conor Newman displayed pictures of three hundred large post-holes found on the hill of Tara. It was the base of a ceremonial circle as big as Stonehenge in England but made completely of wood. "You're felling three hundred trees to erect this monument," he said. "It makes me wonder if the trees themselves didn't come from a single sacred grove. Everything done here had ritual significance, so transforming a sacred forest into a great monument on the hill of Tara would be quite in keeping."

By the end of the Bronze Age, these great "royal" sites were probably already attracting people from far away to the great festivals of the agricultural year, the two solstices—the longest and shortest days of the year—and the four quarter days that marked the start of each new season.

THE END OF THE BRONZE AGE

Toward the end of the Bronze Age, the archaeological record goes strangely silent. From 700 to 300 B.C. is a dark age in Irish prehistory, the period during which iron technology first arrived in the lands around the Irish Sea and, it was once thought, when waves of Celtic invaders arrived from Europe (around 500 B.C.). The coming of the Celts, if they came at all, is the subject of the next chapter, but something was going wrong in Ireland over these dark centuries. Michael Baillie has found evidence in trees from the period that weather was again causing problems across Europe. No obvious catastrophe this time, just an overall worsening of conditions that may have reached its peak in the fifth century B.C. Plague often follows weather change as disease-carrying animals are forced out of their normal habitats in search of food, spreading infection to new areas without natural immunity. In classical Greece, Athens recorded a terrible plague in 430 B.C. that probably spread elsewhere through Europe, maybe even reaching Ireland along the ocean trade routes as did other plagues in later times. Some archaeologists and historians suggest a collapse of the trading networks that had linked Ireland with the rest of Europe. Economic chaos may have heralded the end of the Bronze Age in Ireland. Iron swords found near the coast probably came from sea-raiders, attacking just as Vikings would do more than a thousand years later. Archaeological evidence suggests a lessening of contact with Europe rather than the arrival of new Celtic colonists or invaders.

Just as the 1159 B.C. climate catastrophe changed the structure of Irish society and created a wealthy warrior aristocracy, so bad weather and disease six hundred years later may have caused the fall of previously powerful dynasties and begun a long period of war and instability. In bad times craftsmen do not have the leisure or incentive to create great works of bronze and gold, even if the raw materials are available. Bronze and gold vanish from the archaeological record at this time. Ireland, which for centuries had been one of the richest places in Europe, fades into silence. When it becomes visible again, in the last centuries B.C., the reality of an Irish Iron Age has been overshadowed in popular imagination by legends and sagas, fictional stories about mighty warriors and a heroic Celtic age.

[3]

Ireland and the Celtic Culture

OF ALL THE WORDS now associated with Ireland and the Irish, the most familiar and hackneyed is probably the word "Celtic." Pick up any catalog selling Irish goods and the word is splashed across every page: Celtic music, Celtic spirituality, Celtic crosses—there are even "Celtic" mouse pads. This word coupled with anything Irish is now commonplace and accepted with total validity. But how valid an assumption is this? How truly "Celtic" is Ireland? This question is one of the most significant ones addressed by modern-day Irish archaeologists and historians and has some very interesting answers.

THE NINETEENTH-CENTURY WRITERS

The widespread use of the word "Celtic" in its application to things Irish is actually rooted mainly in the nineteenth century, in what became known as the Celtic Renaissance. This literary and cultural movement was an attempt by Irish writers and folklorists of the period to establish a sense of identity for the Irish people at a time when both politically and socially the country was in a deep malaise. There were valid sociological reasons for this need to establish a sense of nationhood and a legitimacy to Ireland. The forced parliamentary union of Ireland and Britain in 1800 was both an economic and a political failure. The tragic Famine of the 1840s had taken its toll and the Irish landscape was a wasteland of misery and confusion. The population had declined dramatically as a result of death from starvation, disease, and emigration. The slow draining of the countryside from emigration continued for the remainder of the century. The Famine was to leave deep psychological scars on the Irish memory. As one modern Irish historian has written: "The Famine was a crisis of the mind as well as the body."

Celtic revivalists like W. B. Yeats and Douglas Hyde, working in the 1890s, deliberately set about searching out Ireland's ancient past to create a sense of identity and self-respect for the Irish people. In the wake of so much destruction they were determined to establish or re-establish national pride by seeking out the origins of Irish civilization and clearing away as much historical debris as possible. They earnestly sought to discover what Ireland and the Irish were like before the English invasion of the twelfth century and before Christian influence. As one of the protagonists of this movement said, "Ireland is appealing to the past to escape the confusion of the present." The leaders of this revival accepted at face value the writings in the ancient texts, written from the sixth to the twelfth centuries, and used these as historical foundations to create an Ireland that possibly never existed—or at least not as they saw it. They took as valid history these texts written hundreds of years after the events they describe. It was in the nineteenth century that the idealized notion of a long forgotten, homogeneous, Celtic Irish people became the accepted, popular notion of the origin of Irish ethnicity. This idea has persisted into our time, as have other cultural developments of the period.

Much of what we think of as being popular Irish culture originated in the nineteenth century. For example, Irish dance as we now know it was "developed" in the nineteenth century when set dancing was first introduced. Irish dancing masters adapted continental dances, like the quadrille, to the style of solo step dancing, which was introduced into Ireland in the eighteenth century from Europe. The first *céilí* was organized by the Gaelic League in 1894 as a way of gathering people together to promote a sense of Irish culture, but primarily to encourage them to speak the Irish language, which was in serious decline. The oldest known Irish music is hundreds of years old, not thousands, so it can hardly claim to be of ancient "Celtic" times. The Irish language, however, does have a long historical link to the past, and this remains one of the most valid threads in Irish history. Modern archaeological methods and linguistic evidence offer some answers about what life was actually like in pre-Christian Ireland. Through these methods we can gain perhaps a more valid assessment of Irish prehistory.

WHO WERE THE CELTS?

We know that prior to the 1700s the term "Celtic" was not in use in the English language. The eighteenth-century classification came about as a result of linguistic evidence, which linked the native languages of Ireland, Scotland, and Wales to the continental language of the people whom Julius Caesar described as *Celtae*. The word "Celtic" came originally from the Greeks who, around 600 B.C., called the people who lived to the north of Greece *Keltoi*. We know also from references in both Greek and Roman texts that they inhabited a large area in Central Europe. Archaeologists do not believe that the Celts were one homogeneous people but were composed of many tribes speaking a similar language. How these different tribes came to speak a common language is not known, but these various peoples, referred to as Celtic, spoke a language which was a predecessor of modern-day Irish. Thus the word "Celtic" became a way of describing the people who spoke the Gaelic language.

These continental Celtic-speaking people did not commit anything to writing. This is certainly not to say they were an ignorant people. By tradition, information was committed to memory and passed on orally. There are no written records in Ireland before the arrival of Christianity in the fifth century, but there were sophisticated schools of memory where poets, storytellers, and lawyers would memorize what their various disciplines required. So successful was this method that when writing did arrive in Ireland it merely gave form to the rich culture, which had predated it and in many ways survived for hundreds of years after the arrival of the first Christian missionaries. A form of early writing had developed and Ogham, a complicated script based on the Latin alphabet, has survived, but it was usually only used on commemorative pillar stones to identify the dead.

The Romans claimed that the Celts were elitists and would not commit anything to writing for fear that the information would become commonplace and available to all. Julius Caesar, in his description of the Celts in his *Gallic War,* writes that the Celts "consider it improper to commit their studies to writing," and he adds that they knew Greek letters and used these for "all other purposes." The Celtic tribes, Caesar suggests, did not trust the written word because it meant that knowledge could be dispersed and that druids and poets would lose their special status within society. But whatever the reason, it means that when we talk about this period in Irish history we rely on texts written only after the arrival of Christianity. More valid sources for information are the archaeological and linguistic evidence, but the texts reveal some interesting insights about what life might have been like in Ireland so long ago.

THE CELTS AND IRELAND— THE MONASTIC TEXTS

By tradition it was believed that the Celts first came to Ireland around 500 B.C. in one massive invasion. Few Irish scholars now accept this. This myth was based on an Irish document known as the *Leabhar Gabhála,* or *Book of Invasions:* a text first written down in Christian times by monastic scribes around the seventh century and perfected in the twelfth. This is more than a thousand years after the supposed event. Many Irish documents date from these years, which purport to describe pre-Christian life and laws in Ireland. Not only do they depict the arrival of the Gaelic-speaking people in Ireland, they also tell us much about everyday life. These documents are written in the Irish language, and in modern English translations the term "Celtic" is often used as a substitution for the word "Gaelic." The texts also include the great Irish epic, *An Táin Bó Cuailgne* (The Cattle Raid of Cooley). But the story is believed to be older than the period it was written in, and there can be little doubt that it is a descendant of an older, oral form. With its fascinating descriptions of gods and goddesses and druids with supernatural powers, it is obviously rooted in the pre-Christian era. But how much of the original story remains and how much of it is later invention we do not know. This written mythology abounds with stories of heroes and heroines who are said to have lived in Ireland in prehistoric times. There are tales of strong women and warrior men and gods and goddesses who intermarry with mortals and produce extraordinary offspring. They give us wonderful descriptions of love, passion, cattle raiding, poets who have powers to paralyze with their words, women who train warriors for battle, and druids who can foretell the outcome of wars.

WHAT THE LEGENDS CLAIM

For a long time these texts were taken as being the record of actual events passed on through oral memory into historical times and then written down. In the *Book of Invasions* the original inhabitants of Ireland are said to have been the mythological Fir Bolg people. The Fir Bolg play a sociopolitical role in the development of Ireland. They are, for instance, credited with dividing Ireland into fifths: the provinces of Leinster, Munster, Ulster, Connaught, and the royal area known as Meath. They also are said to have established the classic Irish social system of kingship and the notion of its sacred character. These first mythological people are followed by the Túatha Dé Danann—or people of the goddess Danu—who are skilled in magic and druidry. They are said to arrive in Ireland and defeat the Fir Bolg in a number of battles and take over the country. All of this long pseudo-history eventually leads up to the main event, the coming of the Gaels, the Celts.

In the *Book of Invasions,* the Sons of Míl, the ancestors of the Gaels, are described as arriving in Ireland on the feast of Beltine or May 1. They come on shore in the southeast of the country in modern-day Kerry. Amergin, the chief poet, goes on shore first and sets his foot on the soil of Ireland. He then immediately recites a poem in which he identifies himself with the whole of creation. His very words denote the importance of the occasion:

I am an estuary to the sea
I am a wave of the ocean
I am the bull of seven battles
I am the eagle on the rock
I am a flash from the sun

I am the plant of beauty
I am a salmon in the pool
I am the strength of art . . .

This poem is similar to other "foundation" poetry uttered by the mythological founders of other peoples. The mythmakers who first wrote this story knew what they were doing. They were giving validity to the lineage of the Irish. Amergin is claiming the land of Ireland for his people and staking their legitimate claim as the rightful inhabitants. This was an important declaration at the time when the history of Ireland was first being written down.

On the purpose served by these early stories for the society of the time, Patricia Kelly, a historian from the National University of Ireland, explains that "One of the functions of the tales is to say how far back things began. Meaning that this tradition is well established, that is to say it legitimizes it and argues for its retention." A sense of belonging to the land and unity in ethnicity is important in establishing the legitimacy and lineage of a people. In claiming a long and legitimate ancestry these Irish writers were putting Ireland on par with the great classical nations of the known world. The law tracts explain that poets held the highest position in Irish society, so having a poet claim the land of Ireland would have been very appropriate. It would therefore have given a legitimate claim to the present.

THE MYTHOLOGY

The Gaels, the mythology asserts, having come on shore and claimed the land, then go on to defeat the previous inhabitants, the Túatha Dé Danann. The Gaels then set out toward Tara, the principal place of worship in Ireland in ancient times. On the way there they meet, among others, the goddess Ériu, an important deity who gave her name to the island of Ireland. She is friendly and welcoming toward them and foretells that Ireland will belong to the Sons of Míl for all time. A fortuitous prophesy. Ireland thus rightfully becomes the land of the Gael. This beautiful, romantic story remained a part of Irish thinking for hundreds of years. First written down to create and establish a notion of Irishness, it served that purpose well and became a part of Irish identity. It was commonplace then, as now, to trace ancestors back to some declared moment in time—it gave a sense of righteousness to social claims of nobility. Some innovative authors could trace a chieftain's or king's family back to Noah and the flood. This was not a practice unique to Ireland. Origin myths are typical of any society that wants to make legitimate claims to a noble lineage. The Romans did precisely the same thing when their early writers invented a connection with them and the ancient Greek world, giving the Romans a position of legitimacy within classical Mediterranean civilization.

With the spread of the English language in later Irish history, these stories written in Irish were largely forgotten by the educated Irish population who had become almost exclusively English speaking. So when the nineteenth-century revivalists went looking for the roots of Ireland they sought out these old texts and took them to be historically legitimate. The "invasion" of the Celtic-speaking people became a commonly accepted historical fact. It was this influence that cast such a long shadow over the twentieth century, and that continues to shape the ideas in Irish popular culture.

ARCHAEOLOGICAL AND LINGUISTIC EVIDENCE

There is a problem with what is written in these ancient texts. In the mid-twentieth century, when Irish archaeologists went looking for evidence to support the stories, they found no material evidence in Ireland to uphold the theory of a mass invasion of Celtic people at the time claimed in the texts—or at any time for that matter.

The year of the supposed Celtic invasion of Ireland, 500 B.C., is the period known as the Iron Age. The Iron Age artifacts that have been identified as Continental Celtic were found in modern-day Switzerland and are known as La Tène style from the region they were discovered. This was an art form which developed around the middle of the fifth century B.C. The style, often described as the first nonclassical art of Europe, is full of scrolls and spirals and waves of lines which twist and turn in a complex matrix of design. The earliest artifact of this style found in Ireland is a torc (a neck ornament) found at Knock, County Roscommon, which dates to a slightly later time, around the third century B.C. Barry Raftery believes that this piece is obviously an import, but "it is an isolated

piece [found] in the west of the country, so its wider cultural significance should not be exaggerated." In other words, one swallow
doth not a summer make. Many more imported artifacts would
have to be found to support the theory of a mass invasion and they
have not. There are only a few continental La Tène artifacts from
this period in Ireland, and they may have arrived for a number of
reasons. They might simply be the result of trading, or they could
have been brought in by a small elite group. These foreign La Tène
artifacts that have been discovered in Ireland are mostly prestige
objects like horse trappings, scalpels, and trumpets—not the uten-
sils of ordinary people usually found when there is a mass movement of people into a new area. This is precisely what puzzles
archaeologists like Barry who have done extensive work on this period in Irish prehistory. He believes that the few articles found in
Ireland of Continental or British Celtic origin "clearly belonged to
an aristocratic elite who may have traveled to Ireland and settled
there alongside the already established community." He goes on to
stress that "nobody believes in large-scale [Celtic] migration into
the country. At best, we're talking about small-scale intrusions."
Barry thinks that the total absence of what ordinary people would
have used is an indication that no large Celtic invasion occurred.

About a hundred years later, native Irish workshops were producing a local version of La Tène-style decoration. When the La
Tène-style of art came to Ireland, the Irish developed a native version of it, which was to remain a feature of Irish art well into the
Christian period and beyond. How this importation of style happened no one knows. It is possible that it was part of an exchange
pattern of elite goods between people of high status. Contrary to
what the texts say concerning an invasion, for the most part there is
archaeological continuity in Ireland between the earlier Bronze Age
and the "Celtic" Iron Age. This indicates no shift in population
type. In other words, there is no evidence for any change in lifestyle or of a major group of new people coming in. As regards burial
rites for example, there is no change in how funerals were conducted between these periods, and no Continental Celtic-type burial chambers have ever been found in Ireland. Archaeologists
cannot find support for any evident change in lifestyle between the
older period and the period in which the Celts are supposed to have
arrived.

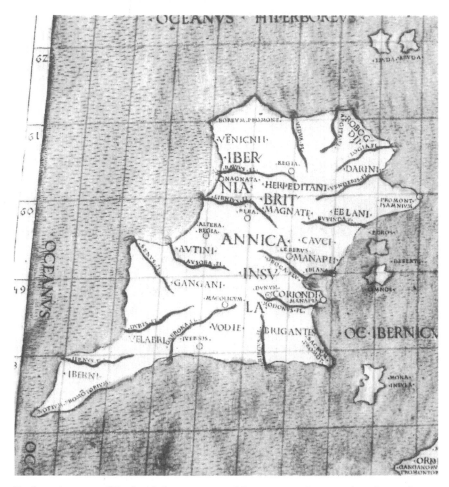

Ptolemy's map of Ireland dates to roughly A.D. 150. It provides the earliest evidence of the Celtic language in Ireland, but archaeologists insist that no Celtic invasion occurred. (*Royal Irish Academy*)

THE IRISH CELTIC LANGUAGE

In spite of the lack of archaeological evidence we do know that the Celtic language and culture came to Ireland. There is ample evidence to show that by around A.D. 100 Ireland was a Celtic-speaking country. One major source in support of this is Ptolemy's map of Ireland dating to about A.D. 150, which shows the country to be Celtic speaking. Ptolemy was a Greek geographer, and Professor Donnchadh Ó Corráin, medieval historian at University College Cork, believes that this is the strongest evidence for the arrival of the Celtic or Gaelic language into Ireland. This is the first absolute proof that the language arrived, and linguistic scholars feel that it must have been well established by this time. In addition, early

Ogham stones bearing the Celtic script and dating to around A.D. 200 can be found scattered throughout Ireland. Written texts from the sixth century show the vernacular language in Ireland to be the Irish language, Gaelic. The pre-Celtic language, whatever it was, was gone by this time, leaving only traces behind. These old texts also describe a Celtic society similar to that found on the Continent with comparable gods and goddesses.

A MIGRATION OVER TIME?

According to Donnchadh Ó Corráin, this transference of language could only be possible by a large number of Celtic-speaking people coming to settle in Ireland. Not just warriors but whole families must have settled, possibly over a long period of time—perhaps as long as five hundred years or more. A once-off invasion as described in the texts is not likely in the face of the lack of archaeological evidence. Donnchadh explains that it takes women with families to transfer a language: "In order to make this country Celtic speaking, a lot of Celtic speakers had to come. This is not a matter of race; this is a matter of language and speech. And if a lot of Celtic speakers had to come they couldn't be just warriors, they had to be full families because the only way to change the language of a country is [for the newcomers] to have families. You need women to rear the children speaking Celtic. Otherwise [the men] go and marry the natives, and of course they don't wind up speaking Celtic at all."

Just as significantly, he also explains that women are more phatic than men: women use language for social communication more than men do. So language tends to travel with women and not with men. Consequently, with male-only invasions the typical pattern is for them to intermarry with the local female population and wind up speaking that language and not keeping their own. This was to happen with the Viking invaders who intermarried with the native Irish women and quickly lost their own language. Similarly, in the twelfth century, when the Anglo-Normans came to Ireland, it was a male-only invasion. Soon after they intermarried into Irish families they also lost their language. Within a generation the Normans were all speaking Irish. They became, as the saying goes, "more Irish than the Irish themselves." So the Celtic language, which did impose itself on the country, could only have done so, according to Donnchadh Ó Corráin, by the arrival of great numbers of Celtic families. That is not to say that there was a massive invasion. The transference of language and culture could have happened over a very long period of time. Some scholars now believe that there might have been a slow trickling in of the newcomers, possibly over half a millennium, and not one huge invasion so romantically described in the texts.

Nevertheless many archaeologists argue that the transference of language could have happened without any Celtic people coming to Ireland at all. John Waddell says, "There was a prolonged and persistent pattern of [sea] contact between the peoples of Ireland, Britain, and the continent extending over perhaps thousands of years. This contact could have allowed a Celtic language to slowly emerge in these various localities." This would explain the total lack of archaeological evidence. Whatever the explanation of this puzzle, there remains no direct evidence for a presence of continental Celtic people in Ireland.

TARA—ANCIENT RITUAL SITE

The hill of Tara was an important site in pre-Christian Ireland. For centuries it was the principal place of ritual worship and had such a status that anyone claiming the high-kingship had first to claim jurisdiction over Tara. The name Tara comes from an obscure old Irish word *Temair,* meaning either "a height with a view" or a "sacred place," either of which is appropriate for describing this location. It is a beautiful, open, breezy site in County Meath. It is a feature of these ancient ritual sites that they are usually on high ground, but this site is particularly imposing. It is not a steep climb to the top of the hill, so it always comes as a surprise to see how high the Hill of Tara sits above the surrounding terrain. It has a very impressive perspective and appears to dominate the central plain of Ireland, commanding panoramic views in all directions. No wonder the ancients chose it as the primary site of worship and kingship. Tara holds especially significant interest and curiosity because of the repeated references to its importance in the texts. The Celtic god Lugh and the goddess Medb are particularly associated with the site. Lugh is one of the most important of the Celtic gods, and he was the divine manifestation of the kingship of Tara. Medb was the goddess of Tara and would rule Tara herself if no suitable candidate for king was presented.

Such an important site as Tara would certainly reflect what was happening in Iron Age Ireland and yield some clues as to the demographics of the society. The results of recent excavations are indeed interesting. Edel Bhreathnach says, "During excavations in 1997 they found enough material to successfully date *Ráth na Rí*, the enclosure of the kings, to 94 or 95 B.C. This is the large oval enclosure that circles the hilltop. When it was just newly constructed the ditch inside its earthen rampart was up to three meters deep. It would have been an enormously impressive monument." This indicates much social activity and an important presence at Tara during the Iron Age. But no evidence was found there to support a Celtic invasion. In fact there is little change between the older Bronze Age and the Iron Age according to the archaeological data. Nonetheless Ogham script of a later date has been found at the site, indicating a cultural presence of the Irish language. The presence of an elite group may explain this apparent enigma. A further piece of evidence for the theory of an elite group is indicated by the finding of prestigious Roman objects dating to the later Iron Age of the second to fourth centuries A.D. Archaeologist Helen Roach explains, "We also found exotic items like a lead seal, glass vessels—objects which are really only found in very special sites. And you can trace them back really to Roman Britain rather than a native object. But that doesn't mean that there were Roman people here. I think it means that they were a powerful elite group who had contacts with Roman Britain and were able to procure these objects which . . . to an Irish family were very special and very prestigious objects to own." Tara had wealthy occupants during this period who may have traded with the Roman Empire or traveled there and returned with some prestige items. But the overall continuity between the older Bronze Age and the Iron Age suggests that if new people came in they must have been very few in number.

The idea of a wealthy elite is one that Barry Raftery also suggests for the presence of imported Roman artifacts found at Tara. Parts of a wine goblet and fragments of several flagons have been found at the site in the area known as the Rath of the Synods. These objects date to the first and second centuries A.D. As these items are not of native origin and are obviously imported, Barry thinks they are possibly "indicative of an affluent elite who held possession of Tara at this time." Such items suggest that the inhabitants could afford wine and owned goblets from which to drink it. The possibility exists that there was a cultural aristocracy here, an upper class who managed to impose their language on the native population. Edel Bhreathnach surmises that maybe "at some stage a group with whatever form of language that ultimately became Irish came to Ireland, and perhaps they took a grip on the part of the country where Tara stands. This is a key part of the country where they may have held key institutions and through their dominance and political astuteness may have managed to impose the language." The entire progression from the older language to the newer one could have taken hundreds of years.

There is much support for this theory of a process of slow, peaceful cultural penetration, as no evidence exists for a violent incursion. In this way there was more than likely a blending in of the Celtic newcomers with the older established population, and in time all became Celtic speaking. Donnchadh Ó Corráin suggests that it is also likely that the Celts "remained a minority in Ireland." They gave their language and culture to the country, but Ireland has obviously more pluralistic roots than previous generations believed. By the late Iron Age the Irish were speaking a Celtic language, but the population was made up of various different kinds of peoples who arrived over a broad space of time, many of whom were certainly not Celtic. The appellation "Celtic" as applied to Ireland can only be used in terms of the language and culture and not as a pure, homogenous, ethnic identity.

THE IRISH TEXTS AND THE GREAT IRISH EPIC

What do the texts tell us of this pre-Christian culture? The stories that were recorded probably originated hundreds of years before they were written down. There was an oral tradition of bardic learning by which stories and poems were handed down through the generations. The Roman conviction that the Celts were elitist might have some truth in it. Making the stories available to a wider audience could possibly have infringed on the special position of the poet in early Irish society. The poets enjoyed such a place of high honor and prestige that they may not have been willing to share this status or see it diminish. Their training was so rigorous that it could take up to twenty years to become a master poet, or *Ollamh*. They would have been very proud of their abilities to remember and embellish the stories and poems handed down to them.

THE GREAT IRISH EPIC— AN TÁIN BÓ CUAILGNE

An Táin Bó Cuailgne, The Cattle Raid of Cooley, is the greatest of all the ancient Irish stories and is the oldest epic written in a vernacular European language. The story is obviously pagan in ethos and origin and it tells us something about life in pre-Christian Ireland, including the religion and politics. However it is not to be taken as historical fact, and a careful reading reveals much about the mythmakers who committed this story to writing in Christian times. It is a testimony to the skill of the early Irish poets that the basic tenet of such a complicated story was probably committed to memory and passed along over many hundreds of years before being written down. Originally written in Old Irish, *The Táin* is now widely available in English translation and remains a popular form of entertainment. Characters from *The Táin* are well known in contemporary Ireland and are still a part of Irish culture. Like all grand epics, it is a great story.

MEDB'S DOMESTIC DISPUTE

The Táin is the story of Queen Medb of Connaught and a family dispute which escalates and eventually becomes a war between the provinces of Connaught and Ulster. In the story, Medb is described as a beautiful, strong, and proud woman who is used to getting what she wants and never questions her right to determine her own destiny. One night, as she and her husband Ailill lie in bed, they get into an argument over which one of them is the more important and more powerful person. Ailill starts the disagreement by his seemingly passive musings that it is well for her to be married to a rich man. "I am thinking," says Ailill, rather foolishly as it turns out, "how much better off you are today than the day I married you."

Medb is somewhat astonished and more than a little angered at this statement and immediately replies that it is he, Ailill, who is a kept man and lucky to have married her. It is Medb's haughty and immediate assertion that she is the one who rules the province and has more possessions than he has that puts the flame to the kindling. Naturally enough, he is not amused at her arrogant response and becomes quite angry. This small domestic dispute would eventually escalate into a war between Connaught and Ulster. A lesson perhaps that there is nothing small about any power play.

COMPARING THEIR POSSESSIONS

Medb's boast is not an idle one. For one thing, she has the law on her side. The old Brehon Laws, the laws of ancient Ireland, allow her to own goods legally independent of her husband. What she brings into the marriage remains hers. Moreover, because she has inherited the throne of Connaught and other riches from her father and Ailill married her and lives in her territory, it is Medb who is legally responsible for him and for his debts. She reminds him that she is responsible for what the law calls his "honor price," the value placed on him under ancient Irish law. If he should get into any kind of legal dispute with someone or into any kind of trouble, Medb would be responsible for paying his fines. In other words, she claims, it is she who is in charge of his life and not the other way around. So it is a legitimate claim that she has to superiority. To compensate for what he probably feels is a social embarrassment, Ailill tries to prove that he has more possessions than she has.

Servants are sent to every corner of their home to painstakingly drag out all their belongings, including even their lowest possessions. Medb's goods are to be put on one side and compared to Ailill's. The descriptions of their possessions are very elaborate and quite entertaining. The ancient storytellers loved to embellish every detail and would probably have held their audience spellbound with the intricate descriptions of the beauty of each valued item. Gold rings, bracelets, great silks, and fabrics of all colors, decorated vessels, pots and washpails, are all laid out. Even livestock is included in this detailed inventory. Herds of sheep and cattle are brought in from the fields to compare side-by-side. We are left to imagine what the servants might be thinking throughout all of this, but life in Medb's household could not have been uneventful, and they were probably well used to such goings-on.

THE WHITE BULL AND THE BROWN BULL

In the way the story unfolds it is evident, interestingly enough, that not only were the ancient Irish a spiritual people but they also obviously held material possessions in high regard. Their wealth and assets were plainly very important to them and to their sense of self-worth. The final "victory," in Medb and Ailill's domestic dispute will go to which one can claim to own more possessions. Medb and Ailill are as proud and possessive of their belongings as any modern-day yuppie. But because wealth was judged primarily in cattle in those days, Medb is upset by the discovery that Ailill has a beautiful white bull called Finnbennach, the white horned. Everything else between wife and husband turns out to be equal except for this beautiful bull. Poor Medb has nothing to compare with this creature. She is far too egotistical and proud to accept this inequality, and she is not to be so easily outdone. Who can blame her—her father had left her the province to rule, and she is queen. Why should she accept second place to her husband Ailill or to anyone else for that matter? So she sends her envoys throughout the whole of Ireland to find a better bull. They find it in Ulster. It belongs to Dáire Mac Fiachna who lives in a place called Cuailgne. So famous is this magnificent creature that he is known throughout Ireland as the Brown Bull of Cuailgne.

MEDB SENDS TO ULSTER FOR
THE BROWN BULL

Immediately Medb sends her envoys into Ulster to ask Dáire to "loan" her the bull for one year. In exchange for this she offers him fifty yearling heifers with the return of the borrowed bull. Medb's chief envoy, Fergus Mac Roth, is known as the chief herald of Ireland and is well received. Dáire is delighted with such a generous offer, so he agrees to give the bull to Fergus who will convey it back to Medb. A large celebration feast follows this agreement, and Fergus and his servants join in the fun. The food is sumptuous and the wine flows, but it also has the effect of loosening the tongue of

Medb's envoys who boast that had they not been given the bull Medb would have sent in her army to take it by force. A proud boast uttered at a moment of unintentional indiscretion, brought on perhaps by relief at getting the bull and a little too much wine. But the indiscreet words bring trouble. Unfortunately one of Dáire's household servants overhears this bragging and goes to him in fury.

There had already been some upset in Ulster at the idea of the brown bull going outside of the province. Much of Ulster's prestige rested on this magnificent creature. Dáire had tried to quiet this unease by pointing out the great deal he had struck with the queen of Connaught. But upon hearing of the boasts of the Connaught men, Dáire's reaction is instant and precipitous: "I swear by the gods my people swear by, that they will not take the brown bull away unless they take him by force." But saying no to Medb is not going to stop her. In response she gathers her sizable army together. She will march on Ulster and take what she wants by force. If diplomacy has failed, a different kind of persuasion will win the day. She intends to challenge the king of Ulster's army and defeat him with her military might. Thus starts the war between Ulster and Connaught over the Brown Bull of Cuailgne.

CÚ CHULAINN—THE GREATEST OF IRISH HEROES

The king of Ulster lives in a place called Emain Macha, now known as Navan Fort, which lies just to the west of the town of Armagh. Situated on high ground, it is similar in appearance to the other royal sites in Ireland. Today all that remains of a once-thriving place is a large grass mound where long ago throngs of people gathered for ritual activities. It was here, so the sagas relate, that the king of Ulster lived, as did the greatest of Irish heroes, Cú Chulainn.

Cú Chulainn was the powerful champion of the Ulster army, and his memory still symbolizes nobility and physical strength. He has both human and supernatural powers as his mother was a human woman and his father was Lugh, the god of the harvest. Cú Chulainn is essentially the all-time Irish superhero, but whether he is based on any real person no one knows. Like Medb, he has been fêted into a quasi-historical figure. It is possible that he was an oral memory of a great hero of long ago committed to writing in the early Christian period, but there is no evidence for this. Nonetheless, his status as an unconquerable warrior remains a powerful symbol in Ireland. The enduring image of Cú Chualainn as the invincible, superhuman warrior was to inspire Irish nationalists thousands of years after he is said to have lived and died. He was the embodiment of indomitable Irish nationalism and guardian of a righteous cause for the early-twentieth-century patriots. W. B. Yeats was to write that the ghost of Cú Chulainn "stalked through" the Dublin General Post Office in 1916 during the Irish rebellion against British rule. In present day Dublin a large statue depicting the noble death of the still powerful and young Cú Chulainn adorns the window of the General Post Office in commemoration of the 1916 Rising.

THE CURSE OF ULSTER

This is the hero Medb's army faces when they march on Ulster. In spite of druidic warnings against success, Medb remains determined, assembling her warriors and war chariots to meet the Ulster army. The war is nasty, with serious losses on both sides. The Ulster soldiers are seized by an ancient curse imposed on the men of Ulster, which renders them powerless in moments of crisis. The hero Cú Chulainn alone is immune to this affliction, and finds himself fighting arm to arm with the pride of Medb's army, the powerful Ferdia. Cú Chulainn finally kills Ferdia but immediately laments it bitterly because Ferdia is in fact his own foster brother. Fosterage of children was a common custom in ancient Ireland and was actually governed by rules in Brehon Law. The moment of victory is marred by the killing of a foster brother—is this an early anti-war cry? Chaos ensues with the two bulls fighting each other. The white bull is killed and the brown bull runs home to Cuailgne and dies, leaving a trail of destruction.

THE CHRISTIAN INFLUENCE

Bearing in mind that what we have of the story comes to us by the writings of Christian monks who lived hundreds of years after the events of the tale, a close reading of the text reveals a bias against Medb and an enhancement of the male hero, Cú Chulainn. These stories in fact are about two time periods: the times of the actual events and the period in which they were written down. Patricia Kelly is quick to point out how the Christian writers determined the outcome of the pagan story. "What they were trying to do was to use these existing legends to tell stories which pointed up morals and provided examples for acceptable or nonacceptable behavior." Medb's boldness, her flair, her sense of self-importance, and her determination to upstage her husband are all recorded but so also is her final disgrace, her ultimate failure to triumph because of her own foolishness. As Patricia says, "Cú Chulainn gets it right all the time, and Medb makes mistakes all along the line, which makes me think that they are talking about [their own] contemporary period. I think that must be one of the elements of the contemporary relevance of this tale, that the monastic scribes are making a comment about queens who take on too much and try to overreach the role that the church would like to have seen them confined to."

Perhaps in the older, oral version, which presumably predated the written form, Medb did triumph and ruled successfully and wisely, without reference to her husband. Perhaps in the pagan version she bested Cú Chulainn, the male superhero. We cannot know for sure: we have only the later Christian version of events. As Donnchadh Ó Corráin observed, the message of the monks would most likely have been: "This [pagan Ireland] was society before the coming of Christianity and God-saving grace, and if Queen Medb was an extremely wanton and headstrong woman, that is the way women were before Christianity got its hands upon them—so [they would have us believe] we have much to be grateful for."

Yet in spite of the obvious male overlay in this great epic, it is easy to see the pagan foundation on which it lies. Here is a woman asserting her independence and superiority over her husband and absolutely sure of her right to do so. If we set aside her eventual failure we can still see the remnants of what was most likely an older, pre-Christian story. The figure of Medb—the strong, haughty, impertinent woman who goes to war in order to assert her supremacy and have a bull better than that of her husband—is the enduring image that stays with us. She was a great pagan queen who never questioned her right to take her army into Ulster and get what she needed in order to establish her dominance over an up-start husband. Her character is so strong that she is sometimes referred to as a goddess in the texts. The Christian monks might have been uncomfortable with a woman with this much power and self-confidence—they surely did not affirm her in her quest to best her husband and prove her superiority.

RATH CROGHAN

One can still go today to see the area traditionally believed to be ruled by Medb. It is in the Province of Connaught in the west of Ireland. Although her legendary dwelling place in Rath Croghan in County Roscommon is long gone, the hill on which it stood is still there to be seen. Driving out the road from the town of Tulsk, the hill is on the left standing open against the sky, verdant but quite deserted, which is the charm of many of these ancient sites. Yet once, so the legend goes, it was thronged with the activity of Medb's court and army. Nowadays you might find archaeologists on the windy hill searching for traces of that ancient life. We went there in search of what we could find out about the site from the latest archaeological evidence.

Joe Fenwick and Conor Newman, archaeologists from the National University of Ireland, Galway, who have explored the hill extensively using geophysical surveying equipment, have discovered some very interesting information concerning the origins of the mound. According to their data, beneath the surface of the mound lie ridges and circles which indicate that from approximately 3000 B.C. there appears to be evidence of ritual activity continuing through the Iron Age and beyond. Yet what exactly that activity was they can only guess. The mound is man-made and is not, as was once thought, a natural hill used by the ancients. It was in fact actually created by them. This interesting discovery gives rise to further questions about the original function of the site. "It was," Conor Newman said, "an important assembly site in ancient times." Yet so far they have found very little evidence of residential life. It seems to have been a very important place for the tribe to gather and meet and conduct religious rituals.

Is the great epic an oral memory of some kind? Is the legendary linking of Medb with the site legitimate? Some archaeologists also report evidence of disturbance in the area bordering Connaught and Ulster around the time *The Táin* was supposed to have taken place. Evidence, perhaps, that the story might be based on some remembered truth and that a war or struggle of some kind took place in the area at this time.

THE CAVE BENEATH THE MOUND

Another part of the puzzle is to be found in the mysterious cave of Oweynagat which lies 765 yards to the southwest of the mound of Rath Croghan. The ancients believed this was the entrance to the Otherworld. It has an extremely small and narrow passageway. Feeling adventurous, we went inside with John Waddell, who insisted that we wear rain suits before we entered. As we crawled along a very narrow muddy passage in total darkness, his advice was much appreciated. This is definitely not a place for the claustrophobic. After crawling for about forty feet through the entrance passage with nothing but John's voice to guide us, we came to the cave itself. What an extraordinary sight as we arrived at the end of the dark passage and stood up: our flashlights lit up the darkness to show a high narrow limestone cave of seemingly cathedral proportions. Much has been written in early Irish literature about this cave, and its association with ancient sacred rites and ceremonial festivals is clear. John described it as "one of the most remarkable monuments in the Rath Croghan complex." The cave itself is natural while the entrance passageway, the souterrain, is man-made. It was obviously a major religious site in ancient Ireland. Just inside the narrow entrance some Ogham script has been carved into the stone which translates as: "The Pillar of Fraech, son of Medb." Queen Medb had a son-in-law called Fraech. No explanation for this inscription is known. The exact date of the Ogham script is unclear, but it is estimated to be perhaps fifth century A.D. This could be further proof that these people actually existed at some time and are the remnants of incomplete memory.

While considering the archaeological evidence and admitting that some questions about these ancient sites cannot be answered, Conor Newman commented, "From an archaeological point of view, we find ourselves reaching a point very rapidly when we run out of things to say that are descriptive. We've said how big it is, we've said how deep it is. So when it comes to the nub of the questions . . . what is it? Why was it built? At that point we have to embrace things like mythology, social anthropology, cultural anthropology to find out what's going on." Perhaps embracing the story of *The Táin,* or the basic tenets of it, gives us clues into an Irish past which continues to haunt and puzzle us. We should consider that possibly the stories are indeed memories, however distorted by the writers, of a time when Ireland, lying outside the Roman Empire, had its own unique form of society.

HOW STORIES LIVED ON IN MEMORY

Stories like *The Táin* would have been told and retold originally by the poets to groups of people eager to be entertained, perhaps at a large tribal get-together or even in the winter evenings as all sat around the large community fire. Craggaunowen, a reconstructed prehistoric Irish village in County Clare, brings visitors back to what life might have been like in ancient Ireland. Crannógs, early Irish homes, have been built there to emulate life as it once was. It was in places like this that Irish communities lived; it is not difficult to imagine a scene in a similar location, long ago, with the community fire lighting up the storyteller's face as all eagerly awaited the telling of the latest story or a familiar yarn told with a new twist. The darkness of night beyond the fire was territory that few wanted to venture into. There would have been comfort in the familiarity of stories told over and over again. Children listening for the first time would be told to be quiet—the poet is about to begin his tale. We can picture that storyteller of long ago, full of histrionics, telling the story in both soft and loud tones as the details unfolded and the fine points were embellished for effect. It would all be there in the telling of the saga: the exaggeration, the elaborate descriptions, and even the sometimes outlandish but often amusing hyperbole. Music would accompany the recital of the tale, giving atmosphere to it—much like some of today's movies. Maybe the storyteller would add something new to the plot or insert a detail not heard before: the brash confidence of Medb, the amazing strength of Cú Chulainn, and the very elaborate and mouthwatering descriptions of Medb and Ailill's possessions, all earnestly listened to. This story of domestic dispute taken to a wider conflict has engendered a lot of interest since its first inception way back in ancient times. Like all epics, it is a story that endures—and a marvel to know that thousands of years after the events are supposed to have taken place the images of Medb and Cú Chulainn are still alive.

The story of a large-scale invasion of Celtic warriors into Ireland might now be relegated to the arena of mythology and pseudo-history, but the legends and myths that have been left behind will probably cast their spells forever.

[4]

Pagan Celtic Religion and Laws

ONE OF THE growth industries that has sprouted up around things Celtic is that of religion. The question of religion and ancient Ireland is a hot topic today. Perhaps in a world weary of crime and instant gratification, searching the past in the hope that back then things were better might seem like a good idea. We know that much of this older religion impacted Christianity when it arrived in Ireland in the fifth and sixth centuries and that even today pagan practices are found mingled with Christian ritual. With such obvious persistence we can speculate with confidence that it must have been a powerful presence in the lives of people at the time. But what exactly was the religion of this Irish world in pre-Christian times?

We do not have what scholars would call "direct information" pertaining to the Celtic religion in that the Celtic people themselves did not commit to paper what their beliefs were. Whether they were on the Continent or in Ireland the Celts left no written texts for us to consult. It was only with the spread of Christianity that writing came to this world. So it is necessary to say that we can only speculate on what the actual practices of Celtic religion were. To gain information on the nature of this religion we must go to archaeology and to the Irish texts surviving from later Christian times. There is sufficient information, however, both from the Irish sources and from the Greek and Roman writers to have a fair idea of what some of those rituals and beliefs were. We certainly do have information on the principal feast days, and we know about some of the various gods and goddesses and the assorted roles they played in the everyday life of people at that time.

WHAT THE TEXTS SAY

In *The Book of Invasions,* a pseudo-history of pre-Christian Ireland which was finally compiled in the twelfth century, the Gaels are said to have come to Ireland in one large invasion. In some modern English translations the term "Celtic" has come to be substituted for the world Gael. Although relegated now to the realm of mythology, this document serves to give us some insight into how religion probably developed in pre-Christian Ireland. Many of the early Christian monks had been familiar with the ancient religion; this is reflected in their writings.

According to this story, the Gaels arrived in Ireland and defeated the previous inhabitants living in the country at the time. These Celtic-speaking people are then said to have taken over Ireland. The previously established residents of Ireland are referred to in the text as the Túatha Dé Danann. The war the Túatha Dé are said to have fought with the Gaels had an interesting outcome, however, because having been defeated these pre-Celtic people are then said to have withheld corn and milk from the Gaels and forced them into a compromise. In the settlement that followed, both sides agreed to divide Ireland between them. The Gaels would take the upper ground and the Túatha Dé Danann would depart underground. The Túatha Dé then became the deities of Ireland. Of course this has no foundation in fact, but the story is nevertheless interesting. It serves as a clear way for the storytellers to explain how the gods and goddesses were resident in Ireland and lived just beneath the surface of the Irish soil.

Throughout the descriptions of this early religion there is always the feeling that the deities are never far away and that the Otherworld, or next life, is only just barely hidden from view, ready to become visible at a moment's notice. Interaction between the living world and that of the departed is commonplace in the stories. This is probably one of the reasons why the heroes and heroines are so fearless. There is such close association with the spiritual world that many of the heroes, like Cú Chulainn, are both divine and human.

THE TÚATHA DÉ DANANN— IRISH GODS AND GODDESSES

After they were banished underground the Túatha Dé Danann became the Irish Celtic pantheon of gods and goddesses. They are said to be the descendants of the goddess Danu. It is in this family of gods and goddesses that we find most of the principal deities of Ireland. Among them is the Dagda, the good god; Lugh, the god of the harvest; Aengus, the god of love, and Brigid, patroness of poets. But there are some exceptions to the main pantheon. Mannon Mac Lir, the god of the sea, is one. Mannon is not part of the Túatha; he is an independent god. In an island society the sea god would be very important as he controls the ocean and the waterways outside of Ireland. So perhaps he had to be accorded a special degree of freedom and uniqueness and could not be hampered by the whims of any other deity. Archaeologists tell us that sea travel was quite common at that time and often easier than travel by land. The prominence of Mannon in many early Irish stories tells us that the society was very aware of the sea and its importance to the people of the time. Communication with the world beyond the ocean was obviously a significant part of life. The Irish were traders and seafarers from an early period, so the sea god had to be independent, strong, and powerful. Mannon incorporates all these attributes.

IRISH DRUIDS

Druids were the priests or soothsayers of the Celtic world. The word is thought to come from an old Celtic word for "oak." Most of the information we have on druids comes to us from the classical writers. The writings of Julius Caesar show that the druids were in charge of the Celtic religion and of overseeing religious rites. We do not know what precisely those roles would involve but there are many references in the Irish stories to druids and their function in early Irish society. In one story the druid Cathbadh seems to have greater power than the king he serves. He prophesies, correctly,

A stone carving known as the Tanderagee idol dates from the Iron Age and is believed to represent a pre-Christian god. (*Leo Eaton*)

that the unborn Deirdre will cause havoc in Ulster. In the great epic *The Táin*, a female druid warns Queen Medb not to go into battle for the brown bull. "I see it crimson, I see it red," she warns. As these all turned out to be prudent prophesies, we can assume that the druids were usually wise and ought to be listened to as they potentially offered a great deal of protection from danger.

Even though the nature of the rituals is hard to discover, from what we can read in the texts it would appear that the Celtic religion was more celebrational than liturgical. There is nothing to indicate solemnity or obligation on the part of the participants. The principal feast days in Ireland were marked with great gatherings of people at the various ritual sites around the country. They were times of joy and festivity, and people often traveled many miles over difficult countryside to reach one of the major religious sites. These religious celebrations were a very important part of the calendar year. But religion was not confined to just these times of the year. There is a strong sense that it also played a central role in everyday life.

RELIGION IN EVERYDAY LIFE

When we were in Craggaunowen, the reconstructed early Irish village in County Clare, we talked about prehistoric religion with Patricia Kelly, a scholar in ancient Irish studies. It seemed a very appropriate place to talk about ancient religion. As darkness fell we sat close to an open fire listening to the sound of horns played by Simon O'Dwyer. We were transported back in time to what religion would have been like in ancient times in Ireland. As the sky around us darkened, the light and warmth of the fire was a comfort. Patricia had come with us on this particular excursion into the past. She reminded us of just how frightening the darkness must have been to an ancient people without the security of modern communication. Looking into the blackness beyond the firelight she remarked, "I think that we can safely say that the world must have been a much scarier place for them than it is for us today. There were forces of nature, there were wild animals, there were stretches of land that were dangerous or had never been traversed." In order to counter this fear, people would seek the protection of elemental gods who could command authority over nature and thereby make life safer. The gods and goddesses, with their various powers over the environment, made the forces of nature more controllable and consequently less frightening.

THE YEARLY RITUALS

The principal feast days and rituals in the Celtic religion were centered on the calendar year and the changing seasons. They were

Tara was originally the most important religious site in pre-Christian Ireland. Because of its immense prestige it later became the ritual site of the high-kingship. (*Office of Public Works, Ireland*)

also usually associated with nature and fertility and especially survival of the tribe. The sense of shared community and the necessity of banding together against whatever odds they faced seem to be paramount in how the religious festivals were observed.

The chief festivals were celebrated on what are known as the quarter days. That was the day in the middle of the cycle of the sun. The mid-winter solstice falls in December and the mid-summer solstice falls in June, so the feasts of the quarter year are February 1, May 1, August 1, and November 1. These were the most important religious dates in the year when the druids presided over events aimed at pleasing the gods and goddesses and ensuring that the tribe would have good fortune shine on them. The texts describe great gatherings at the ritual sites like Tara, Rath Croghan, and Emain Macha. Enormous fires were lit at these celebrations. These were also times of peace and goodwill and what we might recognize as party times. One of the purposes of these religious times was to have a celebration with neighbors and enjoy yourself. We can get an idea of how enjoyable and important these festivals were from an edict which states that a punishment for breaking the law could be exclusion from one of these religious celebrations. Caesar says of this custom that "whosoever does not obey [the law's] decree, is excluded from the sacred rites. This among them is a penalty of extreme severity." Such a law tells us how much these times were enjoyed by everyone: exclusion was punishment. To have been banished from a religious gathering must have felt like ostracism when everyone else was having such fun. To have missed participation might also have been a foreboding omen of bad luck for the coming year, or to be outside the community could also have meant being in the disfavor of the deities.

SAMAIN

The most important time in the Celtic year was the ending of the old year and the start of the new one on November 1. This feast was known as Samain. Celebrations began on the evening before Samain on what was called Oíce Samain or the eve of Samain, October 31. We know from the old Irish texts that on this evening, as the old year ended and a new one began, the tombs in the mounds would be opened to allow the spirits of the dead to emerge and mingle with the living. This was the central feast day in the Celtic calendar. Because the feast of Oíce Samain stood on the boundary between the old year and the new year, there was a belief that the barriers between the living world and the Otherworld temporally disappeared so that each was visible to the other. The two worlds of the living and the dead met at this time. Now this could be a good thing or a bad thing depending on whether a living person had done something to distress the dead or the gods. If this was the case, the dead could return to avenge the wrong, and the living would dress up in disguise to put them off the trail or hide from them. Of course this dressing up also served another purpose. If you were in disguise no living person knew who you were, so you could get up to all sorts of mischief without being detected. In such a close-knit world it probably served as a time of license for letting off steam and relieving tension without incurring the disapproval of the community.

In later Christian times the great feast of Samain was changed to Halloween. It was Oíce Samain, or the evening before Samain, that became the eve of All Hallows, or Hallows' Eve. This important Celtic feast day could not have easily been stamped out, so it was prudent on the part of the Christians to change it rather than challenge it: it became instead a Christian feast day celebrating the saints of the church.

Samain was also a time of sacrificial ritual because the gods and goddesses had to be given special treatment to please them. There is a sense that mischief might occur if the deities were not pleased. In this the Celtic religion seems to be no different from other religions. The supernatural has great power to do good or bad. Yet the idea of festival and celebration seems paramount, and there is a very strong sense of interaction between the two worlds of the living and the dead. Many of the stories indicate an easy relationship between this world and the next, with people often going back and forth between the two. No wonder the Romans described the Celts as fearless in battle—they did not fear death as a separation from this life.

THE DAGDA—THE GOOD GOD

The most important god on Samain was the Dagda, the good god, sometimes referred to as Ollathair, the great father of all the tribe. He is usually depicted carrying a large club, to bash the enemies of his people, and a giant cauldron full of food. His club had great powers, on one end of it he could kill living enemies but with the other end he could revive the dead. His cauldron was a magic vessel because its contents would never become depleted. He truly was the good god. He protected his tribe from any enemy and he also fed them. He is described as having a hostel where hospitality was always available for anyone. The custom of hospitality has a long history in Ireland and has prominent significance in the religion and laws of ancient times.

The chief goddess of this festival was the Morrigan, the tribal mother goddess, who was also the goddess of war and protected her people in battle. She sometimes changes shape on the field of battle to the shape of a raven, a symbol of death. It is as a raven that she comes onto the shoulder of the hero Cú Chulainn at the moment of his death, signaling that he is indeed dead. She is also a prophet and appears in *The Táin* to tell the brown bull the fate that lies ahead of him. On the feast of Samain there is a ritual mating of the Morrigan and the Dagda. Some of the other goddesses and gods in Celtic lore are the offspring of this ritual mating.

IMBOLG

The arrival of spring was marked by a festival known as Imbolg, which was held on February 1. This date celebrated the new season of growth and the awakening of the earth after the long winter. Imbolg is especially associated with the milking of young ewes. The goddess Brigid is the deity most associated with this time. Her name means "the exalted one," and she is one of the most important goddesses of Ireland. Brigid was the daughter of the Dagda and was a triple goddess. She was the patron of poetry, crafts, and healing. She also had a particularly feminine patronage in that she was invoked by women in childbirth for protection and safe delivery of the child. In later Christian times the date of Imbolg was proclaimed as the feast of St. Brigid.

Nowadays the memory of this ancient goddess is still alive in certain parts of Ireland associated with her name. In Lough Gur, in County Limerick, Brigid aficionados gather on the day of Imbolg and celebrate the feast day of the goddess Brigid. Although no one knows for sure what exactly the ancient rituals would have been, this group seems to have no problem in coming up with some interesting innovations. Donned in green branches and leaves, the self-proclaimed "green man" dances around the fields symbolizing the fertilizing of the earth and the start of new growth. Later in the evening the people gather around a community fire and listen to stories of the saint and the goddess. These are old tales dating to a time that no one remembers, so myth and legend thrive. Over the years some of the myths have been added to and embellished such that both saint and goddess seem to have become one and the same person. The Christian story of the saint's birth, for example, is steeped in magic and paganism. Like the goddess, who is said to have been born in a druid's home, St. Brigid is said to have been the daughter of a druid and fed on the milk of Otherworld cows. This presumably gives the saint control over or insight into the Otherworld. It also allows that world to survive but to be Christianized and put under the "safe" guidance of a Christian saint.

THE IRISH GODDESSES

Goddesses were important deities in ancient religions, but Irish goddesses especially played major roles in the lives of people. It was actually a few nights after Imbolg that we sat with Patricia Kelly in Craggaunowen and she talked about the role of the goddess in ancient Ireland. "We do know that there were many female divinities, and they play quite a prominent role. They are not merely associated with what one might call the classical feminine roles; we have [in Ireland] for example, war goddesses. Goddesses make an appearance in the tales of ancient Ireland and they frighten, threaten, or help people. Certainly in the realm of the divine, [in Ireland] women play a quite major role."

Brigid was obviously an important deity to the Irish of the time, and this is most likely the reason why her feast day had to be incorporated into later Christianity. It would probably have been very difficult to eradicate her completely, so it was far easier to substitute a Christian saint and place that saint's feast day on the same day as Imbolg. The fact that this transference from pagan to Christian was necessary gives us some idea of how powerful and enduring the goddess must have been in early Ireland.

BELTINE

The festival on May 1 was called Beltine. Again, as with the other religious feasts, this one is also linked with the season and with nature. Beltine celebrated the beginning of open pasturing. There would have been the customary gathering at the ritual sites. On this occasion a ceremonial bonfire was lit to please the sun and ask it to shine on the crops and the pasture—an imperative request given the nature of Irish weather. This was to ensure new and abundant growth.

The word "*bel*" comes from an old Celtic word for bright light meaning, probably, the sun's light. The Celtic god Belenus is associated with the sun. The word "*tine*" means a fire, so it was the time of Bel's fire or the fire of the sun god. In addition to the great bonfire there were other fires lit at Beltine. Some sources tell of large fires being built in long parallel lines. When the fires were blazing high, cattle would be driven down the burning avenue between the flames, in the belief that they would be purified and freed from any disease. Whether any of the animals ended up being scorched we do not know. With all the feasting and drinking and general merriment that usually went along with these festivals, it is not beyond belief that unfortunate accidents probably did happen.

LÚNASA

The feast of Lúnasa signaled the start of autumn. This was the second most important festival after Samain. It was also one of the longest in duration as it traditionally began in mid-July and lasted until mid-August. The chief day was on August 1 and honored the Celtic god Lugh. He is one of the most interesting and gifted of the gods of Ireland. He is often described as beautiful in appearance and seems to have been much loved. Lugh was said to be youthful, athletic, and handsome. The festival of Lúnasa was primarily a harvest festival and celebrated with all the joy that a bountiful harvest brings.

LUGH'S TALENTS

Lugh could also be described as the god of the arts. Music is particularly associated with this time as is poetry and storytelling. Besides these he is said to have many skills and is the most versatile of all the gods. He is a harpist, a sorcerer, a sports champion, and a craftsman in metal to name but a few of his skills. In this he is very important to a celebration that involves good news: the gathering of the harvest crops. There is a story told of the god Lugh and his importance to Ireland. When Conn of the Hundred Battles, a famous king of Tara, visited Lugh he found him sitting in state as a king of the Otherworld attended by magnificently attired female deities who are identified as the provinces of Ireland. Some stories tell of Lugh actually dying on this day and then resurrecting himself to save the earth from insects that might eat or harm the harvest. He is both the protector of the harvest and the provider of a good time. Of all the Irish festivals, Lúnasa is probably the one most associated with partying and holiday time. The work of the year is complete. The message is that the crop is in, there is plenty of food, and it is time to relax and reap the benefits of a good harvest.

During these religious times of honoring the gods and goddesses, the major ceremonial sites would be thronged with people. But it is especially at Lúnasa and at Samain that major festivals were held at Tara for the whole of Ireland. We are told that people traveled there from all over the county for these important events. The impression is, however, that the sense of festival was paramount to these occasions and that religious feasts were something that brought people together to have a good time. The festive celebration was as important as the religious significance it embodied.

THE WREN FESTIVAL

In spite of the arrival of Christianity in the fifth century, these pagan beliefs did not die out quickly. In fact, many traces of this pre-Christian religion can still be found in parts of Ireland today. The superstitions surrounding the magic of "holy wells" and the power of the water in these wells to effect cures is one example. Many wells associated now with Christian saints have their curative origins in older times. Likewise, there are even festivals that still have strong traces of pagan origins.

One festival that is believed to have survived in Ireland from ancient times is held each year on December 26, the day after Christmas Day. It is known as Wren Day. Held in the town of Dingle in County Kerry each year, the Dingle Wren, as it is known, is the biggest celebration of its kind in Ireland. How or why it came to be associated with the bird is uncertain. What is certain is that it is similar to descriptions of pre-Christian Irish rites. It is celebrated close to the winter solstice and could originally have been a part of that ritual, but it also has a Samain or Halloween feel to it. Dressed and disguised in garish costumes and masks, local people parade through the main street of the town, dancing to the sound of music. Predictably, everyone ends up in the local pub where the fun continues into the night.

Everything we know about religion in ancient Ireland tells us that it played an important and vital role in the lives of people in pre-Christian times. It appears to have been central to their social lives and to their interaction with nature. But nowhere is there a sense that it was viewed as an obligation with severe punishment for failing to observe the correct ritual. Fun rather than fear seems to have been paramount.

Many of these attitudes were brought by the Irish into Christianity after it arrived in Ireland in the fifth century. Irish Christian art would reflect a magnificent enthusiasm and sheer delight in its subject. Irish Christianity was to become a beacon of light in the dark world of Europe following Rome's fall.

ANCIENT IRISH LAW

The everyday life of Irish people in this period was governed by laws referred to as Brehon Laws, administered by people known as brehons. The word "brehon" comes from an old Celtic word meaning a judge or judgment. Although the laws are thought to predate the Christian period, they were first written down in the seventh and eighth centuries, so we do not know for certain how much Christian influence there is in what was finally committed to writing. Scholars debate how much Christian input there is in the laws and how much might have survived from the earlier period, but these laws nevertheless offer an interesting insight into early Irish life. As Fergus Kelly points out in his book *A Guide to Early Irish Law*, "There are often inconsistencies and even contradictions between different sources." Some sources seem to have great Christian influence while others seem to have none. This probably has to do with the different centuries that the surviving texts come from and in which part of the country they originated. The later surviving texts show a greater Christian influence, and many appear to have been based on canon law.

Traditionally the brehons belonged to a legal class that would memorize the laws and pass them on to the next generation by the oral tradition. There was actually quite a lot of organization around this method. Sophisticated schools of learning trained students in this discipline. It took many years, sometimes as long as twenty, to become proficient in the law.

These early laws strongly influenced Irish society. They remained customary in Ireland until the early 1600s when, in the late

Tudor period, England's conquest of Ireland became complete and the ancient laws of Ireland were proscribed in favor of English common law. Brehon Law is interesting for a number of reasons. These laws originally developed without the influence of Roman law and so have origins different from other Western law. Interestingly enough, they are not male centered or even individual centered. Instead they reflect a tribal society where the crime of an individual was the responsibility of the group or family. The law texts state that the basic unit is the *Túath*, (plural is *Túatha*), which loosely translates into English as "tribe." To read these laws is like having a little window into Ireland's distant past. They provide interesting sociological glimpses into early Ireland and what life would have been like at that time.

THE BREHONS—LAWYERS OF ANCIENT IRELAND

There were a number of significant differences between Ireland and Romanized Europe. Unlike the rest of Europe, the laws of ancient Ireland were not instigated by the king. An Irish king did not have control over what the laws were or even how they were administered. In Ireland the king or chieftain was as subject to the law as anyone else. This insight into Irish society highlights the absence in Ireland of a single form of political control. Instead the creation of the law was in the hands of the brehons. The laws were also administered and interpreted by them so they were a powerful class. Like the poets, the brehons were an elite group who sometimes held important positions in the courts of the chieftains or kings. Other brehons traveled around the country administering justice whenever they were called upon by someone to judge a case. Because elite classes like the poets and brehons moved around from place to place they provided a sense of cultural unity. This was important to the cohesion of the society given the fact that political unity in the form of an over-kingship was not a reality in early Ireland.

From the texts we also get a sense of an interdisciplinary connection between the poets, the druids, and the brehons. Sometimes a brehon could also be a druid or a poet and so on. These do not appear to have been always separate classes.

HONOR PRICE

There were no prisons in ancient Ireland. Punishment for a crime was usually by compensation. The basis of the law was that each person had an honor price. A value was put on everyone and if you committed a crime against someone else you paid that person according to his or her honor price. Very often the honor price was expressed in terms of *cumals,* or female slaves. Thus a poet had the value of seven *cumals.* This is not to say that this was the award given to a person when a crime was committed. A *cumal* was used as a value guide only. It is obvious that other goods were substituted for female slaves. It was up to the brehon in the case to determine the equivalent in merchandise to be awarded for compensation.

The value of a person's honor price depended on the status of that person within the group. Thus a poet had the highest honor price, reflecting the very high status of the poet in early Irish society. A child had a lower honor price than an adult. The paying of the honor price could sometimes be the responsibility of other members of a family. In the story of *The Táin,* Medb claims that she is responsible for paying for her husband should he commit a crime or get into any kind of trouble. She also would be paid the compensation if someone committed a crime against him.

Someone's honor price could be lost or lowered if that person committed what was considered a serious offense, like refusing hospitality. Apparently hospitality was an important part of early Irish society, and violating this law was a serious offense. There seems to have been an intense social obligation among all homeowners to provide hospitality for anyone who might need it. As no one was above the law, this obligation applied to all. One law, for example, states that the king, like the rest of the tribe, must not refuse hospitality to anyone.

COMPENSATION

Because compensation was the usual form of redress, it was up to the brehon in charge of the case to determine the value of the offending household, the honor price of the victim, and the amount of compensation to be paid. As cattle had the highest value, the more serious crimes would usually involve the handing over of cattle as atonement for a crime committed. If a crime was heinous, like murder, the compensation could be so large that it might take generations to pay off the fine. So it was possible for someone who was not even born when a crime was committed to be held responsible for paying the victim's family their compensation. An interesting insight into an attempt at fairness lies in a law which states that if ignorance of a law can be demonstrated, the compensation to be paid is cut in half. Accidents are also dealt with in an elaborate way. There are laws which state, for example, that there is no liability if a person accidentally causes a branch of a tree to fly back and injure another, or if someone dislodges a stone and it accidentally hits another.

THE COURT SYSTEM

Although there were no prisons, there was an elaborate court system in which correct procedure was very important. Proper deliberation was necessary, and there were few quick decisions. The accused was given ample time to prepare and defend his or her case. A text describes the proper seating arrangement in court with three chief poets sitting close to the king. But it was the brehon who judged the case and decided it. Others who might be present at the court, like kings or poets, could only give advice on certain matters belonging to their own areas of knowledge. In no way could they, or anyone, interfere with or change the final judgment of the brehon.

BAD JUDGMENTS

If an individual felt that the brehon had made was what called a "bad judgment," objection could be addressed on a separate occasion. In one famous case, a brehon gave judgment against a woman whose sheep had strayed and eaten the grass of her neighbor. The brehon ordered the sheep to be killed and the meat given to the victim as compensation. Under a separate hearing it was declared that this was an incorrect judgment and that the wool of the sheep should have been the compensation, as the wool of the sheep will grow back just as the grass will.

Another way of getting action against an unfair judgment was by way of starvation and fasting, preferably outside of the accuser's house. The wrongly accused would refuse to eat food until the issue was resolved, presumably in his or her favor. This method was also employed against someone who had committed an offense and was getting away with the crime by ignoring it or refusing to pay compensation. The victim would refuse food until justice prevailed. Fasting outside of someone's house was a way of dishonoring a defendant if he ignored the situation. It seems to have been a matter of tremendous shame on a family to have someone sitting outside starving and refusing food. It apparently worked as a way of ensuring a quick response when all else failed.

SOME OF THE ACTUAL LAWS

Some of the laws provide an engaging insight into early Irish society. It seems to have been a flexible, almost easygoing world where there was great trust among the people. For example, on the question of pregnancy a woman could name any man in the community as the father of her child, and this would be accepted. Her word, obviously, was good enough. Another interesting law covering sickness obliges the family of the sick person to keep children quiet and not to feed any honey to the invalid. Honey, the law explains, upsets the bowels of a sick person.

Many of the laws cover the issue of family life. As fosterage was a common practice, some of the laws are concerned with this subject. Fosterage of children within the *Túath* was customary throughout Ireland at the time. Cú Chulainn was fostered by a woman other than his natural mother and raised by her. At the final confrontation in *The Táin* he has to face his foster brother Ferdia whom he actually kills in the battle. Although this section of *The Táin* is a later, twelfth-century addition, Cú Chulainn's lament for Ferdia gives us an idea of how close foster children were to each other. The custom of fosterage remained common in Ireland well after the twelfth-century Norman invasion. Under the fosterage system it was quite usual for children to be raised by others within the community and then return home at a certain age. This custom presumably gave children a sense of belonging to the entire community, not just to one set of parents. It ensured that loyalty and strong bonds within the society were formed at a very young age. The law states that the girls return home to their parents at fourteen and the boys come home at seventeen. These were also the legal marriage ages for each sex.

LAWS CONCERNING POETS

The *filí,* or poets, were considered to be of the highest stature and were feared because of their satire. It was believed that with satirical poems a poet could cause anything from skin rashes to death. So strong was this feeling about satire that laws governed it. Brehon Law was quite specific regarding the use of poetry. Using the weapon of satire to verbally abuse someone was apparently a serious offense. Mocking someone's appearance, making public a physical defect, giving an offensive nickname to someone, or even repeating the satire of another poet could all result in having to pay somebody's honor price. It was even an offense to satirize someone after death. The full honor price of the deceased would be paid to the surviving family in this case.

There was, however, a clear distinction between what was considered justified and unjustified satire. If the satire was unjustified, the full effects of the law would be felt by the offender. But legitimate satire actually played an important role in Irish society. If someone had done something deliberately to offend another or had behaved badly at a public place, the satire would be considered a legitimate way of getting that person to change his or her ways. It seems to have acted as a law unto itself in controlling people's social behavior. It also meant that the poets had great power. They could cause even a king to modify his behavior by encouraging public ridicule for even the slightest form of rudeness or arrogance. One king, who asked his chief poet to celebrate a victory in battle, found that the poet composed a satire on how bad conditions were for the "winning" side. "We are tired and far from home," he wrote. "We have little food, not enough to drink, no rest, too much mud and this," the poet mused, "is victory?" Apparently not even kings were immune to the satire of this class.

WOMEN AND THE LAW

There is much discussion about the status of women under Brehon Law, and the truth is that it is difficult to come to a final conclusion on the issue. Because the laws were written down after the arrival of Christianity, many of these laws show Christian bias and are probably greatly influenced by the imported Christian thinking. Very often, for example, sexual promiscuity by women is condemned while that of men is less so. As Fergus Kelly points out, "Considering that these laws were usually being written down by clerical men, this is not very surprising!" Conversely, it is also clear from the law tracts that a woman could hold the position of highest poet and be the equal of a male poet. There is a reference in the *Annals of Inisfallen* that record the death in 934 of Uallach, daughter of Muinechán, who is described as *Banfile Éireann,* the Woman Poet of Ireland. From this we must assume that a woman could hold the position of a full-fledged poet. It is difficult nonetheless to determine what the legal position of women would have been in pre-Christian times.

The stories may give us some better insight into the status of women. Many of them resound with independent women who are poets and druids and even go into battle. In some stories we learn that women actually trained men for battle. One Roman historian claims that a whole band of warriors could not cope with a Gaul [Celt], "especially if he calls in his wife, [who is] stronger than he by far . . . and she begins to rain blows mingled with kicks like shots." The Irish stories are equally descriptive of the battle role of women. Medb had her own army and has no problem with leading them to invade Ulster. In spite of her final failure, we do not get the impression that her actions are at all unusual. The great hero Cú Chulainn prepared for battle by being trained by three women in the skill of fighting. Whatever we can say about women in early Ireland, they do seem to have enjoyed a status and independence in society that women in later centuries did not.

DIVORCE IN EARLY IRELAND

Under Brehon Law divorce was permitted for many reasons, and there is an entire section of the law which deals with the division of property. There is no early Irish word for "dowry," so we get the sense that goods once owned by a woman were always owned by her; the husband did not become the owner of all. The issue of property division depended on the amount of goods brought into the marriage by each partner and, interestingly enough, the amount of household work done by either partner. The more work done within the household, the greater the share of property after divorce. This law seems to apply to goods obtained after marriage. Divorce was so much a part of early Ireland and family life of the time that it took many centuries for the Irish to abandon this law. Even today in Ireland memories of Brehon Law remain strong. In the first modern-day case of divorce in Ireland in 1996, one of the lawyers involved in the case remarked after the divorce was granted that "we have returned to Brehon Law."

SLAVERY AND THE LAW

Slavery was a common and economically profitable institution throughout Europe at the time, and Ireland was no exception. The Irish had an established slave system, and Brehon Law covers the issue of how slaves were to be treated. The slaves were the bottom class of society and seemed to do all the menial jobs, but we have no way of knowing the percentage of people in slavery. It is clear from reading the law tracts, however, that slavery was an important institution. Slaves mostly originated as foreigners picked up by slave traders, prisoners of war, or people who could not pay a compensation or fine for a crime they had committed and so they passed into slavery. It seems to have been most common and easier to enslave people who were taken from a foreign country and brought into slavery. This was a pattern of slavery perfected by the Romans. When people are captured into slavery and transported to a place far from their own culture and, often, language, it is easier to control them. The Romans did of course experience slave revolts, but considering the centuries of slavery and the numbers of people in slavery, these incidents were remarkably infrequent. For centuries the Irish raided the coast of Britain for slaves. These captured individuals were then shipped back to Ireland and sold into slavery.

The laws governing slavery are quite informative from a sociological and ethical point of view. They tell us that for more than a thousand years before the institution was abolished, there was a sense that it was dangerously inequitable and open to abuse. Some laws attempted to redress this and some tried to establish a legal understanding of the slave's position in society. For example, the master of the slave had to pay any fines for a crime that the slave committed, and if the slave was offended against, the master was paid the fine. One law states that if a slave accidentally injures or kills a passerby while chopping wood, neither he nor his master is liable for a fine or other punishment.

Other laws obviously sought to establish a protective boundary around the relationship of slave to master. A man who impregnated a slave woman had to himself arrange for the rearing of the child. Similarly if a free woman allowed herself to become pregnant by a slave, it was she who was responsible for the rearing of the child, not the slave. There were also attempts to protect slave women from being used for sexual purposes. A sixth-century Brehon Law states that a man who has intercourse with a slave woman is urged to sell her to another, but if she has a child by him she must then be set free. From a sociological point of view, these laws display a sense of justice to what is after all an unjust institution. They also give us a perspective on the ethical unease with which the practice of slavery was viewed by some lawmakers.

LEGACY OF ANCIENT IRISH RELIGION AND LAW

The surviving information on the laws and religion of ancient Ireland allows us the possibility of speculating on what day-to-day life in early Ireland might have been like. Just as important, it also gives us some understanding of the foundation and later development and characterization of Irish society. Both pagan religion and law remained an important part of Irish life for centuries. Their influence on the development of Irish society cannot be denied. Until the early 1600s the Brehon Laws remained customary in Ireland. When Christianity arrived in Ireland in the middle of the fifth century, it had to accommodate the strong presence of a sophisticated pagan religion and learned to adjust to it. It could never hope to overthrow it completely. Traces of the ancient pagan religion are still found today in many Irish Christian practices. Both the law and religion of ancient Ireland were strong forces in shaping Irish society.

[5]

St. Patrick—
Patron Saint of
the Irish

❋

ALL OVER the world on March 17 Irish exiles, descendants of Irish emigrants of long ago, and Hibernophiles celebrate Ireland's most famous saint, St. Patrick. The wearing of the green on that day has become almost an obligatory part of claiming and displaying Irish ancestry. It is also probably fair to say that until recently the day was more important outside of Ireland for the celebrating or proclaiming of Irishness—but even now in Ireland the festival spirit is catching on. While it was always a holy day in Ireland, it is now becoming a day of celebrating Irish identity.

Most people around the world who celebrate the day probably have no idea of who Patrick was or how he came to be the patron saint of Ireland and the curator of all things Irish. The stories and myths surrounding Patrick are so numerous that it is hard to peel back the layers added over many centuries and find the real man. For example, the shamrock, so much a part of the modern St. Patrick's Day, became associated with Patrick only in the seventeenth century as a way of teaching the people of that time about Christianity. The story of the snakes was probably invented in medieval times. Patrick's travels within Ireland are so exaggerated that he would have had to have lived for hundreds of years to have been to the places he is reputed to have visited and founded all the churches he is said to have established. Charlie Doherty, a historian with the National University of Ireland in Dublin, says, "That's the thing about myth, it constantly changes itself and remakes itself, depending on circumstance . . . and what we see nowadays is the cult of Patrick and the contemporary view of it." The cult of Patrick: modern scholars return to this expression again and again. Over the centuries that cult has been added to so many times that it is sometimes hard to separate the myth from reality.

How did this one man become so important to Ireland? Did he really single-handedly convert the pagan Irish to Christianity? The story of Patrick and the Irish is something we can look at from a number of sources, including Patrick's own description of his life. The saga begins on the island of Britain.

IRISH RAIDERS ON THE COAST OF BRITAIN

On the other side of the Irish Sea, by the middle of the fifth century Roman Britain was in decline. Having conquered the island of Britain in A.D. 43, the Roman legions were now leaving the British shores and returning home. Ireland, alone in Europe, lay outside the Roman Empire but was wealthy enough to have traded with it. Roman trading posts have been excavated at the Drumanagh peninsula just north of Dublin. The site sits on the coast across from Lambay Island, which was probably used as a stopping-off port. Barry Raftery, the archaeologist who excavated the site, claims that the Irish traded with the Roman Empire while remaining outside of it. Drumanagh was an important and large trading post, and he explains, "Aerial photographs suggest circular houses and this seems to indicate that this was a place where native Irish were living, trading with the Roman world. They were trading here with Romans and all sorts of other people coming from the Roman Empire." The Irish were very familiar with the Roman world lying just across the sea from them.

They had also figured out that there was valuable bounty to be had by plundering along the British coast and carrying off young men and women to Ireland and selling them into slavery. This was a practice that had been going on for many years, and the Irish had become quite adept at grab-and-run raids. As the Roman armies receded, the British shores were even less protected than before, and Irish raiding increased. The Irish even settled in parts of Britain for trading purposes, and one settlement, that of the Irish Dál Riada in Scotland, grew to become a major one as the Irish established a permanent colony there. The word "Scot" is taken from the Latin word "Scoti" meaning the Irish. In fact the word "Scotland" means the land of the Irish. These Irish settlers gave Scotland its name and the Gaelic language that was brought over with the Irish settlers at this time.

THE IRISH SNATCH THE YOUNG PATRICK INTO SLAVERY

One raid that was to secure a lasting place in Irish history was the taking of a young boy from his British home for slavery in Ireland. The sixteen-year-old boy was called Patrick. He was captured and taken across the Irish Sea and sold into slavery in Ireland. Although British in origin, Patrick was destined to become the patron saint of the Irish; his name would forevermore be associated with the country. Yet the symbol of Patrick, the single-handed converter of the Irish to Christianity, is as much an invention as anything else. Great stories, miracles, and legends have been fabricated and woven around his life. Yes, he did exist, and two documents that have survived from him tell us much about his early life, but it was actually some time after his death that he became the legend we know today.

PATRICK'S OWN WRITINGS

There are more legends about Patrick than actual fact. The two texts Patrick wrote that survived give us an interesting insight into his life and experiences. One document is his own autobiography, usually called the *Confession,* and the other is a letter written later in his life. His *Confession* gives us a lot of information on his early life and his relationship with Ireland and the Irish. One of the reasons why the cult of Patrick survived and grew is because of this extraordinary account of his life written in the fifth century A.D. It is a fascinating way of learning about the adventures of a teenage boy at that time.

In his own words Patrick tells us that soon after he was captured by Irish sailors he was sold into slavery and brought to the west of Ireland. He worked on a sheep farm near the Wood of Fochloch overlooking Killala Bay—part of modern-day County Mayo. The area today looks very much the same as it did in the time of Patrick: rural and isolated, with sheep scattered on the hillsides. Patrick was a Christian boy and had been raised in a Christian country, so Ireland was a very different and strange place to him. Christianity had come to Britain through the spread of this new religion via the Roman Empire. In his *Confession* Patrick also tells of his early life in Britain where he was born around the year 400. He was the son of a deacon and the grandson of a Christian priest. This was long before clerical celibacy became a general rule for the Roman priesthood. The only religion that Patrick would have known in his childhood was Christianity. His world would have been a totally Christian one. In spite of previous attempts to bring Christianity to Ireland, the Irish were still largely a pagan people living with their druidic beliefs and practices. They would still have been celebrating their important feast days with great gatherings at the ancient ritual sites. Likewise the social structure of Ireland would have been very different from the rest of Europe in that there were no towns or urban centers.

THE CHRISTIAN BOY AND THE DRUIDS

Patrick felt a complete stranger to all of this. He was young and frightened. He explains that when he was taken captive, "I was an adolescent, almost a speechless boy before I knew what to seek or what to avoid." He had to grow up fast and survive emotionally. He also tells us in sad, humble tones that he deserved this fate of being taken from his home because in Britain he had strayed from God and did not keep the commandments. He is not specific in details but he mentions a sin which troubled him all his life. We have no way of knowing what he is referring to but perhaps his missionary work was a way of gaining salvation and absolution from this sin.

As a boy slave in Ireland, Patrick had to work hard tending

flocks of sheep on the isolated hill in Fochloch Wood. It was here, in this isolated place that the youth started to pray. He was lonely and he missed his home and everything that was familiar to him. The urban youth must have felt he was truly cast out from all he had known. So he prayed many times during the day and then started to pray into the night. Gradually the young Patrick tells us that he felt the spirit of his Christian God enter into him. We can imagine the lonely youth far from home, living among strangers, turning to the God of his childhood to try to gain comfort. Praying probably also brought him closer to the world of his family. Familiar and remembered words of prayer probably invoked strong memories for him. The rebellious teenager now wanted and needed the security of his parents' world and the God he had been brought up to believe in. Ireland's religious practices were too alien to him, so Patrick could not turn to the druids to guide him spiritually. Their religion was virtually unknown to him, and their rituals must have seemed strange and foreign. Patrick was very much alone in praying to his Christian God. On the principal feast days of the Celts the solitary youth would have ignored the celebrations and was probably even a little horrified at the spectacle of feasting and excess, as he would have thought it. In one Irish text written after the saint's death, Patrick expresses horror at the amount of feasting and merriment at religious festivals and is depicted as chiding the Celtic hero Oisín for being too fond of having a good time. Every aspect of life in Ireland, with no towns and no Roman influence, was very different from what he had left behind in Christian Britain.

PATRICK ESCAPES FROM CAPTIVITY

In his *Confession* Patrick describes how comfort came one dark, chilly night in the form of a voice which said to him, "It is good that you pray and fast and soon you will go back to your homeland." Patrick tells us he was filled with delight and anticipation until finally a few days later he heard another voice telling him that the ship to take him was ready. With great excitement, and convinced that God would guide him, he fled from the mountain where he had spent six lonely years. He then traveled two hundred miles until he reached the eastern shore of Ireland and the ship which was to take him home. After some negotiation with the captain of the ship, Patrick boarded. The youth who came to Ireland left it a grown man.

Yet getting back to his home was not an easy task, and it took some time and determination before he finally reached his family. But Patrick would always have determination and fortitude. His family welcomed him and celebrated his return, as they had not expected ever to see him again. They also made him promise never to leave them again. He assured them that he did not intend to do so. The man who was an urban youth tells us he was glad to be back home. He settled back into the old lifestyle and thanked God for returning him safely to the land of his birth. The story could have ended here, but it does not.

PATRICK REMEMBERS THE IRISH

Time passed and Patrick grew older, but Ireland and the memory of the Irish would not go away so easily. The truth was that he had fallen in love with this island and the people who had once enslaved him. Memories of his life there did not leave him. The feast days with their emphasis on merriment in the form of storytelling, music, and poetry had filled the young Patrick with the belief that these Irish were at heart a good people, even if they were not Christian. Father Frank Fahey of Ballintubber Abbey, who has spent his life studying the life and world of Patrick, describes the Irish of this time as "a very religious people. They had their sacred mountains; they had their liturgies around the wells. There was this presence of the divine in everything. Whether it was the gods, the energies, the spirits, whether it was the embodiment of the chief deity, the sun, whatever it was, they had this sense of religion, spirituality." It is easy to understand why Patrick, with his own Christian background, would be drawn to these people with the idea of bringing his deity to them.

PATRICK RETURNS TO IRELAND

A few years later Patrick himself was ordained a priest, and it was around this time that he tells of a strange experience. Again in his own words he describes how one night he saw a man coming to him in a vision. The man was Irish in appearance, and he gave Patrick a letter which was headed "The Voice of the Irish." Confused but curious over what this meant, Patrick read the letter and said that he could almost hear the voices of the people of Killala Bay speaking to him and pleading with him to return and be with them. He was deeply moved by this request and could not finish reading, but he knew one thing—he would go back to Ireland and bring the message of Christianity with him.

PATRICK NOT THE FIRST MISSIONARY TO THE IRISH

According to later Irish annals, in 432 Patrick arrived back in Ireland to convert the people to Christianity.* In spite of his later reputation, Patrick was not the first to bring the message of Christianity to Ireland. A year before Patrick is said to have arrived, another missionary, Palladius, was sent by the pope to bring the Irish to the Christian faith. There are also references to many others who traveled to Ireland to bring in the new religion. Christian missionaries were fairly widespread in Ireland at the time, but Patrick played an important role in the spread of the new faith among the Irish.

The Irish converted to Christianity without the bloodshed and martyrdom which was de rigueur with conversion elsewhere. How or why it happened this way no one knows for sure. The Irish seemed to have accepted this new deity without a struggle. Probably many factors were involved in the process, but Patrick himself was a clever theologian as were many of the early Christians when it came to introducing the new ideas to pagan people. In his *Confession* he declares, "I have kept faith with the heathens among whom I live and I will continue to keep it." Patrick did not try to stamp out the earlier rituals but rather cleverly blended them with Christian theology. He was fully aware of how the older religion was connected with the seasons and the changes in nature and sought to combine Christian teaching with these elements.

---

*This date is based on annals written one hundred years after Patrick. Consequently, it is more likely to have served political needs than to be historically accurate.

PATRICK'S FUSION OF OLD AND NEW

On a spring morning in Glenstall Abbey in County Limerick, Brother Sean O'Duinn stood near the forest surrounding the abbey and talked to us of the pagan religion that Patrick encountered when he came to Ireland. "You can say that it was bound up with nature, that the Celts spoke of the elemental gods that were concerned with earth, air, fire and water." This contrasted with Christianity. "When you think about it, almost from the beginning Christianity was mainly an urban religion" and not concerned with the changing seasons and nature. It was Patrick's willingness to bring these two different forces together that made him a success at the work of conversion. He did not ask the Irish to forsake their old beliefs but was happy to allow them to blend it all together. This philosophy is explained by him in the *Confession*. Taking the image of the sun, which was worshipped by the Irish, he incorporates that into Christian thinking and belief: "For the sun is that which we see rising daily at His command, but it will never reign, nor will its splendor last forever. And all those who worship it will be subject to grievous punishment. We, however, worship the true sun, Christ, who will never perish." In this way he wove the older icon into the newer Christian one. Patrick artfully allowed the pagan Irish to hold onto some of their old ways but encouraged them to see the icons in another, Christian, light. This convergence of old and new religions was so widespread in the conversion of Ireland to Christianity that hundreds of years later many pagan practices were still quite common. Many have survived to the present day. The reciting of a Christian rosary around a rag tree, for example, is still a common practice throughout Ireland. Rag trees are believed to have powers of healing and are invoked by the hanging of a rag or garment belonging to the person being prayed for.

Patrick traveled mostly throughout northern Ireland in his missionary work. He left no direct record of where he went, so he cannot with certainty be connected with the establishment of any particular church. Later writings on the travels and exact missionary work of Patrick cannot be verified, but he founded many churches including possibly one at Armagh, which was later to become the most important ecclesiastic center in Ireland.

PATRICK'S DEATH

There is no consensus about the date when Patrick died. The Ulster annals state that it was in 492, but the Inisfallen annals say it was in 496, on March 17. In any case, at his death Patrick was just one of many who had been a part of bringing Christianity to Ireland. In truth he never felt at home in Ireland and described the Irish as being "foreigners" to him in his letter to Coroticus, the only other document surviving besides his own simple biography. He wrote this letter on behalf of his converts who were being persecuted by this soldier and his agents, and even taken into slavery. It is believed that Coroticus was a British Roman petty tyrant who appears to have come to the eastern part of Ulster in search of bounty. In the letter Patrick is angry at him and full of anguish for the people he converted who have been mistreated by Coroticus. Patrick's anguish unleashes a whole stream of emotion. He says, in the same letter, that in Ireland he is a "stranger and an exile" from his own homeland. Even though he loved the Irish enough to spend his life converting them to Christianity, he never appears to have felt entirely at home there. In a sense he saw his mission as a kind of martyrdom.

We know that Patrick had not been the only figure involved in the conversion of the Irish to Christianity and that there were many others who came before and after him. Yet Patrick became the great symbol of Ireland, and others who did similar missionary work are forgotten. How did his name become forever associated with the Irish and the coming of Christianity to Ireland? The answer lies in what happened politically some two hundred years after his death.

THE CULT OF PATRICK AND ARMAGH

By the seventh century the monasteries throughout Ireland were competing with each other for status and wealth. The church in Armagh in Ulster, in the northern part of the country, was one of the most ambitious in the Irish church. It wanted to be the primary center of Christianity in Ireland. It claimed to have been founded by Patrick and began to boost him as the primary missionary of the

Irish. There is no direct evidence connecting Patrick with Armagh, but so successful was the propaganda linking the two that to the present day Patrick is known as the founding saint. Two "lives" of Patrick, written by Muirchu and Tirechan in the late seventh century, invented myths and exaggerated his importance. Charlie Doherty says that it was Muirchu who "endowed Patrick with the attributes of a secular hero and ensured that the cult [of Patrick] was elevated to that of a national apostle." Both Muirchu and Tirechan were writing in the interests of Armagh two hundred years after the saint's death and are not considered by scholars to be legitimate sources. But their work played a major role in the development of the cult of Patrick.

Muirchu was a successful propagandist who established the legend of Patrick as the sole converter of the Irish to Christianity. He also established the myth that the Christian church in Ireland was founded exclusively by Patrick. Muirchu succeeded not only in elevating Patrick but he also did a pretty good job in denigrating Tara, which he describes as an Irish Babylon. This denouncement of the most revered of pre-Christian holy sites was done of necessity to enhance Christianity and declare Armagh as the rightful center of Irish spirituality. Tara, with its pagan associations, had to be put down. Muirchu even invented a druid who, in pre-Christian times, foretells at the palace of Tara the coming of a great missionary who will destroy "evil" paganism and all of its gods. With the same ingenuity Patrick's confrontations with druids were exaggerated and downright invented. But the myths were so shrewdly written and often so cleverly detailed in their invention that Patrick was seen as the great Christian hero who vanquished the representatives of paganism and took over as the great new symbol of Christianity. In fact, confrontations with druids were a rarity for the Christian missionaries to Ireland. We know that the Irish converted to Christianity without the type of martyrdom associated with conversion in the rest of Europe, and there are no records of confrontations of the sort described by the mythmakers. But the myths were powerful and popular. They were so successful that Patrick did eventually become the superhero of early Irish Christianity.

RELICS AND PILGRIMS

The church of Armagh had another reason to proclaim supremacy. It claimed to have Patrick's relics. Later it was Downpatrick in County Down that was credited with the status of having the saint's body buried there. In fact no one really knows where Patrick is buried, but it was around this time that relics of saints were becoming an important way of attracting pilgrims. Pilgrimage was something like modern-day tourism. It was a way the monasteries had of making money, and many of them depended on the income they earned from this enterprise. The more pilgrims a monastery could attract, the wealthier it became. Armagh, along with other northern churches, was in direct contact with Rome and managed to convince the Roman authorities to send over to them relics of the church's chief saints. With the precious relics of internationally known saints, Armagh could advertise these as a way of attracting pilgrims. To add to the attraction, a special shrine was built to hold these relics. This gave a sense of uniqueness and authenticity. The pilgrims felt they were in the presence of something special and spiritually powerful.

As Armagh rose in importance, some smaller churches started to claim that they too had been founded by Patrick in order to place themselves under the protection of the growing power of Armagh. Many others were simply willing to recognize Armagh's supremacy and accept its authority in return for protection. These smaller churches and monasteries paid tribute, or taxes, to Armagh, which in turn added to the wealth of the monastery. As the power and influence of Armagh grew, Patrick's status as a cult figure also took on major importance. Patrick and Armagh were inexorably linked.

THE UÍ NÉILL INFLUENCE

There was another influence in the development of the cult of Patrick. At this time the most powerful family in Ulster, the Uí Néill (later called O'Neill) were expanding their territory. The Uí Néill were the most ambitious and influential family in Ireland and would remain so until well into Elizabethan times. They systematically defeated some smaller dynasties and took over the area of

Armagh. Thus Armagh now fell within their territory. The Uí Néill also claimed the high-kingship of Tara and had aspirations of being the most important dynasty in Ireland. There was a tradition of linking the high-kingship to the possession of the ancient site of Tara. So it was important that they claim rights over Tara. The high-kingship was not a position of absolute power as kingship was in the rest of Europe at the time, but it was nevertheless a prestigious position. The Uí Néill were determined to secure that prestige. They were also making their own province in Ulster the most important in Ireland, as this was certainly a way of declaring their own prominence to the whole island. If they were to be the primary dynasty in Ireland, their homeland would have to be the most important. Armagh, lying within Uí Néill territory, became part of that importance. They set about this task in a very systematic way by having their own annalists invent records of their successes and therefore their right to the Tara kingship. The Uí Néill were very clever at self-promotion. They managed to take over the hill of Tara, Ireland's ancient capital as it is sometimes called, and therefore declared themselves to be high-kings of Ireland. They had their scribes promulgate the importance of Tara and thus their right to the self-proclaimed title of high-king. The appellation "high-king" had no political significance but it did carry social prestige, and for centuries the Uí Néill considered themselves to be the most important dynasty in Ireland.

TARA—THE SACRED PLACE

Today Tara is still an exposed and windswept place and has remained visually impressive. It is about thirty-five miles from Dublin. Once you get off the main Dublin/Navan road, the winding country road takes you right up to the site. Sitting on the grass on this ancient hill in County Meath on a windy spring day, Edel Bhreathnach talked to us about how the Uí Néill took over this ritual site and made it their own. Looking around at the wide view of surrounding counties, it is not hard to understand why this site was such an impressive one to the ancients. It feels like the top of the world. The Uí Néill annalists invented the story of their family ancestry in order to justify their claim to this most prestigious of ancient Irish sites and to the early high-kingship of Ireland. Edel described the Uí Néill political machine: "Well, the Uí Néill were absolute masters of propaganda. Indeed, such masters that we as historians are only beginning to unravel their propaganda which really began and was put together in the eighth century." Part of that propaganda was the promotion of both Patrick and Armagh. Having taken over the ancient pagan site of Tara, they also promoted their church at Armagh as being the center of Irish Christianity.

CROAGH PATRICK

Sites associated with Patrick also grew abundantly in number. His missionary activity was greatly exaggerated. He would have had to have been a very energetic man to have climbed all the mountains and blessed all the wells associated with his name! The site of Croagh Patrick (Patrick's Mountain) is just one example of the growth of the Patrick cult. Croagh Patrick is in modern-day County Mayo in the west of Ireland and was once under the jurisdiction of the powerful Armagh. Each year at the end of July thousands of pilgrims climb the mountain associated with Patrick, attempting to emulate his climb and thereby earn penance and remission from sin. Many walk in bare feet—most starting out at dawn. It is quite a sight. But few of the people who make the climb realize how old a ritual this is and that the roots of Croagh Patrick go very far back in time. In fact they go back before the time of Patrick.

Many modern-day pilgrims at Croagh Patrick might wonder and marvel at Patrick's ability to climb such a difficult terrain. The truth is there is no evidence that Patrick ever visited the site, much less climbed the mountain. Scholars doubt he was ever there. The name of Patrick was "imposed" on the hill around the year 800, according to historian Peter Harbison. The church knew that it was an important pre-Christian ritual site and wanted to claim it for Christianity. Scholars believe that the mountain was once the domain of the Celtic god Lugh, whose feast day was August 1. This may be the reason that the annual climb is on the last Sunday in July. This date falls within the pagan feast time of Lúnasa. Peter Harbison also points out the sense of festival and fun about the modern pilgrimage. "I think what we are seeing in Croagh Patrick, is a Christianization, a very diplomatic Christianization of an old pagan festival in honor of the good god Lugh. And if you look at the pilgrims to this very day who climb Croagh Patrick, you notice that there are also a lot of young people who are telling stories and laughing as they go up and down," very much in the tradition of the older pagan feast day.

PATRICK'S ENDURING LEGACY

Patrick remains a strong and very real figure for us. His surviving texts give him this credibility. His words connect us to him in a way that is vibrant and surprisingly immediate, given the amount of time that has passed since his death. It really is quite extraordinary that his autobiography, written in the fifth century, serves as a testament of his own personal experiences with Ireland and the Irish. His writings are unique in that they are the only surviving manuscripts that describe Christian missionary work outside the boundaries of the mighty Roman Empire. Patrick is a singular voice coming to us in words that express his humanity, his humility, and his personal struggle to spread the Christian gospel to a people he first lived among as a slave.

A striking aspect of his personal writings is that Patrick is never conceited when he speaks. In fact he is reticent and uncertain about his own abilities because, as he explains, "I have not the education of others, who have absorbed to the full both law and sacred scripture alike, and who have never, from infancy onward, had to change to another language but rather could perfect the language they had." The education he missed while he was a slave in Ireland haunted him all his life. He never felt that he caught up with his classmates in spite of the fact that he went on with his education and was ordained a priest. In his writings he humbly apologizes for his poor Latin. Patrick's own language would have been a vulgar form of Latin, which would have been polished had he remained at school and not been taken into slavery in Ireland. He is conscious of the fact that he did not learn Latin grammar and syntax as a boy. Instead he found himself among the Gaelic-speaking Irish as a slave struggling to understand their foreign language. He also refers to his own "lack of knowledge and slow speech." Patrick apparently had a stammer. With all of these apparent obstacles in his path, it is remarkable that he persisted. He writes that his *Con-*

fession "may not be elegant but it is assuredly and most powerfully written on your hearts not with ink but with the spirit of the living God." The interesting thing about this passage is that it is a paraphrase of Paul's "Letter to the Corinthians." Obviously in spite of how little schooled he felt himself to be, Patrick was very familiar with the scriptures. Even at a distance of almost sixteen hundred years we can feel the gentle and self-doubting nature of the man. Fortitude may have been a part of Patrick's nature, but arrogance never was.

Although he was not the sole converter of the Irish that later documents would have us believe, his dedication to the Irish cannot be doubted. What kind of companion was he? He was probably not the kind of fellow who would sit around the community fire at night swapping stories. He was not Irish, after all, and by his own testimony declares that he always felt like an outsider in Ireland. His infamous mythological rebuttal of the pagan hero Oisín tells us just how stern storytellers considered him to be. We can only imagine how he must have shaken his head in wonder at the Irish propensity to enjoy a good time. But the letter he wrote to Coroticus in defense of his own converts is remarkable in its sincerity, tenderness, and the earnestness it expresses. In this letter Patrick cries out, "I grieve for you; I grieve, my most loved ones!" on hearing that some of his Irish converts have been robbed and killed by these British bounty hunters whom he describes as "rebels against Christ."

PATRICK THE PATRON SAINT

Armagh triumphed and finally emerged as the most important church in Ireland. So successful was the promotion of Armagh that to the present day both the Roman Catholic church and the Protestant Church of Ireland each have their primacies there. Two large cathedrals stand against the sky, one Protestant and one Catholic, both named after St. Patrick and both claiming descent from the saint. Summing up the phenomenon of both Patrick and his relationship with Armagh, Charlie Doherty says, "It was good fortune and astute politics, rather than any status conferred on it by Patrick, that allowed Armagh to emerge as the most important church in Ireland by the end of the seventh century." With the

Patrick first came to Ireland as a slave. Propaganda and clever politics would eventually make him the patron saint of the Irish. (*National Library of Ireland*)

emergence of Armagh as the principal ecclesiastical center of Ireland came the cult of Patrick, which has survived down the centuries to the present day. This cult has gone far beyond the domain of Christianity. Patrick is now the symbol of universal Irishness and in that role he seems to be unshakable. In modern terms his feast day has more to do with national or ethnic identity than religion.

ST. PATRICK AND HIS FEAST DAY

Does it really matter if most of what we hear of St. Patrick is simply fable or clever invention? His own writings are enough to tell us that he was humble, self-effacing, and persistent in his mission. He was a gentle and sincere man who gave his life to Ireland and the Irish. His elevation to the status of Ireland's chief apostle may be the cleverest piece of propaganda to come out of early Irish Christianity, but Patrick never sought this status for himself. He would probably be amazed at how his name has been remembered.

The celebration of the feast day of St. Patrick has been going on since the ninth century. Irish scholars who traveled and settled on the European continent all that time ago are credited with starting the tradition, possibly as a way of staying linked to their homeland. Even then Patrick had already become a symbol of Ireland to those exiles far from its shores. Nowadays many of the Irish at home and around the world who celebrate St. Patrick's Day on March 17 probably do not realize just how ancient a tradition this celebration really is. They are repeating a pattern first started almost twelve hundred years ago. In referring to the modern parade and the enormous worldwide celebration of St. Patrick, Charlie Doherty said: "The very idea of this huge celebration is something I don't think could have been contemplated even in the wildest dreams of the people who created the myth of Patrick in the first place." St. Patrick's Day is a rallying point for Irishness and a good excuse to have a party—and, in a twist of irony, it is probably true to say that it has become more of a pagan feast than a Christian holy day.

[6]

The Rise of
Celtic Spirituality

WHEN PATRICK DIED in 492—or 496, depending on whichever version of the annals one prefers—he had been spreading Christianity among the Irish for more than sixty years. But Ireland had not changed much over that time. Pockets of Christianity existed around the royal courts and local centers of power, where Patrick and other early missionaries had been successful, but the vast majority of the country was still pagan. There are faint echoes of an organized Christian province that may have existed in the southeast of Ireland, where Palladius had probably been sent by the pope in 431, the year before Patrick is supposed to have arrived in the north. With direct sea links to the Roman provinces of Gaul and Hispania—modern France and Spain—raiders would have been bringing Christian slaves into the country for more than a century. And some native Irish fighting as mercenaries for Rome on the Continent could also have been converted and brought their new faith back home.

THE FIRST GENERATION OF
CHRISTIAN MISSIONARIES

In spite of the best efforts of Patrick's later propagandists to ensure that Patrick received full credit for converting Ireland to Christianity, a number of other contemporary fifth-century names survived Armagh's campaign to spread the Patrick cult across the country and obscure any challenge to Patrick's supremacy. Along with Palladius in the south, a priest called Auxilius founded a church near present-day Naas, southwest of Dublin, a site long associated with the kings of Leinster. A man called Secundinus may have set up a Christian community close to the great royal site of Tara, while a third man—Iserninus—is associated with the founding of a church at Kilcullen, close to the royal center of the kings of Leinster at Dún Ailinne. Patrick's probable first foundation was at Downpatrick in County Down, a royal site of the kings of Ulster, while Armagh—center of the Patrick cult—was near Navan Fort, greatest of all pre-Christian kingship sites in the north. "Armagh" is only a different pronunciation of the ancient "Ard Macha." Church leaders in Europe must have had excellent information about the political setup in Ireland. It was probably deliberate policy to send missionaries directly to the local centers of secular power. From the beginning, Christianity in Ireland spread from the top down, a religion of the upper classes in Irish society.

Enough other names survive in early monastery texts to suggest that there were many bishops, priests, and missionaries from outside Ireland who operated both before and during the time Patrick evangelized the north. All must have tried to re-create in Ireland the same Roman model of Christianity they knew in Europe. Christianity may have started as a freethinking and populist offshoot of Judaism, but it had taken on an authoritarian Roman structure soon after the Emperor Constantine's Edict of Milan in 313. Bishops controlled all junior priests and subsidiary churches within their jurisdiction, just as magistrates and regional governors controlled lesser officials in secular Roman society. In the church this was and is still called the diocesan model. Unfortunately it did not work in Ireland where every petty king and tribal leader considered himself independent in his own territory, even if he acknowledged a more powerful regional king as his overlord.

A UNIQUELY IRISH CHURCH

Brother Sean O'Duinn, an authority on the early Irish church and a monk at the modern Benedictine Abbey of Glenstall in County Limerick, explained the difficulty facing early missionaries in Ireland. "From the beginning, Christianity was an urban religion," he said. "When the apostles left Jerusalem to preach the faith, they went to the great cities of the time—Antioch, Rome, Lyons, and Odessa. Even in the heart of the empire it took a long time before country people were evangelized. The word 'pagan' comes from a Roman word meaning 'countrymen,' so pagans were just people in remote areas who had not yet been Christianized. It was not like civilized Europe when the first missionaries came to Ireland. There were no towns or cities, no central administration. Instead you had dozens of tiny little states called *Túatha* and each, in theory anyway, was independent. The early missionaries had to go around to all the kings and leaders one by one. It must have been a difficult piecemeal kind of operation."

The first churches were built on tribal lands given by local kings. The first converts and the first native Irish priests often came from within the royal families themselves. The unique monastic form of the Irish church evolved because of this link between local church and local king. Church lands had to stay within the tribe, so giving spiritual authority to an outside bishop was acceptable only if authority on the ground remained tied to the local royal dynasty. The first missionaries were pragmatic men, organizing their church to suit the conditions in which they found themselves. Within a century of Patrick's death, a monastic model of Irish Christianity was firmly established where individual monasteries, linked to local or regional dynasties, were the centers of religious power in Ireland, ruled by abbots who might not even be priests but would be closely related to the local king. Abbots and monasteries feuded and fought amongst themselves just as kings and *Túatha* did, trying to increase their wealth and power and bring other monasteries under their control. In later centuries this would become full-scale warfare, with abbots leading their monastic troops in attacks on other monasteries.

Why did the kings and chiefs of Ireland accept Christianity so readily? No early Irish saints seem to have died for their faith; Ireland produced no Christian martyrs. As we have seen, the Celtic pantheon of deities was highly inclusive, and druid priests probably thought the Christian god would fit in well. We know from Patrick's own writings that he incorporated many pre-Christian beliefs and traditions into the Christianity he preached; other early missionaries obviously did the same. More important, Christianity carried with it the seductive aura of Roman power and civilization, and the heady promise of literacy. Ireland might have been an illiterate land, but its leaders were well aware of what was happening on the Continent. They would have seen the power of reading and writing and realized how it could be used to enhance their control. In the constant jockeying for position among Irish tribes, shrewd leaders understood that a monastery under their protection was worth its weight in gold. Where kings and their advisors—the druids—understood the political advantages of Christianity, previously pagan sites probably became the first churches and druids the first priests, bringing many of their ceremonies and traditions with them into the new faith. Local deities turned overnight into saints as saints took on the miraculous powers of pagan gods and goddesses. Nowhere is this process more evidence than in the story of St. Brigid, one of the three founding saints of Ireland along with St. Patrick and St. Columba.

WHEN GODS BECAME SAINTS

Today the word "saint" is associated mostly with Catholicism and a process of canonization by the pope of especially holy men and women. In early Christianity a saint was simply a man or woman who through his or her own character or actions seemed that much closer to God than ordinary people and so had power to act as an intermediary between the human and heavenly realm. Founders of monasteries were invariably considered saints by later generations. Their relics—such body parts as might have survived—became the most valuable treasure of any monastery. Sometimes it is difficult to know whether some of the saints described in later monastery annals from Christianity's earliest period in Ireland are real people or just pre-Christian gods and goddesses adopted into the new faith.

"The Irish eventually accepted Christianity," Glenstall monk Sean O'Duinn said, "but it was a very long process, taking hundreds of years. Over this time there was a certain convergence, a blurring of belief at the border of old and new faith." Many saints existed in this blurred no-man's-land between Christianity and paganism.

St. Brigid is a favorite source of argument among scholars. Was she a real person living in the sixth century A.D. who founded the first great woman's monastery in Ireland, the convent of Kildare, or did later monastic writers simply take the Irish earth goddess Brigid, whose name comes from the old Irish *Briganti*, meaning "the exalted one," and turn her into a Christian saint? The cult of the goddess Brigid was closely associated with the Kildare region, where a religious community claiming St. Brigid as their founding abbess was a major Christian center for a thousand years. There is evidence from Celtic Europe that priestesses in charge of certain shrines took on the human attributes of the goddess by taking her name. So the priestess of Brigid might be called "the Brigid."

Brigid scholar Paurigeen Clancy sees no difficulty in reconciling the Christian and pre-Christian stories. "If there's a strong cult of a pre-Christian goddess," she said, "it would make absolute sense to Christianize it and bring it into the new faith by having a holy woman take the name and so 'inherit' the mantle of the goddess." This is just the sort of convergence that Glenstall Abbey's Sean O'Duinn was describing. The founder of the church at Kildare may have been born into a druid family who had looked after Brigid's shrine for generations. The goddess turned into a saint but retained all the female archetypes of the divine. St. Brigid is called Muire nan Gaol, "Mary of the Gael." She is portrayed as the healer, the wise woman, speaking with animals and controlling the forces of nature. The list of miracles she performed, according to Cogitosus, who wrote *The Life of St. Brigid the Virgin* around A.D. 650, included hanging her cloak on a sunbeam, protecting crops from a storm, causing rivers to flood or change direction, and providing meat, butter, and bread in abundance whenever her people were in need. These are stories more relevant to a fertility goddess than a Christian abbess, protecting her people just as she had done for untold centuries before the coming of Christianity.

ST. BRIGID'S DAY AT LOUGH GUR'S STONE CIRCLE

February 1 is Imbolg in the pre-Christian calendar. The first of the four "quarter days" celebrated the reawakening of the land after its winter sleep. At the center of a great stone circle in Lough Gur—a place of ritual and worship for at least four thousand years—a present day Imbolg festival gave clues to those first Christian centuries when old and new faith were learning to live together. We had come to Lough Gur to meet a *seanchaí*, a traditional Irish storyteller who was known locally for her tales of St. Brigid.

The stone circle at Lough Gur, built around 2000 B.C., is one of the largest and best preserved in Ireland, 113 standing stones bordering a circle more than 150 feet in diameter. About 30 adults and children had come on a cold and damp winter evening to honor the ancient festival of Imbolg. Most came from the local area, including the priestess. These were not the sort of people one normally expects to be celebrating pagan rites, just local farmers and villagers, even a local schoolteacher. Catholicism has lost so much of its grip on Ireland in recent years that a growing number of people are looking back to their Celtic roots for spiritual meaning. The ceremony itself was a modern innovation since pre-Christian druid priests left no record of their rituals. There were prayers, singing, and a procession around the central fire, not so different from many Christian festivals across the ages. In the early dusk of a winter evening, with candles flickering against the standing stones on the perimeter of the circle and a fire blazing brightly in the center, it was not hard to imagine Patrick and other early missionaries attending similar ceremonies, watching and planning how best to incorporate native beliefs into their missionary teaching. The fire blazed brighter as the night grew darker, a damp mist blowing in across the standing stones that ringed the ancient circle. All the children carried candles as they circled the fire. The singing ceased and the worshippers gathered close to the fire as the *seanchaí* came forward, helped by two of the older children and leaning on a stout stick. She was settled in a chair beside the fire, and the priestess came forward to wrap a warm blanket around her to protect her from the chill. In a soft but clear voice, she started telling the story of Brigid, the Christian saint.

THE SEANCHAÍ'S STORY OF BRIGID

"It was Christianity's earliest time in Ireland," the *seanchaí* said, "and a high-king of Ireland got one of his slave girls in the family way. When the girl-child was born, she was the most beautiful child in all the land. And they say that Brigid, who was the fertility goddess of Ireland, came in and looked at the child in the cradle and gave her blessing. So they called the child Brigid. And the high-king said to the mother, 'You have been so good and given me such a beautiful daughter, I'm giving you your freedom.' So Brigid grew up in the house of the high-king, and when she reached the age of fifteen, the king said it was time for her to marry. But Brigid had other ideas. She was a very beautiful girl and many people wanted her hand. So she said to the Lord above, 'The king wants me to marry,' she said, 'but I do not wish it. I wish to take the veil and be single all my life.' So she said to the Lord Above, 'Will you make me hideous so I don't have to marry?' And the Lord thought so much of her that he gave her a terrible carbuncle over her eye. Her face swelled up and she became so hideous that no man would touch her. So the king said to her, 'Right! you've got your wish. Go away and take some women with you and take the veil.'

"So Brigid went away with a group of virgins and widows, and together they started a farm and did very well. In those days the bear and the wolf and the wildcat roamed Ireland, and after a few years the villagers came to Brigid and said, 'There's a wolf taking our sheep. We can't do anything about it. He kills our dogs and when we went to shoo him away, he almost took one of our children.' So Brigid walked out into the night and called the wolf to her, and she said to him, 'Wolf, have you taken sheep belonging to my people? We need those sheep for milk and meat and clothes.' 'Well,' said the wolf, 'I'm old,' he says, 'and not as fast as I used to be. But I too must live, and that's why I've killed your dogs and I will kill your sheep.' And Brigid stood and looked him in the eye and said: 'You won't; come here and stand by me.' And he came and he stood at the heels of Brigid, and she gave him a big plate of meat and a big bowl of milk. 'For that,' said she, 'wild animal that you are, you will guard the flocks from dogs like those you have killed, and from all of your kind, and you will be with me as my servant and guardian for the rest of my life.' And the wolf agreed and he was.

"And Brigid called the birds of the air and they came to her. And when times were hard and she had no flour, she called upon her namesake who was the goddess of fertility and the harvest, and the goddess ensured her crops were fruitful and that all who were under Brigid's protection flourished. Now the Devil saw all of this and didn't think very much of it and he said, 'I'll put paid to all this,' he said. But Brigid made a cross out of rushes, and she held it up and said, 'Let this cross be the sign of my God,' she said. 'And no devil will come near any house where this cross is held.'

"And so," the *seanchaí* concluded, "every year we make the Brigid cross fresh with rushes, so that every year we have fresh protection and a bountiful harvest. And so long as this is made, both St. Brigid and the goddess will guard Ireland."

Pagan and Christian beliefs, still coexisting side-by-side. A generation ago there would have hardly been a house in Ireland without a Brigid cross hanging on its wall, fresh every year. But Ireland is changing; old customs and old beliefs have lost their power among the Internet generation, although in the west—from County Kerry in the south to County Donegal in the north—it is still possible to find communities that honor the old traditions. At the tiny two-roomed schoolhouse of Dunquin, right at the tip of the Dingle peninsula, children gather rushes and weave their Brigid crosses every year under the guidance of a Gaelic-speaking schoolteacher who tells them stories of both saint and goddess. When they have made sufficient crosses, the children hand-carry them to every house in the village. The cross itself represents the Christian Crucifixion, but the four arms spreading out from a woven square of reeds at the center also suggest the rays of the sun, the ancient pre-Christian religious symbol. Clearly the origin of Brigid crosses is much older than the coming of Christianity to Ireland.

WOMEN LEADERS IN THE EARLY IRISH CHURCH

When an Irish monastic scholar called Cogitosus wrote the *Life of Brigid* in the mid-seventh century, he had little to draw on except ancient folk tales, although he linked Brigid with Ibar, another missionary bishop who preached the Gospel in Ireland at the time of Patrick. Ibar's association with Brigid suggests the possibility that he was a missionary working in the Kildare region. There are enough stories about the abbey in Kildare to suggest that women played a more central role in the early Irish church than is often thought. There was clearly a major church there as early as A.D. 500 that was both the seat of a bishop and under female control. A later *Life of Brigid* tells how Brigid was consecrated a bishop "by mistake," since a woman bishop would have been unthinkable in the Christian church at that time. Cogitosus suggests she was "bishop in all but name." Yet the fact that the story survives at all argues for a powerful female leader of the church in Kildare. In later centuries Kildare became a dual monastery for men and women, one of the most important centers of Christianity in Ireland. Liam de Paor, one of the most respected of all early Irish historians, wrote that while there is no good evidence of male monasteries in Ireland before A.D. 535–540, female foundations appeared as much as forty years earlier. "It may well be," he wrote in his landmark book *St. Patrick's World*, "that the great Irish monastic movement, that would dominate the ecclesiastical history of the country from the 7th through the 12th centuries, was pioneered by communities of women from as early as the 5th century."

The argument for strong women church leaders has precedent. There is clear evidence of important women deacons and leaders of religious communities during Christianity's initial spread across the Roman world. Only later did a patriarchal church leadership relegate women to second-class status. In Ireland Patrick himself wrote about women coming forward as "virgins for Christ." He went on to write: "They do not do it with their father's consent; on the contrary they endure harassment and false accusations from their parents, but nonetheless their numbers increase, as well as those of widows and women living in chastity." Later monastery annals say that Brigid was born in 452 and died in either 524 or 526. Whoever founded the abbey at Kildare would therefore have been converted by the first generation of missionaries to come to Ireland.

There is no question that the status and independence allowed women under early Irish Brehon Law may have contributed to their importance in the early church. Brigid herself, in most of the legends, stands up to her father when he wants her to get married. Women were usually of lesser value than men, but some women poets warranted the highest honor price while queens like Medb of Connaught clearly had a status equal to their husbands. Women in Ireland seem to have enjoyed an independence that women elsewhere in the world might have envied. Paurigeen Clancy sees these early Christian women as Ireland's first feminists. "Women were expected to get married," Paurigeen said, "but the church offered an alternative; not just going out and founding monasteries but literacy as well, the opportunity to learn how to read and write. It's no wonder they jumped at it." Yet Patrick's own words, and the story of how Brigid defied the high-king, make it clear that becoming a virgin for Christ often did not happen without heated opposition from family and tribe. So little is known about this first century of Irish Christianity, but women certainly played a far greater role in spreading Christianity through the country than later histories of the Irish church ever suggest.

THE SECOND GENERATION

Sometime around A.D. 500, a new group of founding saints arrived from Britain to galvanize the Irish church into its second growth spurt. Why it needed galvanizing is not known, although the efforts of Patrick and the other early missionaries may have been exhausted. Probably only a small percentage of the country had been converted. Farsighted kings saw advantages to the new faith, but many others ignored it. Christianity had yet to reach a critical mass in Ireland. A catalyst would be needed before the monastic explosion could begin.

If the first generation of Christian founders of the Irish church came from the Roman province of Gaul, it was Britain—especially Wales and Scotland—that birthed the second generation of Irish saints. St. Enda was Irish born but came from the abbey of Whithorn—in a part of Scotland known as Galloway that directly faced the Irish coast of Ulster in the north—to found a monastery on the Aran Islands. A key British figure was St. Finnian, from Llancarfan in Wales, who founded the monastery of Clonard in the Irish midlands. Another saint—St. Mochta—apparently crossed the Irish Sea to establish a monastery at Louth on the east coast.

Everything is hazy about this "Dark Age." What sources exist were written centuries after the events they were describing. Although Rome had abandoned Britain to its fate decades earlier, the province was able to hold out against barbarian invaders for a long time—the sixth century is also the time of the legendary King Arthur—and the British church appears to have been strong and vibrant over this period. It is frustrating to know so little about such an important time but there are occasional flashes of knowledge. Recent excavations at the site of Whithorn in Scotland show that this was a major Christian site, set right in the heart of country settled by Irish—the Dál Riada—sometime in the final centuries of the Roman period. The Christian abbey of St. David in Wales had been producing scholars and monastic founders for more than a century. If Patrick and the first generation of founders attempted to set up a diocesan model of Christianity like the one they had known on the Continent, it seems likely this second generation of founders from Britain were the ones who firmly established the monastic model that ultimately created such a uniquely Irish church. The torch was being passed, and St. Enda of Aran was probably the most influential of the new generation, the "young Turks" of Irish saints.

ST. ENDA OF ARAN

Like all early saints, what is known about St. Enda is more folklore than history. The only known description of his life was written more than eight hundred years after his death. Yet his monastic school on Aran seems to have been the most important center of religious training in the early sixth century. The founders of most of Ireland's greatest monasteries are said to have studied under Enda: Ciaran of Clonmacnoise, Kevin of Glendalough, Columba—in Irish "Colmcille"—who went on to become the third of Ireland's founding saints, and a whole lot more. Even Brendan the Navigator apparently stopped off at Aran to get Enda's blessing before heading off into the Atlantic and—so it is suggested—sailing as far as America. Like the Patrick cult, most of the stories about Enda were later propaganda designed to build up the importance of the saint and his monastery on Inismor, the largest of the Aran Islands that lie in the Atlantic off Ireland's west coast. But propaganda aside, St. Enda was clearly a very important figure.

Enda was probably born around A.D. 450, somewhere in the north of Ireland. Legend says he was a king's son who later became a king himself. After a particularly bloody battle, King Enda supposedly arrived at a convent run by one of his sisters where he decided to ravish one of the young novices who had caught his eye. Before he could touch her, the young girl, being both virtuous and a bride of Christ, died piously in the bedchamber where she had been sent to await the king's pleasure. Enda, so the story goes was "struck to his soul" in horror at her death. His sister the abbess, clearly not one to pass up the chance for a good Christian homily, told Enda he would die too if he did not repent and accept Christ. The king became a devout Christian and traveled to Scotland to complete his religious education at the *Candida Casa*—the White House—at Whithorn. Eventually he settled on the Aran Islands, arriving on a stone boat, the only kind a holy saint could ever consider using. A rock in a small bay on Inismor's east coast is still pointed out today as the boat of the saint.

There are a large number of early Christian church sites on Inismor, which was an important religious center by early in the sixth century A.D. "Aran of the Saints," as it was known, continued to be a major center of Christian pilgrimage for the next thousand years. Nothing remains of the monastery that Enda founded; early monasteries were of wood and wattle and daub, just like the farmsteads and home sites of everyone else. What remains today dates from a later period when monastic buildings were made of stone, although most of those were torn down in the sixteenth century to build the fort used by the forces of English dictator Oliver Cromwell to control the island. The tiny half-ruined church of *Teaghlach Einne*—the church of Enda—still survives, built in the ninth century, perhaps on the site of Enda's original wooden church. Legend says that Enda's tomb was to the north of the church, but the whole area is now covered by drifting sand. While the church itself is half-buried, enough has been cleared for a visitor to walk inside and stand—perhaps—where the man most responsible for introducing monasticism to Ireland once preached and taught.

The monastic regime of St. Enda seems to have been appallingly severe, with constant fasting, discomfort, and continuous study and prayer. One story tells how he tested the holiness of his students by having them put to sea naked in just the frame of a currach—the traditional Irish boat where the frame was usually covered with animal skins. If the water came in, they were still in a state of terrible sin. Oddly enough, hundreds of disciples seem to have been attracted to this ascetic life. Legend says that no less than 120 saints are buried in the monastery graveyard near today's village of Cill Einne, no doubt having died of exposure after St. Enda's rigorous tests of faith. Enda himself comes across in the stories as a cantankerous and argumentative man. He kicked St. Columba off the island, denying him the use of a boat so the future saint had to swim 8 miles through stormy seas to the mainland. He also argued with St. Brecan, who had a monastery at the other end of the island, about who would control the biggest part of the island. On Inismor today, islanders still tell the story of the contest between the two saints. Enda and Brecan agreed to each say mass before dawn in their respective monasteries and then ride out toward each other. The island would be divided between them at the place where they met. Brecan, according to the Enda legends, cheated and set out before dawn, but God caused his horse's hooves to stick in the sand so he could not go on, allowing Enda to claim the lion's share of the island. There is little of the "pious monk" about early saints like Enda, more likely to curse an enemy than bless a friend, but this is typical of early Irish saints. A later Welsh scholar wrote: "The saints of this land are more vindictive than the saints of any other region." Perhaps we see dim reflections of earlier figures in these monastic records, druid priests who carried with them the power and fury of the old nature gods, hidden behind the mask of a new Christian faith. Brecan, the saint who tried to stop Enda from controlling Inismor, is also the name of a pre-Christian god on the island who was destroyed by another early saint. These ancient legends give hints of real people and real events at the beginning of the sixth century A.D.

Christianity was taking root in Ireland; the critical mass was forming. But it still needed a catalyst before Ireland could change from a pagan country into the Land of Saints and Scholars. At the end of the fifth century, Christianity was still restricted to small pockets of faith around some of the royal courts. By the start of the seventh century, dozens of wealthy and powerful monasteries—like Glendalough, Clonmacnoise, Inisfallen, Finglas, and others—dominated the land. What happened in between?

THE DENDROCHRONOLOGIST'S STORY

Michael Baillie provided clues to life in Bronze Age Ireland when he showed how oak trees preserved in bogs pointed to a great climate catastrophe in 1159 B.C. Now dendrochronology offers clues to why the Christian church became so successful in sixth-century Ireland. In his laboratory at Queen's University, Belfast, Michael unrolled a piece of graph paper more than twenty feet long that held tree ring measurements across seven thousand years of Irish history. The tree rings suggest that catastrophic climate disasters devastated Ireland several times over this period. A serious climate problem occurred in 2345 B.C., around the time Neolithic Irish farmers were first raising great burial mounds to honor their ancestors. The 1159 B.C. event ended Ireland's early Bronze Age and created a warrior society. Trees also suggest the climate was terrible around 430 B.C., the time when the Irish archaeological record goes silent at the transition between the Bronze and the Iron Age, the legendary period when the Celts are supposed to have first come to Ireland. In the Christian era another climate event with worldwide repercussions occurred in A.D. 540, according to tree-ring evidence. As Michael explained, "It shows up in trees in Ireland, Scotland, and England, right across Europe and up into Scandinavia. It's in American, Siberian, and Chinese trees. We're seeing the local symptoms of a massive environmental event that's tied right into the Dark Age period."

Archaeological journalist David Keyes, in his book *Catastrophe*, puts the disaster five years earlier in 535–536 and suggests that the massive volcanic eruption of Krakatoa in Java—many times bigger than its later 1883 explosion—caused the catastrophe. While not ruling out the volcano theory, Michael Baillie prefers the possibility of cometary bombardment, fragments of comet breaking up as they hit Earth's atmosphere. The dust and ash they would put into the atmosphere is equivalent to a massive volcanic eruption. "Based on an analysis of meteor showers by some British astronomers, the earth was at increased risk of bombardment between 400 and 600," Michael explained.

He put one of his bog oak samples under the microscope. "This tree's pretty typical," he said, "wide rings from A.D. 500 through the next three decades but in the late 530s the rings change character; they get incredibly narrow." He replaced the sample with a different slice of bog oak. "But this is the really interesting example." It showed a ring for A.D. 540 so narrow as to be almost invisible, then big fat rings for the next few years. "This is almost certainly reaction wood," Michael explained. "The tree was surrounded by other trees which were blown down at the time. So the tree's released and puts on massive rings afterwards. I've seen events of this sort in quite a number of trees."

It is an image of the apocalypse, acres of forests dead and dying with just a few trees struggling to survive through that terrible year; birds and animals mostly gone, the people in shock, wondering what had become of their world. It was a planet-wide disaster with catastrophic results. There is evidence of crop failures and widespread famine around the world; everywhere societies were in turmoil. In Byzantium the historian Procopius described an eighteen-month darkening of the sun. In China there are records of frost and snow in midsummer; the country erupted in violence and rebellion, spawning new dynasties that finally resulted in the reunification of China under the Sui dynasty thirty years later. On the other side of the Pacific, Teotihuacan, greatest of all pre-Columbian cities and center of a mighty Mexican empire, collapsed in anarchy and revolution.

JUSTINIAN'S PLAGUE

Bubonic plague usually follows climate disruptions as disease-carrying animals move outside their usual territory in search of food, infecting animal and human populations with no natural immunity. Just two years later, in 542, Europe was hit by plague. Once such a conflagration starts, there is no stopping it until the outbreak has burned itself out. Justinian's Plague—named for the Roman Emperor of Byzantium—quickly engulfed his capital of Constantinople and spread across Europe like a forest fire to reach Ireland by 544. A writer in Spain recorded dismally, "The world we knew died." Irish monastic records—the *Annals of Ulster*—for the year A.D. 544 record the arrival of "the first mortality called *blefed* [bubonic plague]." Four years later the records have upgraded it to a *mortalitas magna*, a great death, and provide a long list of the important people who died that year, including kings and abbots.

Across the Christian world, people thought of these disasters in biblical terms. "The sun goes dim—a dust veil effect of some kind—the crops die and then plague follows." Michael Baillie summed up the sequence of disasters. "You put that package together," he went on, "especially when you add in some strange evidence that suggest earthquakes, and it begins to bear a striking resemblance to God's anger against the land of Egypt in the book of Exodus. Almost a generation later, Zacharias of Mytilene wrote in 556 that 'the sun was darkened by day and the moon by night' and adds that what they lived through was like the plagues of Egypt coupled with the destruction of Sodom and Gomorrah. This would be a selling point for Christians, a trigger for the wholesale Christianization of Ireland."

Trees and crops recover relatively quickly from the initial climate disaster, but plague has a much longer-lasting effect. It may carry off only 10 to 15 percent of the population in the first attack, but it has a nasty habit of staying around, returning again and again to infect those without natural immunity who either survived or were born after the first attack. For some reason, plague is most devastating to those in the prime of life. The able-bodied—the backbone of society—die in the first outbreak, but children and old people die in greater numbers next time around. And when a society loses its children, it loses any hope for the future.

Plague spreads faster in crowded conditions. With no towns in sixth-century Ireland, the royal courts were probably major centers of contagion. As traders, scholars, poets, priests, and warriors traveled across the land, the disease spread from Túath to Túath. The great quarter-day pagan festivals, drawing people together from a wide region, would also have accelerated the spread of the disease. Although Christian monks certainly died just as fast as their pagan neighbors, it is easy to imagine church leaders explaining the plague as divine retribution against a sinful people who had not yet accepted Christianity. People turn to religion in times of stress. The *mortalitas magna* remained endemic in Ireland for more than a century, returning generation after generation, the worst outbreak of bubonic plague until the Black Death almost a thousand years later.

ST. EIMIN'S STORY

There is a revealing description in the *Caen* (law) *of Eimin Bran* about the seventh-century saint Eimin. Plague was raging through Ireland again, as it had at regular intervals since the first outbreak in 544. The king of Leinster came to the saint, accompanied by all his chieftains, and offered that they would all become monks if only the saint would save his people. After praying all night, St. Eimin made a bargain with the king. As evil filled the land and plague was the result, the saint could not stop the deaths but he agreed that his holy monks would sacrifice themselves in such a way that God's anger would be set aside; one monk would die for every Leinster chieftain who died from the plague. The deal was considered important enough to be set down as a *caen*, a law jointly made by priests and kings to govern the land. In return the king and his chiefs were to obey God's laws, protect Eimin's monastery from all enemies, and agree never to collect taxes or rents from it or its dependent churches. If the king broke the bargain, those monks still alive would curse him and his people, and Leinster would no longer be under the saint's divine protection.

St. Eimin sounds like a modern pragmatist, knowing nothing could stop his monks dying of plague and so making use of their deaths to advance the Christian cause. But it is wrong to apply modern attitudes to ancient times. St. Eimin's story offers a glimpse of what probably happened in many places across Ireland after 540: terrified people believing the old gods had failed them and converting to Christianity in hopes that the priests of the new religion would save them, while the priests truly believed that the

plague was a sign of God's anger against the wickedness of the people. St. Eimin's promise was doubtless fulfilled. Since plague does
not discriminate between Christian and non-Christian, probably as
many monks died as did people from the Leinster royal court, but
their deaths would be seen as holy sacrifices. This is a common
theme in the lives of sixth-and-seventh-century saints, how in time
of plague they would give up their lives so others may live. This was
a deeply superstitious age. A catastrophe like the climate disaster of
540 and the ensuing outbreaks of plague would have been seen by
non-Christians as the anger of the gods while Christians would
genuinely have believed that prayer and the holy intercession of
saints could make a difference. Saints were taking over the role of
pre-Christian gods and goddesses as intermediaries between people
and the forces that ruled their lives.

Historian Elva Johnston tells a story about a sixth-century
saint who was begged by the people down in County Kerry to save
them from a terrible monster that was killing people all over the
place. The saint's name—Mac Creiche—happens to be an Irish
word used for a type of bubonic plague. So the saint calls down the
fire from heaven and destroys the monster, but it keeps returning in
different forms, once like a monster with terrible claws, next like a
giant badger that breaths out a deadly poison. And each time the
saint fights in single combat with different forms of the monster
until it is finally defeated.

"You can see," Elva said, "how the idea of a saint defending the
people against a natural catastrophe that's come to Ireland from
outside, like a monster, would be very appealing. Everyone's going
to want that sort of heavenly power on their side."

Monasteries also held the relics of the great founding saints,
and the mid-sixth century is when the cult of relics began to take
hold. Relics, usually any remaining body parts of particularly holy
saints, were viewed rather like spiritual antibiotics. You would go to
a particular monastery because it might have the tooth of St.
Patrick, and maybe if it was brought out, you would be cured.

FILLING A POWER VACUUM

Elva Johnston believes these few decades in the middle of the sixth
century were one of the most important times in Irish history.

"Everything we now think of as early Irish society was coming together then," she explained. "Historical records aren't very good, but it's clear many important earlier royal dynasties disappeared in the sixth century and new power structures were forming. Society broke down because people who died from the plague tended to be prominent, important people at the royal courts where contagion was far worse than out in the wilds. Who or what would fill the vacuum? Around this time we begin to see a very powerful monastic church emerging, with monasteries emerging as major landowners."

Within a generation of the worldwide climate disaster in 540, most of the monasteries that gave rise to the Golden Age of Irish Christianity were already in existence. Among them the great monastery of Durrow, supposedly founded in 543 by St. Columba, Clonmacnoise, founded in 545 by St. Ciaran, and Clonfert, founded—according to legend—in 547 by St. Brendan (the Navigator). All these monasteries were closely linked to local kings, many from ambitious new dynasties who had taken advantage of the power vacuum existing in mid-sixth-century Ireland.

In the south an ambitious dynasty—the Eóganacht—burst out from their royal site on top of the Rock of Cashel—in County Tipperary—to become the new kings of Munster. The Uí Néill, who would dominate Irish kingship for the next five hundred years, expanded out of original homelands west of the Shannon in Connaught. In the north they and their allies took over most of present-day Donegal, Derry, and Antrim, pushing the once-mighty rulers of Ulster back to the sea. In the midlands the Uí Néill took over the ancient kingship site of Tara, exploiting the symbolic power of a religious site in use since Neolithic times to claim the high-kingship of Ireland. Religious leaders in Armagh, who were as ambitious as any secular ruler, were quick to ally themselves with the rising power of the Uí Néill. It gave Armagh the protection of the most powerful dynasty in the land while the Uí Néill got the blessing and protection of St. Patrick in heaven, important for any new dynasty trying to legitimize its hold on power. This link between Armagh and the Uí Néill helped ensure that the cult of Patrick would take precedence over other Irish saints, just as Armagh itself came to dominate the Irish church.

[7]

Saints and Scribes

BY THE END of the sixth-century, Ireland was very different from the way it was when Patrick died a century earlier. New dynasties ruled the land and dozens of wealthy and powerful monasteries, closely allied with local or regional kings, were changing the structure of Irish society. Ireland was, for all intents and purposes, a Christian land. Already it was putting its own unique stamp on Christianity, a Celtic Irish church that it would export first to Britain and then right across the ancient Roman provinces of Europe, a vigorous new growth to infuse new life into a tired and archaic faith which existed primarily in the decaying towns of a now-vanished empire.

CLONMACNOISE—PORTRAIT OF A SEVENTH-CENTURY MONASTERY

Donnchadh Ó Corráin is professor of history at the National University of Ireland in Cork. A puckish figure with a shock of white hair and a cherubic grin, he is one of Ireland's leading early Irish scholars and brings an infectious enthusiasm to his study of early Christianity. He had come to the monastery site of Clonmacnoise where a number of ruined stone churches and two slender round towers now share several acres of lush grass with hundreds of gravestones and a modern concrete and glass open-air church built for the pope's 1979 visit. The River Shannon flows right past the monastery in a great lazy loop, full of pleasure craft on a hot summer afternoon. St. Ciaran chose his site well; the Shannon had been a route up and down Ireland from Neolithic times. There was a bridge over the river at Clonmacnoise at the beginning of the ninth century; before that would have been a ferry, part of the important road between Uí Néill lands to the east and the kingdom of Connaught in the west. In good weather Clonmacnoise has a pastoral beauty with sheep grazing in the water meadows below the monastery and a ruined Norman castle perched lopsidedly on a nearby mound, its walls leaning so far off center that it seems the slightest breeze will send it tumbling down into the Shannon. But in bad weather, when rain comes hissing off the river in gray sheets, sluicing from roofless church walls, puddling around the graves and flowing in waterfalls off the round towers that rise through the gloom like God's fingers pointing the way to heaven, Clonmacnoise shows a harsher face. Life in a monastery might be good for the soul, but sixth-century Ireland was neither comfortable nor safe.

Round towers are the most distinctive of all Irish monastic landmarks, topped with conical stone caps—those at Clonmacnoise broke off long ago—with entrances as much as twelve feet above the ground, reached by exterior wooden steps or ladders. The Brothers Grimm must have seen such towers before they wrote their fairy tale about Rapunzel, letting down her long hair like rope so her lover could climb to her chamber at the top. Round towers are unique to Ireland, but they were not built until the eleventh century, half a millennium after St. Ciaran founded Clonmacnoise and long after the Viking attacks for which people once thought they had been built. Yet this is how most visitors imagine the monasteries looked throughout their existence.

"There were no stone buildings here before 800 A.D.," Donnchadh said as he scrambled up the ladder placed against the tower to reach the entrance. Entry to the Clonmacnoise tower is forbidden to visitors, and Donnchadh had been beaming in delight ever since he had been told he could climb all the way to the top. It was his first time, and he squeezed through the narrow outside door and puffed his way up three interior ladders with the enthusiasm of a schoolboy on a holiday adventure. The narrow stone parapet on top offered a panoramic view over the whole Clonmacnoise site, swarming with summer tourists. "It would have been even busier back then, lots of people, lots of small boats on the river," Donnchadh said. "You'd see a large enclosure, surrounded by a big circular ditch, probably with a wooden fence or palisade on top. It would have enclosed a number of wattle-and-daub and wooden plank buildings. The Irish word for chapel is *domhachteach,* which simply means an oak house."

Some of these buildings were churches and chapels, some monkish cells, others specialist offices like the scriptorium, where monks spent their daylight hours copying manuscripts. There were no large buildings at all. Outside the palisade or ditch were dozens of other huts where the lay servants of the monastery lived. Out beyond that were the farmers. For much of their early existence, monasteries looked no different from farmers' homesteads, built within defensive ring forts whose outlines are still found everywhere in the Irish landscape—fairy-forts as they are known in folklore. But as they grew in power and wealth, the larger monasteries took on a more distinct form. "The Irish thought of their monastic site as a series of concentric circles," Donnchadh said, "a place that was holy, a place that was holier and a place that was most holy. In the most holy place in the center they allowed only clerics and definitely no women. In the holier place they allowed people of proven good reputation, while in the place that was simply holy, they permitted sinners, hawkers, merchants, and whores."

Later on, carved stone High Crosses were set up to mark boundaries between these different areas, assembly points for open-air services since churches were too small for community worship. Even the term "monk" is misleading in respect to early Irish monasteries. They took no vows of poverty or chastity, although most probably took some vow of obedience to their abbot. Many were married and had children. Some were warriors, fighting for their abbots against competing monasteries. Aristocrats lived as comfortably within the monastery as they did in the royal courts; even kings built houses there. Slaves were as common as they were elsewhere in Irish society, and an individual's status within the monastery was regulated by the same honor price that applied outside. As monasteries grew wealthy from their lands and herds—and offerings brought by the faithful—they attracted the finest craftsmen in the land.

There were plenty of devout Christians who disapproved of this increased secularization of the Irish church. Saints would go

St. Kevin's Church and round tower in Glendalough. This church, believed to date from the twelfth century, was built on the site where St. Kevin founded one of the first great Irish monasteries. (*Carmel McCaffrey*)

off into the wild to worship God as solitary hermits. Unfortunately they seldom managed to get away from the world for long. Disciples followed them, drawn by a particular saint's reputation for ascetic holiness. Then more and more arrived, building huts and shelters around the hermitage, until the saint woke one morning to find himself the center of yet another large monastic community. Off he would go again, seeking an even more remote hermitage, but the same thing would keep happening until a string of new monasteries had evolved, all claiming the holy saint as founder and squabbling over his relics. Glendalough, in the Wicklow Hills, had such a beginning. Legend says that St. Kevin came here in the sixth century to live as a hermit in a lakeside cave. By his death—at the miraculous age of 120—his hermitage was one of Ireland's leading monasteries.

Many early saints left Ireland altogether, settling on remote offshore islands or traveling to foreign lands. Sixth-century Ireland, still reeling from the aftereffects of climate disaster and plague, was birthing two very different monastic ideals that together would define the Irish church. One was the growth of wealthy centers of Christian power and scholarship big enough to be described as towns. The other was the desire for remote and desolate places— often outside Ireland—where holy saints could withdraw from the world to worship God in isolation. The creative pull between these two opposing forces would make the Irish church the powerhouse of all Christendom, carrying faith and scholarship back to a Europe recovering from its Dark Age. Whether in the great monastic settlements of Ireland's agricultural heartland, or perched on remote and inhospitable monastic islands far out into the Atlantic, the heart of this powerhouse was the scriptorium.

THE POWER OF LITERACY

Although plague and the collapse of Irish society in the sixth century may have been the catalyst for Christianity's success in Ireland, it was literacy that made the new faith so attractive to Ireland's secular rulers. Christianity arrived in Ireland trailing the power and prestige of the now-vanished Roman Empire. Since Ireland had never been a part of the empire, Irish kings envied and desired its civilization. Literacy and scholarship were viewed as central to Rome's power. Learning to read and write became a growth industry in Ireland. Within a short time the Latin of Irish scholars and theologians was the purest form of the language existing anywhere in Europe. Donnchadh Ó Corráin explained why.

"Irish Christians knew that only Latin gave them access to God's own words," he said. "But Ireland was outside the Roman-language area, the first non-Roman country to accept Christianity in the West, so the Irish had to learn Latin as a foreign language. In the beginning they learned it properly from the best European grammarians and the best books. And when those books didn't suit them, they wrote even better ones. By the sixth century the language was already corrupted elsewhere in Europe. People who thought they were speaking Latin in France and Spain didn't realize they were actually speaking early French and early Spanish. But in Ireland the language remained pure because it was for an educated elite alone, uncorrupted by colloquial use."

As Roman civilization faded and barbarian conquerors built new kingdoms in the ruins of the old Roman provinces, Ireland became the guardian not just of the Latin language but its literature as well. The vast bulk of Latin classical texts were preserved by scholar monks in Irish monasteries founded in the middle decades of the sixth century. Literacy was the information technology of its age, a necessary foundation for secular activities like law, government, propaganda, and poetry, in addition to Holy Scripture. Just like today's Internet, everyone in authority wanted a piece of it. As the church controlled the new tools of literacy, kings and aristocrats were happy to send their children to study at monasteries that now became Ireland's first schools and universities. These students from the royal dynasties—sometimes kings themselves—were the next generation of monks and scholars, building even closer ties between church and state.

"The church penetrated Irish secular society more deeply than anywhere else in Western Europe," Donnchadh Ó Corráin explained. "It framed all intellectual thought and regulated all professional instruction. By controlling education, the church controlled the people who advised the rulers. This gave it unprecedented power to fashion Irish society within a Christian framework."

There were no books in Ireland before the arrival of Christianity, so books were special from the start. As churches and monasteries spread, more books were needed. But the supply of books from continental Europe dried up after the barbarian invasions, so Irish monasteries had to create their own, copying each by hand. Thousands of ordinary books—prayer books, hymnals, scripture, books of grammar and vocabulary—were essential to the running of a monastery. Masterpieces of calligraphy and illumination like the *Book of Kells* were exceptions, the result of years of work by teams of artists and produced only for special occasions. Transmission of all written knowledge depended on the craft of the scribe, which meant that handwriting—calligraphy—was the single most important skill taught in the monastic schools.

THE CALLIGRAPHER'S STORY

Tim O'Neill is a calligrapher, still successfully practicing his arcane craft at the start of the twenty-first century. Tim's work is on display around the world; his calligraphy chosen as a tail design on British Airways planes. Once a week he teaches a senior class in a Dublin high school. Sitting at the back of the classroom, watching Tim write out the Roman alphabet on a blackboard and talk about how thickness of pen nib determines the height of the writing, it is not hard to imagine a sixth-century scriptorium full of similar boys, rebellious sons of local royalty, clumsily struggling to master unfamiliar writing techniques in a language that must have initially been incomprehensible. When a cell phone went off in a boy's pocket, it drew as much scorn from his teacher as any scriptorium master might have leveled at a sixth-century novice who dared talk when he should be copying.

"Silence was important in the scriptorium," Tim explained. "When you talk, your attention's not on the page and you make mistakes. Teachers kept rigid discipline. If you made noise, you were punished. You might be beaten with a rod, sent out to stand in the cold, jump in the lake in winter, maybe walk barefoot through stinging nettles—all punishments designed to make you realize that life was suffering and how much better things were in heaven."

Other boys in the class quickly turned off their cell phones, worried that Tim would enforce such sixth-century punishments. Although Ireland's last hereditary scribe died in 1880—the end of an unbroken line stretching back more than a thousand years—the study of calligraphy has recently found new and enthusiastic converts. Tim has no difficulty filling his classes. As the boys set to work copying a page from the *Book of Kells*, the calligrapher talked of life in the scriptorium. "They worked on vellum—calf skin—that the young scribes had to prepare," he explained. "They'd skin the animal, scrape the hair off one side and the fat from the other, then bury it in the ground for a while to soften, soak it in quicklime, take it out, stretch it, scrape it down, and finally let it dry in the sun; altogether a very messy and smelly operation."

A trained scribe could write around 150 words an hour. It took Tim half an hour to copy 25 lines from the *Book of Durrow*, a beautiful seventh-century edition of the Gospels. He estimated it would take another 60 days to copy the entire text if he worked 6 hours a day. If a simple copy of the Gospels, without illumination, took 360 scribe hours; it is not surprising that books were so precious. Copying was done in daylight—it is difficult to do good calligraphy by candlelight—and the best pens were cut from the flight feathers of swans, each quill trimmed with a penknife to produce a good nib.

Every scribe had his penknife, using it to score lines in the vellum—to write in a straight line—and scratch out copying mistakes. Black ink came from soot mixed with gummy tree sap, but Irish monasteries preferred a dark brown ink made by crushing oak apples—small growths on oak trees—and mixing the resulting oak gall with water.

Copying for hours on end was immensely tedious. A comment written in the margin of a manuscript says, "Three fingers do the work but the whole body labors." In other words, the scribe's back was killing him, his feet were cramped, he was stiff all over, and probably half frozen into the bargain. Hundreds of such comments are scribbled in Irish on the margins of Latin manuscripts. The monks of early Ireland sound just like us, grumbling about a supervisor or working conditions. One complains about a cold wind blowing off the lake, "It's chilling me on a Friday." Another writes, "A curse on the man who makes me work on a Saturday night." Normally they would not work over the weekend. Sometimes the scribes pose little questions in the margin, like, "What do you think of my writing," or "I'm trying out my pen, isn't it nice?" They show a great sense of humor. One monk cut his hand with his penknife, and when it bled onto the manuscript he wrote a little note, "This is the blood of Sean." Another laments, "Oh what a pity the cat has strayed and hasn't come back." Monks could have bad days. "Don't blame me for the bad writing today," one wrote. "The day is very dark, the ink is bad and the vellum is in bad condition, it's not my fault the writing's bad."

The primary purpose of the monastic scriptoria was the copying of sacred texts, but by the end of the sixth century they had also started recording history, writing down events that happened within the monastery and across Ireland. At Glenstall Abbey, a modern Benedictine monastery near Limerick, which still keeps a handwritten diary of each day's events, the abbot explained why. "The monasteries' interests were so all-embracing that all sorts of secular events affected their activities and were recorded in the annals. Records of battles, the succession of kings, plagues, good or bad weather, the success of the harvest, all become the bits and pieces of history." These monastic annals are why so much is known about Ireland between the seventh and eleventh centuries. They provide the most detailed history of any country in Europe over this period.

History was not the only thing they wrote. Donnchadh Ó Corráin believes the Irish church took over the training of poets early in its existence. In pre-Christian times the poets—*filí*—had been druids. Under Christianity they remained a very powerful and influential elite. Retainers of kings, they had an honor price almost equal to kings. They wrote inaugural odes for the king's accession, laments for his death, and in between publicized the dynasty, creating the sort of propaganda that allowed the Uí Néill to claim an ancestral right to the kingship of Tara. They were consummate public relations professionals, guardians of Irish culture. Once inside the church, with the power of literacy at their command, they were able to change how the Irish saw themselves and their place in a Christian world.

THE INVENTION OF IRISH PREHISTORY

"It's one of the reasons why the church was so interested in writing down sagas in Irish," historian Elva Johnston said. "It gave them another way of controlling how the culture imagined itself. The whole idea of what Ireland meant, or what it meant to be Irish, was created by monks. They were creating the idea of a place called Ireland and putting it in the context of world history. They looked at the Bible and found there was no mention of the Irish there, and they said, 'Isn't this strange, it must be an oversight. We know we're linked to the Bible, but we've also got our own past which is just as worthy to be written down and celebrated.' So they created ancient mythologies that tell the story of the Irish all the way back to Noah's Flood. These scholar monks were totally self-confident about what they were doing, putting Ireland on a par with the great classical cultures of the world."

Starting in the sixth century, scholars in the monasteries adapted the Latin alphabet to the sounds of Irish. It was a huge intellectual achievement, the first place in the world where the vernacular—the colloquial native language—was written down. Elva's favorite piece of early Irish arrogance comes from a manuscript describing an Irish scholar who was present at the Tower of Babel. "God got angry at humanity for daring to build a tower to reach heaven. He made everyone speak different languages so no one understood anyone else. But this Irishman went around and talked to all the different people—unfortunately the story doesn't say how he did this—but he and his colleagues took the best bits of all the newly created languages and put them back together to create Irish. The inference is, 'We should write in Irish because it's made up of all the best bits of language created by God at the Tower of Babel. It's really the original language, so they must be speaking Irish in heaven.' "

The writing of sagas may have begun as early as the sixth century, although the versions known today came from much later, every new generation of copyists adding extra detail and invention. Writing in the vernacular made the stories accessible to ordinary people. Scholars in the monasteries were drawing on old tales from a nonliterate past but giving them a clear Christian slant, making them serve a Christian purpose. For all their propaganda, these monks were great storytellers, successors to an oral tradition stretching back at least a thousand years. One scholar, after copying out Ireland's greatest saga, *The Taín,* realized his story was not up to expected standards of Christian morality, so he justified himself by adding a note at the end that said some of it was okay, some of it was "devilish lies," and some of it was "for the enjoyment of idiots."

By the end of the sixth century, monastic scriptoria were creating scripture, religious texts, history, and the beginnings of a great written poetic tradition that continues unabated in Ireland today. The Irish church was first and foremost a scholarly church and its first scholar saint was St. Columba—in Irish Colmcille—the third of Ireland's founding saints along with Patrick and Brigid and one of the most important historical figures of the sixth century.

ST. COLMCILLE—DOVE OF THE CHURCH

Some time in A.D. 521—legend says Thursday, December 7—a boy was born into the dynasty of ruling families known collectively as the Uí Néill, all claiming descent from the legendary pre-Christian warrior Niall of the Nine Hostages. Niall was one of the triumphs of Uí Néill literary propaganda, designed to justify their claim as Ireland's senior dynasty. Their scholar scribes had rewritten history, glorifying this great ancestral hero—probably fictitious—who they claimed ruled from Tara as high-king of Ireland generations earlier.

The boy's immediate family ruled much of Donegal. There is a tradition he was originally called Crimthann, meaning "fox," or "sly, deceitful one" but this was not a suitable name for a future saint so his boyhood friends were "inspired by angels" to call him Colmcille, which meant "dove of the church." (Columba is simply the Latin form of Colm, the word for dove.)

Legend has a lot to say about St. Colmcille. Apparently St. Patrick and St. Brigid each prophesied his birth, and a ball of fire seen hovering above the sleeping child proved the presence of the Holy Spirit. His greatest biographer Adomnan, one of Colmcille's successors as abbot of Iona—a monastery island off the west coast of Scotland that became a leading center of the Irish church—wrote his *Life of St. Columba* toward the end of the seventh century, one hundred years after the saint's death. Writers in those days were not concerned with historical accuracy. They were creating propaganda to inspire fellow Christians with the sanctity of their founding saint and his power to perform miracles.

In the seventh century Iona ruled a large federation of churches on both sides of the Irish Sea. Even as holy a biographer as Adomnan—later venerated as a saint himself—was not above using his *Life of St. Columba* as propaganda for his own ideas on how the church should go about its business. There is little real information about Colmcille's activities prior to his leaving Ireland in 563 to sail to Iona. What exists is a rich tapestry of folklore and legend with a few threads of truth mixed in along the way.

COLMCILLE'S EARLY YEARS

The Grianan of Aileach is one of the largest and most spectacular circular stone forts anywhere in Ireland, built high on a mountainous neck of land leading to the Inishowen peninsula of northern Donegal. Inside dry-stone walls—fourteen-feet thick at the base and still standing sixteen-feet high—is an open area large enough for the residence of a king. Built sometime after 500—it is almost impossible to date a dry-stone wall—this fort was a center of power for the Northern Uí Néill. Donegal is Uí Néill country, and Colmcille was probably born just a few miles to the west, beside Lough Garton in the shadow of the Glendowan Mountains. Here can still be found a low earth mound, topped by a U-shaped group of standing stones, beside which is a stone slab. The monument's origins are probably Bronze Age, but local legends insist the stone slab was the floor of the hut where Colmcille was born. The slab is known as *Leac na Cumhadh,* or the Stone of the Sorrows. Throughout the nineteenth and early twentieth centuries, local people immigrating to America or other foreign lands slept here on the night before departure. They believed that since Colmcille went into exile on Iona, sleeping on the spot where he was born would help them bear "with lighter hearts the burden of an exile's sorrow." Of course there is no proof Colmcille was born anywhere near Garton—the earliest historical source linking him with the area is from the twelfth century—but there is a pilgrimage every year on the anniversary of the saint's death.

Presumably Colmcille was educated by Christian priests; Adomnan says he studied with a Christian poet called Gemman, probably a druid who had converted to the new faith. This is reinforced by other accounts suggesting he received formal training in the techniques of the *filí,* the hereditary poets of Ireland. When druids tried to stop Colmcille from chanting vespers near a king's fort for fear he would upset the "heathen masses," the saint chanted the forty-fourth Psalm ("Deliver me from my enemies, Oh my God . . .") so loud that "his voice was raised up in the air like thunder, and the king and his people were stricken with unbearable terror." Quite an oratorical technique! Years later, when converting the Picts of Scotland, Colmcille apparently used his voice as a weapon against Pictish magicians. He is also credited with writing many poems. Scholarship, literature, and poetry are closely linked with Colmcille throughout his life.

There is also the legend he studied under St. Enda of Aran and angered the cantankerous saint enough to be thrown off the island without a boat, forced to swim eight miles back to the mainland. If born in 521, he was nineteen when the A.D. 540 climate disaster hit, followed by the first outbreak of plague. One version of his life says he studied at Glasnevin monastery—near present-day Dublin—until plague forced the monastery to be evacuated and the students sent home for safety. Family and friends may have died, an impressionable age to experience the power and wrath of God.

Colmcille was forty-two when he left Ireland for Iona, so there are unaccounted decades in his story. It is likely, although not mentioned by biographers, that he was ordained a priest. A close relative of Uí Néill kings, he was eligible for kingship himself and probably intimately involved in the affairs of the family dynasty. It is said he founded monasteries before leaving Ireland, including Durrow—in the Irish midlands—and Derry on the Donegal coast. Adomnan refers to him during this period as "the father and founder of monasteries." At Glencolmcille, on the western tip of Donegal, there is still an annual pilgrimage—often barefoot—across several miles of mountain, bog, and open countryside, following stations of the cross supposedly laid out by Colmcille when he lived here as a young priest. There is nothing except local legend to link him with the site, but the pilgrimage is earlier than the ninth century, when the beautifully carved Christian pillar stones now marking the stations of the cross were first erected.

THE WORLD'S FIRST COPYRIGHT CASE

A famous legend about Colmcille's life tells why he had to leave Ireland. Sometime around 560 he was visiting St. Finnian, one of the second generation of Irish saints who had come from Wales to found the monastery of Clonard. Colmcille wanted to make a copy of a beautiful manuscript of the Psalms that Finnian possessed but was afraid the Welsh saint would not let him do it, so he copied it secretly at night, his fingers "shining as brightly as candles" to give him light. After Colmcille had finished, Finnian demanded the new copy since he had not given permission for it to be made. Colmcille appealed to the reigning high-king, who came from an opposing branch of the family—the Southern Uí Néill. After lengthy deliberation, the high-king pronounced judgment against Colmcille, saying, *"le gach boin a boinin, le gach leabhar a leabhran"*—to every cow its calf, to every book its copy. It is the world's first recorded copyright case. Colmcille was furious, demanding revenge for such an unjust decision and, with family honor at stake, Colmcille's relatives from the Northern Uí Néill declared war on the high-king.

At the Battle of Cul Dreimne in A.D. 561, thousands died and the Northern Uí Néill defeated their rivals to seize the high-kingship themselves. Apparently Colmcille was guilt-ridden at the slaughter he had caused and vowed to go into exile. It is a late legend—Adomnan never mentions it—but it offers clues to what was happening in Ireland at the time. It reinforces the importance of books in Colmcille's life and links him directly to the Battle of Cul Dreimne, a critical battle where the Northern Uí Néill defeated their southern cousins and took over the high-kingship. Another legend of the battle says that the high-king and his army were protected by a magic "druidic" fence that was destroyed by "the prayers of Colmcille." The battle took place at a time when factions within the Uí Néill were consolidating power and jockeying for supremacy. Perhaps we are glimpsing a war between Christian and pagan forces, with Colmcille and his relatives on the side of the new faith.

The following year there was mention of a church synod trying to excommunicate Colmcille, an action prevented only by a passionate defense from St. Brendan. Since the synod took place in lands controlled by the Southern Uí Néill, perhaps the king was pressuring local church leaders to punish the saint for whatever role he played in the Battle of Cul Dreimne.

THE PILGRIM FOR CHRIST

For whatever reason, in 563 Colmcille and a group of companions left the northern Irish coast, supposedly near present-day Derry, to sail a currach to the tiny island three miles long and a mile and a half wide off the west coast of Scotland now called Iona. He would be a pilgrim for Christ, searching for a suitable island out of sight of Ireland—a condition of his self-imposed exile—where he could worship God in the wilderness. Thick layers of myth and legend surround Colmcille's journey and arrival on Iona. It is said he traveled with twelve companions, possibly a detail added by later biographers although it may reflect a practice of consciously imitating the model of Christ and his twelve disciples. There are indications that other offshore monastery settlements—like Skelligmichael off the western tip of Ireland—were first settled by "an abbot and twelve monks."

Iona is less than ninety miles away from Derry as the crow flies. In 1963, on the fourteen-hundredth anniversary of Colmcille's voyage, a group of Church of Ireland priests and laymen—a skipper and twelve men—set sail in the saint's footsteps in a currach specially built in the ancient style. It took them eight days, headland hopping up the coast of Scotland. Twenty-seven years later Cannon

Barry, one of the leaders of the pilgrimage and now in his eighties, ran his hand along the oar he had pulled—the boat is still preserved in the Derry Harbor Museum—and talked about how the voyage helped him understand Colmcille as a man rather than a saint. "That sort of voyage is dangerous even today in an open boat, especially when the sea's running high," he said. "We found we couldn't use the sail much, the wind was wrong, so we had to row pretty much the whole way. If Columba was skipper, he must have had previous sailing experience. You need to know what you're about in those seas. And there can be only one boss; you do what the boss says immediately, otherwise you endanger yourself and everyone else aboard. We weren't a terribly religious crowd, quoting scripture and stuff like that, but I don't think Columba was like that either. He was a tough guy and we could well imagine him bawling out the lads when they needed it, just like our skipper did. They said he had a loud voice you could hear five furlongs [two-thirds of a mile] off. He must have been a big rough guy." Cannon Barry smiled at the memory. "Yes, it's a great way to get to know Columba, getting in a boat with twelve of the lads."

IONA

Cannon Barry and his twelve fellow pilgrims stepped ashore on Iona to be met by a large crowd that included the archbishop of Canterbury. Colmcille and his fellow monks probably arrived on an uninhabited island, although archaeologists have found evidence of human settlement from prehistoric times. Iona was owned by Irish Dál Riada kings who had settled Scotland's west coast more than a century earlier. Ultimately the Dál Riada kingdom would grow into the kingdom of Scotland. Colmcille was hardly going into exile. Maire Herbert, a leading Colmcille scholar, thinks it likely there were already links between Colmcille's Uí Néill relatives and the Dál Riada kings.

"I think he left Ireland with a very definite goal," Maire said as she stepped off the small ferry that links Iona with the larger Hebridean island of Mull and the rest of Scotland. "He probably went first to the local Dál Riada king and got permission to settle on the island. I suspect he left his homeland because he was too close to the seat of power and perhaps got embroiled in the political intrigues of his family. We think of him coming to Iona to retire from the world, but he remained very much engaged with the world. Just because he renounced political status to become a monk doesn't mean he gave up his contacts with high-placed people. He remained a friend and adviser of kings all his life."

Today the ferry docks just below a medieval abbey built on the site of Colmcille's original monastery. Nothing remains from this time except a tiny part of the defensive ditch. The settlement would have been like other early Irish monasteries—a small plank church with huts of wattle and daub for the scriptorium and monks' cells, surrounded by a circular ditch topped by a palisade. But in a twelfth century *Life of Colmcille* there is a curious story— dismissed by most modern scholars as scurrilous fiction—that the saint offered a pagan human sacrifice before he built his first monastery on Iona. Maire Herbert translated the passage:

> Then Colmcille said to his company, "it would benefit us if our roots were put down into the ground here. Someone among you should go down into the soil of the island to consecrate it." The obedient Odran rose up and said: "If I be taken, I am prepared for it." "Odran," said Colmcille, "you will be rewarded for it." Then Odran went to heaven."

Human sacrifice was part of pre-Christian Celtic culture. Bodies like one under the walls of Dún Aengus, a great stone fort on the Aran Islands, were clearly sacrificed to encourage the goodwill of the gods in such a sacred place. While the story of Odran's death does not fit the behavior of a holy Christian saint, it reminds us how short a time Christianity had been in Ireland. Whether practiced by Colmcille or not, such pre-Christian customs may not yet have been stamped out.

Once the monastery was established, it grew quickly into a leading center of scholarship and missionary activity. Colmcille traveled widely, visiting and being visited by important rulers from across Scotland and northern Britain—even returning to Ireland on several occasions—as he established his federation of churches on both sides of the Irish Sea with Iona as its head, the spiritual heart of the Dál Riada kingdom. Iona reinforced the Gaelic identity of Dál Riada, monastery and kingdom growing together in power just as Armagh and the Uí Néill did back in Ireland. There was clearly rivalry between Columban churches and those under Armagh's control, and Colmcille may have overshadowed Patrick as Ireland's senior saint for some while. He converted the Picts to Christianity and in 574 inaugurated a new Dál Riada king on Iona, the first recorded Christian inauguration—coronation—of a king anywhere in Europe. Because of the political influence of its founder, Iona attracted royal refugees from the outset. Osbold, king of Northumbria in northern Britain, spent time on the island as an exile. When he regained his kingdom, he invited Colmcille's missionaries to Christianize his kingdom.

As Maire Herbert said, "The Iona enterprise spanned Ireland, Dál Riada, Pictland, and Northumbria. It crossed cultural and language barriers; it was the seed from which Christianity spread southwards into Britain. And the organization Colmcille set up was extremely durable because he linked it directly to his own family, stipulating that all future abbots be drawn from the Northern Uí Néill."

It is known the saint read the great classical Roman writers. Scholarship was a central part of his vision. Annals kept on Iona form the core of surviving Irish annals, the basis of all knowledge about Irish and north British history before the eighth century. Colmcille's successor abbots maintained this focus on scholarship. Most scholars now accept that the *Book of Kells*—a mixture of decorative influences from Ireland, Pictland, and northern Britain—was created on Iona, perhaps as a special edition for the two-hundredth anniversary of the saint's death. There are clues to suggest that the high art of Celtic illumination itself began on the island; Celtic artistry inspired by a unique painting style found in an early Byzantine gospel manuscript called the *Diatessaron* that may have reached Iona from the eastern Mediterranean in the seventh century.

Visitors to the cloisters of Iona Abbey today can still see the sculptured grave slabs of dozens of Dál Riada and Scottish kings who were buried on the island, "the resting place of lawful kings, but not usurpers." It is an impressive total: four Irish, eight Norwegian, and forty-eight Scottish kings, including Kenneth MacAlpine, who united Scotland in the ninth century, and Shakespeare's Macbeth, who died in 1057. The medieval abbey was restored in the 1930s and is now home to the Iona Community, an ecumenical

Christian organization involved in worldwide social issues like racism, land mines, the environment, and third-world debt. "Iona was never just an Irish community," Maire Herbert said, "and Colmcille never saw himself as only just ministering to his own people. He was looking outward all the time, involved in all the issues of the world about him."

WHITE MARTYRDOM

Colmcille's "exile" on Iona was part of an overall pattern of behavior common in the Irish church between the sixth and ninth centuries when holy monks deliberately cut themselves off from family and society to seek God in harsh and distant places. Long before the arrival of Christianity, forced exile had been a punishment for serious crimes against society. Survival in Ireland was so tied to position in society—honor price, status, law, family, and tribe—that having these social connections cut and being exiled to the wilderness was often a fate "worse than death." Outlaws could be killed on sight, even if they survived a lack of food and shelter and the wild animals and malevolent gods who ran wild in the forests outside the Túath's protection. By the sixth century the church had seized on a form of this punishment as a way to achieve greater holiness. Historian Elva Johnston explains why.

"One of the problems the Irish church faced was that conversion had been so peaceful they didn't have martyrs from the period when Christianity was first introduced into Ireland. This was embarrassing because everyone really revered the early martyrs; they were the superstars of Christianity. So the Irish invented different types of martyrdom. There was Red Martyrdom, the good old-fashioned kind where you were killed off in quite an unpleasant way. Then there was Green and White Martyrdom that involved renouncing your home, renouncing your kindred, and living a very holy life. It counted when you just left your home within Ireland but it counted even more when you left Ireland entirely. So if they went out into the ocean, went off to a remote island, or left their homeland forever, this was a form of martyrdom on a par with being thrown to the lions in the amphitheater."

Monks seeking White Martyrdom settled dozens of tiny islands off the coast of Ireland. Some, like Rathlin Island off the Antrim coast, Tory Island off the northwest coast of Donegal, and Inish-murray, west of Sligo, developed into quite large monasteries with ruins that can still be seen today. But none of Ireland's other monastery islands matches the spectacular austerity of Skellig-michael, the peak of an undersea mountain that rears up like the point of a spear, seven hundred feet out of the Atlantic waves. This must have been the extreme edge of White Martyrdom in Ireland. Even in good conditions the island is an uncomfortable ninety minute boat ride in heavy Atlantic swells from the fishing village of Portmagee in southwest Kerry. A twenty-foot rise and fall in water level makes landing hazardous, timing one's leap onto the jetty to when the boat is at the top of its rise. Six hundred steps carved into the mountain rock lead up to where the monks built their monastery. In windy conditions the climb can be dangerous; in 1999 a German tourist fell to his death. There is no flat ground anywhere on the island. The main monastery buildings, a cluster of beehive huts built five hundred feet above sea level, stand on a man-made platform.

Bob Harris is a guide for the Irish Heritage Association who has spent the past thirteen summers living on Skelligmichael. His experience is as close as it is possible to get to how monks who chose White Martyrdom lived here fourteen hundred years ago. "The monks wanted to be close to God, but at the same time they were practical men," he said. "They chose the most sheltered place on the island to build their huts. Storms blow up out of the blue, and you can be cut off for ten days at a time; the mainland can ac-tually disappear for days on end. They didn't just come here for their own salvation. They had an important task to do, praying for the souls of all mankind. They felt they were waging war against the evil of the world, and prayer was their weapon."

There is no water on Skelligmichael, so they had to build cis-terns to catch rainwater. Their diet would have been fish, eggs, sea birds, and whatever plants they could grow in the small garden they constructed beside the monastery. Walking through the cluster of beehive huts that make up the tiny monastic village, it is easy to forget that when they first arrived, there was nothing here but an angled surface of bare rock with no access from sea level. Every-thing had to be built from scratch. "When you think of the work, the quarrying, the intensive amount of labor," Bob marveled, "of

The island of Skelligmichael, several miles off the southwest coast of Ireland, holds the bleakest and most inhospitable monastery anywhere in the country. (*Leo Eaton*)

course they'd have seen it as an act of devotion, a sort of rebuilding the City of God but it must have been incredibly difficult. Much of this island is sheer rock. Think how many must have been killed during the construction; that's real martyrdom. It certainly took many generations of monks, perhaps a couple of hundred years after those first ones arrived before it took the form we see now as a permanent monastic village."

If Skelligmichael represents the most austere of monastery islands, it was still in sight of Ireland. Many monks choosing White Martyrdom sailed further away. Colmcille—legend says—stopped at Iona because it was the first place from which he could no longer see Ireland. Irish monks settled on the Shetlands and Orkney Islands off the north coast of Scotland, established a monastery on the Faeroe Islands—now part of Denmark—and reached as far as Iceland. There are sailing instructions in old Irish describing how to navigate between Iceland and Ireland. The experience of countless Irish monks, along with stories from Irish fishermen who had been sailing currachs west into the Atlantic for centuries, were combined into a story credited to another sixth-century saint which became a medieval best-seller across Europe, the *Navigatio Brendani,* or *Voyages of Brendan the Navigator,* who some claim reached America four hundred years before the Vikings and nine hundred years before Columbus.

BRENDAN THE NAVIGATOR

In 1976 the British explorer Tim Severin, fascinated by the idea that St. Brendan might have sailed to America in the sixth century, constructed a large currach in the traditional style—which he called the *Brendan*—and set sail from Brandon Creek on the Dingle peninsula of County Kerry, an area traditionally linked to St. Brendan. Through the summer and fall of 1976, Severin and his crew followed the path of Irish saints north to Iceland, where they stayed for the winter, before heading west in spring to pass Greenland and reach Newfoundland by the end of June 1977. Severin proved that an Irish leather-covered currach could have reached America in the sixth century, although he admitted it was the most dangerous adventure of his life. It is possible Irish sailors did sail this far, but Severin's voyage proved nothing about Brendan since the *Navigatio,* like all sagas of Irish saints, was written centuries after his death—probably initially in the ninth century—drawing together stories and folklore from many different sources that were then expanded and embellished by generations of later storytellers and scribes.

The *Navigatio* is entertaining even today. Brendan takes two different voyages into the Atlantic, seeking the promised Land of the Saints. Along the way he visits many strange and wonderful islands that each display unique characteristics, some of heavenly perfection and others of temptation and damnation. There is a flat island without grass that shudders when they light a fire on it and turns out to be the back of a whale. There is an island filled with ravenous man-eating mice, and another where the inhabitants throw burning slag at Brendan's boat but miss, causing the sea around the boat to boil. The saint sails past a great white crystal pillar floating in the ocean and lands on an island of fire, where he meets Judas and protects him from the fires of hell for a day. One island offers three choirs of monks ceaselessly singing, another a place where Christians never age. The boat passes through a "coagulated sea" to reach an island where water from the well puts Brendan's crew to sleep. Only after many years and terrible hardships does Brendan reach the Land of the Saints. He returns to Ireland as an old man to pass on the story of his travels before he dies.

As historian Elva Johnston said, "The monks who wrote the *Navigatio* knew Homer; they'd read the *Odyssey* and they knew the Sumerian epic of *Gilgamesh* and his quest for eternal life. Story traditions used in the tales of St. Brendan are just as popular today. C. S. Lewis drew many of the events for *The Voyage of the Dawn Treader*—in the Narnia books—directly from the *Navigatio,* which he knew well. *Star Trek* follows the same pattern, only the Enterprise goes from planet to planet rather than Brendan going from island to island. The writers of the *Navigatio* were following pre-Christian Celtic storytelling traditions called *echtra* or "voyage" tales, in which heroes like Conle and Bran were lured out—usually by beautiful women—to islands in the Western Sea from where they could never return. Those who tried were turned immediately to dust on touching Ireland's shore, since hundreds of years had passed while they'd been away."

What makes the Brendan stories so unique is the wealth of observable details. The white crystal pillar is clearly an iceberg; the Island of Fire probably one of Iceland's active volcanoes. "There's a level of realism in the description," Elva said. "They face miraculous events against this backdrop of reality. The information must have come from a variety of different sources—fishermen who knew the Atlantic waters, wandering monks who'd certainly sailed as far as Iceland. But I don't think America is the promised Land of the Saints. If you actually read the text, it describes Brendan's travels west into the Atlantic to find this amazing number of islands—like the western isles of Ireland and Scotland—but then he turns back east to find the Land of the Saints. I think it's pretty clear it's meant to be just off the coast of Donegal. It's a much more interesting notion, that you can travel the world for years to find the Promised Land but what you want ultimately turns out to be much closer to home."

The real St. Brendan seems to have operated primarily in the Galway area on the west coast, founding monasteries at Annaghdown and Clonfert, where he was buried in 577. His connection with the Dingle peninsula and Mount Brandon appears to be a later invention, his cult imposed hundreds of years later after local church leaders realized that the fame of a "superstar" saint would attract more pilgrims than any lesser-known local saint. Brendan was clearly one of the important leaders of Irish monasticism in the sixth century. He was a contemporary of Colmcille—whom he supposedly visited on Iona—and may have been respected as a sailor in his own lifetime, visiting the islands of Western Ireland and Scotland where fellow monks had sought White Martyrdom. His activities are now so encrusted with fantasy that it is impossible to know where truth ends and fiction begins, but there is no question that Brendan represented a common type, the Irish monk ranging far afield between the seventh and tenth centuries, sailing north and west into the Atlantic or traveling east and south through Britain and on into Europe.

COLUMBANUS AND IRISH MONASTERIES IN EUROPE

The old Roman provinces of northern Gaul were still nominally Christian in the sixth century, with bishops based in the ancient cities; the Roman church had always been an urban religion. Many of the new barbarian rulers found it useful to convert to Christianity, but outside the cities, the countryside was almost entirely pagan with Christianity unknown in huge areas of Northern Europe. Rome was the center of the Latin church, and Roman monasteries were common in Southern Gaul and Italy, where St. Benedict founded his Benedictine Order around 540, following a set of rules he developed to regulate the disorganized chaos existing in monasteries at the time. Benedict is one of two fathers of European monasticism, a title he shares with the Irish St. Columbanus.

Irish monks who came to Europe in search of White Martyrdom were not seeking Christian communities and never planned to become missionaries. All they really wanted was a wilderness where they could seek God in solitude, although most hoped someday to travel to Rome because so many early church fathers had been martyred there.

Columbanus was born in 543 and spent much of his adult life in the monastery of Bangor. He was already forty-eight when he chose White Martyrdom and left Ireland, a headstrong, argumentative, and difficult man, not one to suffer fools gladly, particularly if they did not agree with him. In 591 he arrived in Europe with twelve fellow monks—again a parallel with Christ and his twelve disciples—where the king of Burgundy gave him an old Roman fort in which to build his first monastery.

Rulers in north and eastern Gaul were happy to welcome monks from Ireland and encourage them to spread Christianity in the pagan countryside. Although the customs and practices they brought from Ireland horrified the local Roman bishops, they fascinated everyone else. People flocked to Columbanus, attracted by the discipline, austerity, non-conformity, and spiritual independence of his community. His Irish church must have been a welcome change for anyone used to the archaic Roman religion then existing, especially since—as in Ireland—literacy and scholarship were central to his monastic activity.

Columbanus ran out of space in the Roman fort and built another monastery close by, at Luxeuil, but disciples kept arriving and a third monastery soon became necessary. Local Roman bishops were furious at Columbanus's growing power, not least because bishops were supposed to outrank abbots in the Roman Church, a fact ignored by Columbanus. He wrote letters to the pope, defending the practices of the Irish church and—like Benedict—came up with a set of strict rules for his monks that relied heavily on corporal punishment. "Spare the rod and spoil the child" was an expression that would have appealed to the Irish saint. He raged at the immorality of the royal court and had a running feud with Brunhilde, the dowager queen, who became his implacable enemy.

After twenty years in France he was arrested and forced to leave, placing a curse on the young Burgundian king and prophesying that he and his children would be dead within three years. Unfortunately the curse did not work. Columbanus moved on up the Rhine and into Switzerland, founding new monasteries along the way and managing to antagonize the locals each time. After many such moves, he finally arrived in Italy in 612 where a sympathetic king gave him land in Bobbio, between Milan and Genoa, to build a new monastery. He died and was buried there in 615, his tomb still a pilgrimage shrine for Irish abroad. Columbanus is the most important of the many Irish saints who founded monasteries in Europe. His followers from Luxeuil alone are credited with founding more than one hundred additional monasteries in France, Germany, Switzerland, and Italy, while Bobbio remained a leading European center of scholarship for the next thousand years.

IRISH OR LATIN—WHICH CHURCH RULED IN ENGLAND?

While Columbanus and his successors were founding monasteries in Europe, events in Britain would have a profound effect on the church as a whole. As the Columban Irish church spread its influence and missionary activities south into Britain from Iona, the pope in Rome—Gregory I—sent a mission to Kent in southern England in 597 to convert the Saxons. Its leader was Augustine, a Benedictine monk from Rome who set up his first bishopric at Canterbury—still the senior church in Britain. This was a Roman church, celibate and under the control of bishops, unlike the decentralized and noncelibate Irish church where abbots held the real power. Latin and Irish churches also argued about the date of Easter, each calculating it differently, a serious matter in societies where so much depended on the correct celebration of Christian feast days.

As Irish and Latin areas of influence came into conflict, each pressured England's kings to accept their viewpoint. Things came to a head in 664 at the Abbey of Whitby in Yorkshire. Scholars from both sides made their arguments in front of King Oswy of Northumbria. Oswy had previously supported the Irish but now acknowledged the supremacy of Rome, persuaded by the fact that the pope was in direct line of succession from St. Peter. His words were recorded. "I dare no longer contradict the decrees of him who keeps the doors of the Kingdom of Heaven, less he should refuse me entrance." The Roman church had won a crucial victory with far-reaching repercussions. It meant that the Anglo-Saxon missionaries who left England for Europe in the eighth century to convert the Germans—like St. Boniface, St. Swithbert, and St. Willibrord—were Benedictines, loyal to a Roman pope.

THE PERIGRINI

From the sixth century on, Irish pilgrims traveled to Europe in increasing numbers. By the ninth century, one European monk noted that the practice of traveling to foreign lands had become second nature to the Irish while another wondered if any Irish were left behind in Ireland, since so many were in Europe.

Dagmar Ó Riain is a historian who takes modern Irish pilgrims on tours of the shrines of early Irish saints in Europe. Standing in the crypt of St. Columbanus's monastery in Bobbio where Irish pilgrims have gathered for almost fourteen hundred years, she watched an Irish priest perform mass in front of the saint's tomb. "It seems to be in the character of the Irish to wander, to want to go abroad, to go southward," she said. "Maybe it had something to do with the Irish weather, but they all began with the idea of going south to Rome. Most never got there, stopping off along the way. Often the travel itself was more important than getting there. In France, Germany, Switzerland, Northern Italy—everywhere we have places associated with these Irish *perigrini*."

Perigrinus was originally a Roman word meaning "stateless person," but it evolved over time to mean anyone who journeyed away from the country of their birth, so the wandering Irish in Europe became known as *peregrini*. In the eighth century a backlash started to build against the Irish as the Benedictine missionaries from Anglo-Saxon England—such as St. Boniface—began stirring up public opinion against them. Apart from ongoing disputes between the Irish and Latin church, Celts and Anglo-Saxons had never liked each other. Following the Anglo-Saxon invasions of Britain in the fifth century, Celtic monasteries in Wales and the West refused even to try to convert their pagan conquerors "for fear they'd meet them again in Paradise."

As early as 730, attempts were made to restrict the activities of Irish priests in Europe. Benedictines insisted on a stability and order that ran counter to the Irish desire to wander freely, so Anglo-Saxons were preferred by the ambitious Carolingian dynasty taking power in Northern Europe in the eighth century. The dynasty reached its crowning glory in 800 when Charlemagne was anointed as Holy Roman Emperor by the pope. Footloose Irish priests who refused to accept outside authority were a thorn in the side of this new European Order as kings and bishops tried to govern Europe more efficiently. Boniface had no use for wandering Irish bishops, probably doubting they had even been properly ordained. But the Irish kept coming. This was religious tourism on a grand scale with a complete network of Irish pilgrim hostels throughout Europe and in Rome itself. Anti-Irish sentiment was hardening, enflamed by Roman churchmen who considered some Irish priests little better than pagans. Some towns even barred their gates to the *perigrini*.

At the Council of Chalon-sur-Saone in 813, the ordination of "irresponsible people as priests and deacons by Irishmen without authorization who say they are bishops" was declared null and void. Soon afterwards the Irish were expelled from their European monasteries and hostels, forced—as one chronicler reported—"to beg from door to door." But the *perigrini* were not without influence; Irish scholars were established in all the royal courts and crowds of pilgrims were a rich source of what is today termed "tourist dollars" wherever they went. By 845 the pilgrim hostels were being returned to their Irish owners, although patterns of Irish pilgrimage were changing.

Throughout the ninth century, pilgrimage back in Ireland was growing in popularity. The *perigrini* continued to travel to Europe, especially the intellectual elite—always welcome—but overall their numbers were declining. As scholar and archaeologist Peter Harbison explained, "The church came up with a pithy little phrase in the ninth century which said, 'To go to Rome, much labor, little profit.' This was obviously a way of saying, 'Stay at home and we'll give you good pilgrimage in Ireland.' Europe's problem had become Ireland's opportunity. Local pilgrimage routes, especially those connected with famous and powerful saints like Patrick, Brendan, Brigid, and Colmcille, were now drawing the big crowds and the big money. Monasteries that controlled the relics of the most popular saints were becoming wealthier than ever.

[8]

Irish Monasteries and Scholars

THE IRISH MONASTERIES for which wealth and prestige became bywords were to be found in the rich grasslands that lie mostly to the east of the River Shannon. The monastery system that developed in Ireland was unique in European Christian terms, yet these atypical monasteries were the wellsprings from which Irish art and learning spread throughout Europe. Many consider this to be the most magnificent period in Irish Christianity.

Clonmacnoise, arguably the greatest of the Irish monasteries, which surpassed even Armagh in scholarship and learning, was also probably the most beautiful of all. It came into its full flowering of scholarship in the eighth to ninth centuries, a period of great learning and artistic development in Ireland. Today its ruined buildings stand as testimony to the significant position this monastery once held in European scholarship. Even now it is a place of beauty, peace, and tranquility. It is sited right next to the River Shannon in the center of Ireland, in an area still pastoral and idyllic. When we visited Clonmacnoise one early spring morning, Irish medieval historian Donnchadh Ó Corráin walked with us through the ruins. Experiencing firsthand its pastoral serenity, it was easy to understand why this location was chosen as a place of community and spirituality. To the ancient Irish, a people without towns or urban centers, the connection to nature was important, and beauty in a place would have had a top priority. It could not have been difficult to persuade people to live in Clonmacnoise. It became one of the largest communities in Ireland and a center of Irish and European learning. Looking at the still impressive ruins of round towers and ancient church walls, Donnchadh remarked: "Clonmacnoise was one of the great ecclesiastical centers of the [Irish] golden age. Its abbots and governing cadre were amongst the great ecclesiastic nobility of the land. It was a great center of literature and art." Like other Irish monasteries of the time, its influence spread way beyond the confines of its own parapet. Walking around the ruins with the crisp air blowing off the River Shannon, it was hard not to feel nostalgic for the long-lost Irish monastery system which was destroyed by the reforms of the twelfth century.

IRISH CHRISTIAN LIFE

In the early days of Christianity in Ireland there had been an attempt to establish dioceses with bishops in charge of whole areas. But this was an urban model based on the experience of European Christianity, and Ireland had no urban centers. So Christianity in Ireland developed along the lines of the way the population lived at the time—in small communities, which eventually developed into large monasteries. But to use the word "monastery" is a bit of a misnomer as the monasteries that developed in Ireland during these centuries bore little resemblance to what we now think of as religious communities. They were religious, but they were not ascetically monastic as we would understand the word. They were not like modern-day monasteries or even monasteries of the Middle Ages where monks observed a regular order of life.

As Christianity in Ireland spread, the monasteries became large nucleuses of population. This is a significant part of the story of later Irish monasticism. They were much more than monasteries; they became whole communities developing along the lines of the society that had founded them. It used to be said that the Irish founded monasteries because they wanted to isolate themselves from others and be closer to God, but in fact the Irish monastery system was not a place of isolation. Monasteries were large, thriving centers of activity and worldliness.

THE MONASTIC CITIES

By the end of the seventh century great monastic towns had sprouted all over the country, but they did not espouse austere monkish lifestyles. They referred to themselves as "monastic cities," and they certainly were the closest thing that Ireland had to urban centers. Within the monastic towns were workshops and markets filled with the hustle and bustle of daily life. The monastery was not just one large building as it would be today but was made up of many structures including work areas, living quarters, and places for trading and bartering goods. Irish monasteries were in fact thriving communities incorporating all aspects of secular life.

By the eighth century the monasteries had been almost completely secularized while remaining Christian in ethos: they celebrated the life of Christ but were also very much integrated into the material world. They had moved away from the Roman or European idea of monasticism as isolation and developed a system and living style unique to Ireland. Whole families lived and worked within the monastery town. The abbots who ran the monasteries were usually married men and had families of their own. Celibacy was not considered a necessary component of monastic life in Ireland. The monks themselves were also usually married, and it was these families that made up a large part of the monastery town. On the death of an abbot the usual practice was for one of his sons to inherit the monastery and become the new abbot. Although there was no exact order of succession, the monastery and its wealth all stayed within the family.

THE ROYAL ABBOTS

Extensive writings survive from this period which allow us to know quite a lot about Irish society and the monastic system that became the most important feature of Irish life at the time. We know that the monasteries were very closely connected and integrated into the upper ranks of Irish society. The abbots belonged mostly to the royal families and were wealthy and influential men. The land that the monastery was originally built on had often been donated by a royal family, and one of the family's sons or brothers would likely have been the first abbot. It was not unusual for an abbot to hold the title king and abbot, often the abbots had brothers or fathers who were kings. This traditional connection with a particular family line sometimes continued for many centuries. For instance, the king of the Uí Néill had a house at Armagh and lived there for part of the year. The Leinster king lived sometimes at the monastery of Kildare where his brother was the abbot and his sister the abbess. The abbots themselves, being aristocrats, frequently married women from the royal houses and led lives like princes.

CHURCH STRUCTURE

Some larger monasteries controlled or "owned" other smaller ones. Armagh and Iona were the two most powerful ecclesiastical centers of the Irish church. Iona had dependent churches both in Ireland and in Scotland and owned monasteries at Derry and at Kells, in modern day County Meath. Armagh had a whole network of dependent churches across Ireland. It claimed to have been founded by Patrick, and from the seventh century linked itself to the rising dynasty of the Uí Néill. Armagh therefore claimed primacy over the whole of Ireland. This supremacy was generally acknowledged by the end of the seventh century. Clonmacnoise likewise sat at the head of a number of smaller communities and all of these lesser monasteries would pay taxes to their head monastery.

This is not to say, however, that Ireland had a church hierarchical system like the rest of Europe. It did not. Individual churches and monasteries enjoyed a great deal of independence. Some churches were allied to the larger monasteries but many were free, that is, they were under no obligation to a higher church or monastery or even to the original owner of the land. Others were not so free and had to pay taxes to the family that had originally donated the land to them. This payment might persist for many generations. At the top end of the scale were the largest monasteries, with their royal alliances, with dependent churches and smaller monasteries paying taxes to them. At the bottom of the scale the smallest church would consist of a church and perhaps a graveyard serving a local community. The average person living on the land at this time was not bound to an overlord as he might have been in Romanized Europe. The commoners were freemen and usually owned their land and had rights under the law. So the smaller churches served these people and very often were independent of the larger ones. There might only be one priest in such a church and his son would inherit the job on his father's death.

WOMEN IN IRISH CHRISTIANITY

The position of women within Irish Christian society is very interesting and one that has been given much scholarly attention recently. We know that the abbesses were an important and vital part of Christianity in Ireland during its developing process. In the early days of conversion the Christian missionaries and converts had more or less tried to live separately from those who were still espousing the pagan gods and goddesses. But these early Christian converts were not gender conscious or biased in that both men and women in Ireland worked together to bring the Christian message to others. Ireland differed also from the rest of European Christianity in that women neither became separated from the mainstream of Christian preaching nor were they forced to go into enclosed convents.

The Irish abbesses were as much a part of mainstream Irish Christianity as were their counterparts, the abbots. The abbess in Kildare for example, was for some time also a bishop. The legendary St. Brigid was said to be the original abbess there, but as the medieval historian Elva Johnston explains, "Brigid is given the status of bishop for the first time in a ninth-century life of the saint, but it probably dates from at least a century earlier. At first it was believed that this rank only applied to Brigid, but then it was claimed that her successor abbesses would also be awarded the status of bishop." It seems that the abbesses of Kildare held the title of bishop for hundreds of years. Many religious women served as wives to priests and monks and fulfilled their roles in religious life through the men they were married to. But the influence of a wife cannot be discounted easily. The wife of a priest or an abbot must have had quite an influence on the running of the monastery and the direction of Christianity in general. Although the actual power that women held in the early Irish church is debated, it does appear that they were certainly not as marginalized as they would become after the later twelfth-century reforms.

MONASTIC WEALTH AND THE FLOWERING OF THE IRISH CHURCH

Although the sixth century saw the heroic age of the Irish church when famous founders like Colmcille did their work, it was not a time when art flourished. It was at approximately the beginning of the eighth century that the great Irish artworks come into prominence. This significant period in Irish history heralded in a time of tremendous achievements in the arts and in scholarship. Monastic worldliness contributed to the great flowering of the Irish church. The monastery towns had the wealth to maintain vast workshops to attract craft workers of the highest skills.

The wealth of the monasteries lay in many sources. They owned extensive rich farmland which formed the basis of their wealth. They also encouraged pilgrimage, and the pilgrims paid very well for the privilege of staying in the monastery. Pilgrimage in those days was as popular and profitable as tourism is today. In fact pilgrimage became a significant part of the income of many monasteries. Although some monks had it prescribed for them as atonement for sin, most of the lay people who went on pilgrimage did so for fun. Saints' feast days, especially the founding saints of monasteries, became days of celebration and pilgrimage. From early on we know, for example, that March 17, the supposed date of Patrick's death, was a day of celebration at Armagh. Another source of income lay in relics. The larger monasteries had valuable relics which were carried around in times of plague or sickness, and people would pay quite an amount to have a relic brought to a sick friend or relative in distress. The lesser monasteries paid taxes or rent to the larger monasteries they were governed by. The wealth of the large monasteries formed the backbone of the Irish economy of the time.

IRISH ART IN METAL, SCRIPTORIA, AND STONE

In these rich monasteries the demand arose for exquisite liturgical vessels and for beautiful gospel books to grace the altars of these wealthy establishments. The rich abbots living in the prosperous monasteries had the resources to pay for the creation and develop-

Dating to approximately A.D. 700, the Ardagh Chalice is considered the greatest of all early Christian metalwork in Europe. Richly ornamented, the real genius is in the magnificent design. (*National Museum of Ireland*)

ment of the beautiful manuscripts and chalices associated with this time. The monasteries seemed to have a taste for opulence in design, which was perhaps a part of their worldliness. Whatever the reasons, this is the period of great Irish art in manuscripts, metal, and stone. The large wealthy monasteries ran scriptoria and workshops in stone carving and metalwork where aestheticism in design was held in very high regard.

One of the greatest examples of exquisite Irish artwork from this era is the Ardagh Chalice. On display in the National Museum of Ireland in Dublin, this chalice is considered the finest example of Irish metalwork of the eighth century. It was given its name because it was discovered in a bog in 1868 in Ardagh in County Limerick. It actually dates to approximately the year 700 and is regarded as the epitome of Irish craftsmanship of the period. This extraordinarily beautiful chalice is made of silver and bronze and orna-

mented with gold filigree. But it is in its design that the aestheticism and genius lies. When we visited the museum in Dublin we
were privileged to see the chalice outside of the protective glass
case where it is usually displayed. It is a marvelous achievement in
metal work. Pat Wallace, director of the museum, described it for
us as "The best quality in Europe of its day: gold, wirework, so-
called filigree in the girder around the top. The bowl and the base
are separate, silver, cast bronze dipped in a kind of a gold in the
middle of the stem, and then gold foil work. Then there are the
studs around it, underneath the handle, in the handle, and studs
around the girder. All of those have blue and red enamel. That's a
technique that originated in the Roman world and was perfected
and developed here by the Irish."

Another achievement in Irish art of this period is the Tara
Brooch, so named because it was discovered on a beach close to
the hill of Tara. The interesting thing about this item is that it is
not a Christian object but has been made with the same skill and
care that is found in the chalices of the day. This is a brooch that
was obviously made to be worn by a wealthy person as a prestige
object. As Pat Wallace pointed out, "It just shows us that great art
and great metalwork skills were lavished as much on everyday artifacts for the nobility and for a king as they would be for early Christian objects." This is an interesting observation and is an indication
that Irish Christianity of this time seems to have made no distinction between the spiritual and material world. Both were accorded
the best work of the superior craftsman.

GOSPEL ILLUMINATION

Part of the daily routine of monastery life was the transcribing of
the gospels and other manuscripts, including grammars. In an age
before the printing press it was the only way to get a copy of a book.
Many of these copies were for personal day-to-day use and written
without much decoration. Transcribing was such a commonplace
practice that often the monks wrote poems and notes in the margins of the pages they were copying giving us interesting insights
into their daily lives. While the gospels or psalms were usually written in Latin, these margin notes, and poems, were written in Irish.
Many interesting pieces of information can be gleaned from these

annotations, from complaints about the cold conditions they were writing in, to love poems. One poem, written by a scribe about his cat, *Pangur Bán,* or White Cat, is an amusing and charming piece of ancient doggerel. The opening lines are:

> I and Pangur Bán, my cat
> Tis a like task we are at;
> Hunting mice is his delight
> Hunting words I sit all night.

But some gospel books were important works of art. Manuscript illumination in Ireland saw its major development in the eighth century. Irish contact with scriptoria in Britain and continental Europe brought about an interplay of diverse influences to this art form. Still, the general tendency in Irish illumination was towards a greater increase in ornamentation and design developing into a uniquely Irish form of abstract artistic expression. Scriptoria were to be found in all the large Irish monasteries, and many of these manuscripts have also survived. They represent fine examples of how highly skilled the Irish monastic scribes had become.

The *Book of Kells* is the greatest of these manuscripts; it has no rival for decoration, skill, and beauty. It is a brilliantly illuminated copy of the four gospels written in Latin in a text form known as Irish majuscule. Although there is no direct evidence regarding its precise provenance, it is thought to have been designed and written by Irish monks on the island of Iona some time in the late eighth century. It may have been created to mark the two-hundredth anniversary of the death of Colmcille, the founding saint of Iona. It is believed that it was subsequently carried to the monastery at Kells in Ireland, possibly as a result of the Viking attacks in the later centuries. The book was unfinished at the time it was brought to Kells, and work was done to complete it there, although it was never absolutely finished.

This magnificent manuscript is said to be the work of an entire scriptorium working together in its production: scribes and painters collaborated in its inception. Nevertheless, creative license is apparent on every page of the manuscript. There was considerable artistic freedom permitted in the creation of this work which differs from continental manuscript illumination of the time. It is extremely ornate and much more elaborate in design than its European counterparts. Francoise Henry, an authority on the *Book of Kells* and its origins, says of the Irish scriptorium which produced the book, "Like the scribes, the painters belonged to a scriptorium where there was no watertight compartments and there was sufficient give and take to produce a common flavor in the work, whatever the individual tendencies of the artists." The basic design is complex yet delicate in its intricate ornament and mastery of artistic patterns. Capital letters are filled with circles, spirals, animals, birds, and small human figures which sometimes protrude menacingly above the text. The symbolism of it all remains unknown, but it is without doubt the greatest illuminated book found anywhere in Europe of this period. Today the *Book of Kells* is housed in Trinity College, Dublin, where it is displayed to tourists in its own interpretive center at the university. The book is in a protective glass case, and a new page is turned each day.

HIGH CROSSES

The most distinctive, visual feature of Irish monasteries of the ninth century were the enormous High Crosses, sometimes referred to as Celtic crosses. These impressive, large, freestanding stone crosses are still to be found scattered across Ireland on the sites of many of the ruined monasteries. Some stand as high as twenty feet. They are the product of the fine stone workmanship common in Ireland at a time when stone carving was rare in the rest of Europe. The crosses are elaborately carved with images from the Bible. The stonework designs are comparable to the contemporary Irish metalwork and illuminated manuscripts and display similar abstract designs and ornamentation.

The unusual design of the cross is the most notable feature: a ringed cross head is mounted on a solid stepped base. The ring is the most distinctive and familiar feature of the cross, yet its origin is uncertain. Some scholars believe that the ring on the High Crosses has a practical origin and may have been developed for structural purposes. The large stone cross head, they suggest, would be unsound without the help of the ring to support it. But this theory fails to take into account the possible symbolism of the ring design. Earlier ringed crosses were found on slabs, and the ring design may have connections to the older pagan icon the sun.

The *Book of Kells* is a brilliantly illuminated manuscript of the four gospels. Shown here is a page from the gospel of St. Mark. (*Trinity College, Dublin*)

There is a ringed cross design on a linen wall-hanging from Egypt dating to around A.D. 500 which foreshadows the design on Irish crosses. The ring may also be a symbol of triumph as it was in ancient Rome, and it may be a representation of Christ's triumph over sin. Perhaps the true origin of the cross motif is best understood as a necessary structural design which also had some symbolic meaning, possibly inspired by earlier circular icons.

When we view these enormous stone monuments today we see them in gray stone, but this is not how they once were. It is now believed that originally they were painted with bright colors to enhance their appearance: a representation in stone of what was being painted in the illuminated gospels. Over the years the paint on the crosses was eroded from exposure to the elements. In their original colorful glory they must have been an extraordinary sight for a visitor to encounter when they came on a monastery and saw such a marker for the first time.

Remnants of more than two hundred stone crosses are to be found in Ireland today, representing only about half the number believed to have once existed. The crosses seem to have served a number of purposes. They might have acted as boundary markers to the monastery for pilgrims and others who came to visit. It has also been suggested that they could have been status symbols, and the elaborate designs and impressive size of some of them suggest this. Yet one of the main functions was to act as a sort of bible of the poor in that they depict scenes from the Old and New Testament and therefore "told" these stories to those who could not read. For this reason they are sometimes described as "sermons in stone." But they do not depict the stories of the Bible in any systematic way. Images were carved for their spiritual or symbolic meaning to emphasize some fundamental aspect of Christianity. They sometimes also contained specific references to the monastery where they stood. The great cross at Clonmacnoise, known as the Cross of the Scriptures, has a representation of the founding of the monastery. Carved on one side is the Uí Néill king who granted the land, and on the other side is St. Ciaran, the founder of the monastery.

IRISH SCHOLARSHIP

A major attribute of Irish monasticism from the eighth century on was that of scholarship. Irish monasteries became large centers of European learning. Many foreign princes and scholars traveled to Ireland to attend Irish schools for their education. At the height of its influence Clonmacnoise had about 2,500 students within its

Historian Maire Herbert stands next to the ancient St. Martin's cross in front of the rebuilt medieval monastery of Iona, St. Columba's holy island. The cross dates from the original monastery and may have been the forerunner of all other Celtic crosses in Ireland. (*Leo Eaton*)

parapet, many of whom had come to Ireland from Europe to be educated. They studied the Psalms and the Gospels, but they also developed a culture of Latin grammar and of Latin scholarship. Greek was also studied. This love of linguistic erudition passed into the vernacular, the Irish language, and the Irish were the first people in Europe of any vernacular language to write their own grammars. From the year 700 there were excellent written grammars in the Irish language. This is when much of the ancient literature of Ireland was first written down from the oral sources. Ireland has the oldest literature in Europe in a native language. Stories of heroines and heroes and Celtic gods and goddesses were all committed to writing at this time. The scribes probably saw in Queen Medb and Cú Chulainn champions of their own past whose deeds might be described as the equivalent of the Old Testament of their own people.

But the work did not consist only of copying down older stories. At this time a lively literature in the Irish vernacular flourished, and much of that written literature was new. The Irish took the traditional metrical Latin verse and made it their own. A new syllabic form of Irish lyric poetry was created. Poets still held one of the most honored positions in Irish society, and the poets of this period left behind a legacy of poetic originality and greatness.

Likewise, as they were writing books on Christian canon law the scribes also wrote down the ancient Irish laws—the Brehon Laws, which continue to be a source of keen scholarly interest; they supply us with a fascinating insight into early Ireland.

IRISH SCHOLARS IN EUROPE

The Irish were eager and enthusiastic about education, and out of this passion came the desire to spread their learning abroad. While in the past they had gone overseas as Christian missionaries, now they went to Europe as learned scholars to spread knowledge. The character of the movement of Irish scholars into Europe during this period is different from the great missionary movement of the seventh century. Whereas the earlier missionaries had eventually been discouraged from preaching because of their independent spirit, by this time the Irish had gained a solid reputation for scholarship. The superior learning of the Irish schools had become an established and widely acknowledged fact. These scholars traveled from Ireland bringing learning and knowledge with them at a time when European scholarship had all but vanished. During this period, known in Europe as the Dark Ages, the continent was thronged with the Irish who were now going abroad in droves to take up positions as advisers, scholars, and astrologers in the royal courts.

For hundreds of years Irish scholars were to be found at the European courts, particularly in the Carolingian and Frankish empires. Irish scholars like Dicuil, who wrote tracts on geography, grammar, and astronomy, and the poet Sedulius, who was the leading scholar-courtier at Liége, became a common feature of court life. Dicuil's great work, *Liber de Mensura Orbis Terrae* (Concerning the Measurement of the World), contains an important summary on geography and gives concise information about various lands. He drew on many earlier sources but added the results of his own investigations. Dicuil is the first source for information on Iceland because of reports he obtained from Irish monks who traveled there sometime before A.D. 795. He recorded their descriptions of the landscape and the midnight sun some fifty years before the Vikings arrived there and settled the country. The Irish poet Sedulius has left behind some ninety poems and a significant treatise on an introduction to the logic of Aristotle. Irish scholarship was held in such high esteem during this era that no European court considered itself to be well served without the presence of at least one of these Irish scholars.

JOHANNES SCOTTUS ERIUGENA

One of the most outstanding of all these learned scholars was Johannes Scottus Eriugena, or John the Irishman. The word "Scottus" means the Irishman, and 'Eriugena" means born in Ireland. During the ninth century, Scottus was one of a number of Irish scholars working in the area of Reims in France. The philosophical writings of Scottus were so far beyond his time that his work was not appreciated until the time of the early Renaissance philosophers. His true contribution to Western philosophy and the recovery of his writings in recent times has been a major source of interest. Bertrand Russell called him "the most astonishing figure of the early Medieval period." Scottus's mind grew and flourished in the Ireland that he was born into and grew up in. The freedom to think and go beyond the accepted teaching of the time was part of the Irish scholastic ethos of this period. With monastic worldliness came curiosity, and with that came innovative thinking. This is one reason why Scottus is so remarkable—he was able to swim intellectually beyond the accepted Christian norms of his own era.

Johannes Scottus Eriugena was born around the year 800 and was resident at the French court in the middle of the ninth century. He was appointed by King Charles II of France (known as Charles the Bald) to his court at Compiegne near Laon as supervisor of the court schools. His mind belonged to a later age, and he was condemned by various church councils for espousing such radical thinking as free will and questioning established Christian thinking on the origin of the universe. Scottus taught that man should not be completely dependent on any authority for spiritual direction but that free will plays a role in salvation. He was pantheistic in his theological tendencies and believed in accessing God through direct revelatory experience. In this way he foreshadowed later Christian mystics. He also maintained in his writings that reason does not need the sanction of authority but that reason itself is the basis of authority.

His Greek was unusually fine for the period he lived in. In Ireland at this time, Greek was studied and learned whereas in the rest of Europe it was virtually unknown. Consequently Scottus translated into Latin the work of Pseudo-Dionysius and added his own commentary. He was the only scholar of that period to produce a complete philosophical synthesis, *De Divisione Naturae*, the first great work of its kind in Western Europe. He came into conflict with Pope Nicholas I for his radical thinking and Neo-Platonism but was supported by Charles and remained at his court. His original thinking would not endear him to the establishment of his day or for many days to come. He died in approximately 875, but as late as 1585 Scottus's work was condemned by Pope Gregory XIII as heretical. In 1681 his *De Divisione Naturae* was placed on the "Index of Forbidden Books" by the Vatican. By the twentieth century, however, he was being recognized for the genius that he was.

Understanding Johannus Scottus and his ability and willingness to think beyond the confines of orthodox dogma is perhaps a way of understanding the Ireland of his time. The plethora of philosophers and scholars produced in Ireland in this period is a testament to the level of learning cultivated by the Irish schools. That Ireland could produce thinkers like Scottus shows the broadness of mind and intellectual range typical of the Irish centers of learning. Like the scriptoria and the other art forms that flourished at the time in Ireland, scholarship was not confined to convention. As Europe stagnated, the Irish schools grew to maturity with the power of freethinking. The Irish scholars are evidence of a sense of erudite confidence and belief in intellectual exploration which seems to have been nurtured in the country during that period.

MONASTIC BATTLES

Life within this monastic system was not always peaceful. As the large monasteries became increasingly wealthy they found that more and more they were the targets of both the kings and other monasteries. Very often the rich monasteries were attacked and plundered for their wealth. In later centuries the Vikings were to do this on a grand scale, but years before the Vikings came to Ireland there were monastic raids and battles between the monasteries. One of the earliest records of a monastic battle is written in the *Annals of Inisfallen* in 664, about fighting at the monastery at Birr. In 760 Birr went to war with Clonmacnoise to settle some differences. Four years after this there is a record of a large battle between the monastery of Clonmacnoise and that of Durrow in which the records tell of two hundred of the monastery community of Durrow being killed. In other words, these monasteries were behaving very much like city-states and fought over issues between them. Donnchadh Ó Corráin describes these battles: "We do know that there were monastic troops, of course, and even before the Viking period we find pitched battles between monasteries. That is to say monasteries had contentions and quarrels, presumably over property and income. There's a pitched battle between [the monasteries at] Cork and Clonfert, in which there was an innumerable slaughter, the annals say, of the ecclesiastical heads and superiors of Cork."

These battles were not just fought between monasteries. Monasteries were also often the targets in political disputes. In 780, for instance, the *Annals of Ulster* relate that in a war between Leinster and the Uí Néill, the over-king of the Uí Néill "pursued them [the Leinstermen] with his adherents, and laid waste and burned their territory and churches." In 793 Armagh, the chief ecclesiastic center of Ireland, was attacked and plundered by an Irish king. From all of these accounts it is obvious that the monasteries had armies with which they would defend themselves, or they would attack other monasteries or kingships if the need should arise.

The monasteries had become so rich and powerful that in times of crisis in society, especially in times of crop failure or any shortage of food, secular violence against the monasteries escalated. A cattle plague in 777 was followed by raids on the monasteries of Kildare, Clonmore, and Kildalkey. This type of attack in times of need continues for hundreds of years, and in 1015 the *Annals of Inisfallen* report that most of the churches of Munster were vacated because of the scarcity of food. In the same year they tell of much looting of the monasteries in the area.

What is very clear from all of this is that the monasteries had become well-known as populous centers of wealth. The attacks on them had nothing to do with anti-religious feelings. It was simply that the monasteries had the resources and the means of survival. Consequently, in times of societal stress or need they were the obvious targets of attack and plunder. For this reason the Irish kings attempted to dominate the monasteries or place their close relatives in the position of abbot or abbess. As the violent assaults on monasteries predated the Viking plundering, it is incorrect to say that the Irish were following Viking example, as has sometimes been claimed. Native attacks had more to do with the perceived economic growth of the monastery towns; they were not the result of imitating Viking patterns.

KINGSHIP IN IRELAND

In spite of the wealth and prestige of the monasteries, the kings and their families remained a vibrant force in Irish society. It is difficult to say exactly how many petty kingships there were in Ireland at the time, but it is estimated that there may have been around a hundred. But the position of an Irish king was not like that in the rest of Europe. A king in Ireland had no real power. An Irish king did not "own" the land as he did in Europe, and, unlike European kings, he did not have the authority of a judge or a lawmaker. He was simply the representative of his people or a leader of his people in times of war. The high-kingship was a title without any real meaning. The Uí Néill had claimed the title high-kings of Ireland for centuries, but it did not mean much beyond the prestige of such a title. Irish high-kings were first among equals, rather than rulers of the entire country. Significantly, Irish kings were not above the law. Their authority came from a mixture of their own personality and charisma, military strength, and an ever-changing network of alliances with lesser kings or chieftains. Another important difference between Ireland and the rest of Romanized Europe was the absence of order of succession based on birthright. In Ireland primogeniture, the heir being the oldest surviving son, was not the practice. Instead, on the death of a king or a chieftain, senior members of the court would meet in what was called a *dáil*, or discussion group, to decide the next leader.

INAUGURATION OF KINGS

The precise details of the inauguration of a king are not clear, but we do have some idea of who would have participated and how the ceremony might have been conducted. The chief poet was an important presence at the event. He (or she, perhaps) was usually there to recite in verse the genealogy of the new king and give some credence to his fitness to be respected in his role. A ruler's genealogy, real or invented, was important because it established the sense of his "Irishness" and his family line going back to prehistory. The poet would have also been there to recite poems giving advice to the new king on how to rule and how to be a just overseer of his people's affairs. There is evidence to suggest that it was the chief poet who was the actual officiant of the ceremony and not the ecclesiastics who were also present. The calling aloud of the name and title of the new ruler was an essential part of the ceremony. This proclamation of the actual name of the king was vitally important, and the chief poet, who was the master of the word, as it were, was therefore the true kingmaker. The *Lia Fáil*, or stone of destiny, is said to have cried out at the inauguration of a true king.

This apparently happened with some frequency. It is easy to assume that some kind of precaution must have been made to assure that the stone would cry out at the appropriate time.

In Ireland, as in many places in Europe, the king was seen as a sacred person. People believed that with a rightful king the crops would grow, the cattle would be disease free, and the rivers and lakes would be full of fish. To cement this sacredness, part of the Irish inauguration ceremony involved a "sacred marriage" of a king and a goddess, very often the goddess of the territory. The feast of Tara, in which the king of the Uí Néill was solemnly wedded to the goddess of Tara, was a ceremony that went on for hundreds of years into the Christian period. Some time in the early part of the ninth century the "ordination" of high-kings began, perhaps as a carry-over from the pagan practice of godly marriage. One of the Uí Néill kings, Áed Ingor, was probably the first king of Tara to be ordained at his inauguration. This practice of Christian ordination was to spread to Europe as Irish scholars brought the idea abroad.

Later descriptions of the inauguration of Irish kings, from the twelfth century on, describe in more detail the actual rites of the ceremony, but these descriptions lack validity. They are based chiefly on the work of Giraldus Cambrensis, the Norman chronicler who wrote a history of Ireland in the twelfth century and who shows a marked prejudice against the Irish. He was, after all, writing in part to justify the Norman invasion. His descriptions of incest and bestiality are most likely barbarous propaganda against the pagan practices of the Irish. By the twelfth century the Irish were being portrayed in Europe as being in need of religious and moral reform.

CHIEFTAINS AND KINGS

Socially by the eighth century the lesser kings were on their way down in society, and their importance had greatly diminished. Some of them would not be referred to as king but as *taoiseach* or chieftain. It was the five or six kings of the provinces who were the real players in Irish society. Many of them had managed to extend their territories beyond their traditional lands by winning allegiances with smaller kingdoms. The annals are full of the battles and deeds of these few provincial kings. In many ways they had become the celebrities of their day. In the north the powerful Uí Néill had extended their territory to include all of modern-day Donegal and had also expanded east and south through Leitrim and Longford into the midlands. For centuries they had claimed the kingship of Tara, which always remained the most prestigious kingship. In a sense central power was developing slowly, and it was inevitable that a king would emerge who would try to make himself true king of all Ireland. Such a man emerged in Munster and he was the first to try to become a meaningful high-king. To do so he would have to challenge the power of the Uí Néill. That he failed is not surprising, but the methods he employed were sometimes so outrageous and seemingly excessive that they ensured that his name would not be forgotten.

FEIDLIMID MAC CRIMTHAINN

As religion and politics were closely linked together, the royal houses often played major roles in the running of both church and state. Some royal families combined the power and the aspirations of both kings and bishops. One man who held both a civil and ecclesiastic title was Feidlimid Mac Crimthainn. He was certainly one of the most colorful and interesting characters to emerge from early Irish history. He was at the same time both king of Munster and bishop of Cashel. Feidlimid was king of Munster from 820 until 847 and Cashel, his bishopric, was the primary seat of Christianity in Munster. It was also the ancestral royal seat of the kings of Munster, and King Feidlimid was one of the Eóganacht family who had ruled Munster for generations.

By the eighth century the Eóganacht were second only to the Uí Néill of Ulster in prominence and were almost as clever at inventing ancestors. The Eóganacht claimed that angels pointed out the site of Cashel to their founding ancestor and that their king had been baptized and blessed by St. Patrick. It was fairly predictable, given the climate of prestige and competition which prevailed among monasteries and kings alike, that sooner or later one of the Eóganacht would challenge the Uí Néill to the position of high-king. In spite of the fact that the high-kingship was not a powerful political position, the title carried a great deal of prestige. Feidlimid wanted the prestige for himself and his own dynasty, the Eóganacht, but he also had ideas of kingship which were beyond his time in Ireland. He was ruthless and unrelenting in his pursuit of his objective. Ironically he was one of the *Céli Dé*, an ascetic group within Irish Christianity which espoused strict observance. Considering how he went about achieving his goals it is difficult to understand this, but perhaps he was driven by conviction. Whatever his private beliefs he made no allowance for anyone who got in the way of his ambitions.

CASHEL

Even today the rock of Cashel is an impressive sight. Situated close to the town of Cashel, its steep incline can be seen for miles around. It was originally used as a fortification for the Eóganacht dynasty as early as the fourth century. Cashel was taken over by Christian influence early on in Irish Christianity, and it had always considered itself to be second only to Armagh in Irish ecclesiastic affairs. It had at one time aspirations of being the main center for Irish Christianity. A number of Munster kings also held the title bishop of Cashel, and it was here that the kings of Munster were traditionally inaugurated. The site was formally given to the church in 1101, thus ending any pagan or political associations with it. Today, a ruined thirteenth-century cathedral stands on the top of the rocky hill where once kingly inaugurations and Christian ceremonies took place. The climb up the rock is quite steep, and legend has it that it was abandoned as a religious center when an archbishop could no longer make the climb to his cathedral. But during the time of Feidlimid Mac Crimthainn it was a thriving community and the proud capital and ecclesiastic center of Munster.

FEIDLIMID'S POLITICS

King-Bishop Feidlimid led quite an active life by all accounts. The annals include numerous references to his antics which make for startling reading in our time. He plundered monasteries for their wealth and carried off untold bounty. He is credited with plundering the monasteries at Kildare, Durrow, Fore, and Gallen. He fully understood the economic and political power of the monastic communities, and in his attempt to gain the high-kingship of Ireland made various attempts to get the larger monasteries on his side. He put in a candidate for abbot in Clonmacnoise and went to war with the monastery when it appeared his man would fail. He attacked the monastery a number of times and plundered it. Feidlimid's candidate ended up being thrown into the River Shannon by the monks of Clonmacnoise. Being a candidate for abbot in those days obviously sometimes had its downside.

Feidlimid was not daunted by these events. He then interfered directly with the politics of Armagh. The support of Armagh was of primary importance to him and his ambition. He was astutely aware of the political significant of this center in both secular and ecclesiastic affairs. A strong high-kingship of all Ireland was favored by Armagh as a necessary corollary to its own claim of ecclesiastic primacy. But Armagh was riddled with disputes over succession and experienced many bitter struggles over the question of rights to the abbacy. At the time of Feidlimid two rival candidates were fighting over the abbacy there. When the Abbot Diarmait was expelled from Armagh and Forannan was installed in his place Feidlimid attacked the new abbot and imprisoned him in the hope of having him set aside and replaced by his own supporter, Diarmait.

Feidlimid's ultimate aim was dominance over the powerful Uí Néill, and on numerous occasions he raided the lands of the Uí Néill in Ulster. He led serious attacks against the Uí Néill in 823 and again in 826 by invading their territory, but he did not make the gains he wanted. Finally in 827 he managed to persuade the king of the Uí Néill to meet him at Birr for a peace conference. Its outcome is unclear. The Munster annals record that it was at this time that the Uí Néill recognized Feidlimid's supremacy, but as no other annals record this, it is difficult to conclude that this in fact happened. The Munster annalists were probably reflecting their own bias in what they would have wished to happen or, it has been suggested, they might even have been told by Feidlimid what to write. It is doubtful that the Uí Néill, under relatively little pressure, would grant such an honor to a Munster king. Some time after this in 838 Feidlimid met with the king of Tara, Niall. The meeting turned very nasty, and Feidlimid is described in the annals as seizing Niall's wife, Gormlaith, and her female retinue. This was obviously an insult to the entire Uí Néill dynasty. Gormlaith was an important woman in her own right and was later described in her obituary in 861 as *"Regina Scotorum,"* the Queen of the Irish.

THE END OF THE DREAM

But these outrageous and flamboyant gestures would not gain Feidlimid the high-kingship, which at the time depended also on the favor and respect of the lesser kings. Shows of power alone were not enough to convince the Irish that someone should be high-king, and Feidlimid did not gain the allegiances he would have needed. Niall is reported in the Ulster annals as defeating Feidlimid in a battle in 841 and again stopping his progress into Ulster, but this still did not put an end to Feidlimid's ambition. Two years later, in 843, he burned and attacked the monastery town of Clonmacnoise and according to their annalists it was done "without respect of place, saint or shrine." In the *Annals of Clonmacnoise*, St. Ciaran, their long-dead founding saint, is described as being so angry that he is said to have appeared to Feidlimid after he returned home to Cashel and to have given him a poke with his staff which eventually caused Feidlimid to die of the flux.

Yet is has to be acknowledged that Feidlimid was the most powerful king (and bishop) of his time. The fact that he ultimately failed to gain the high-kingship of Ireland was not entirely indicative of his personal failure but rather that the times were not quite ripe for such a king. The Uí Néill remained a dominant power in Ireland and it was shortly after this time that they produced one of their most powerful leaders, Máel Sechnaill. It would take a stronger personality and another set of circumstances to topple the Uí Néill from their superior position.

Remarking on Feidlimid's career Donnchadh Ó Corráin says, "He engaged in very clever politics . . . and it's quite plain that Feidlimid Mac Crimthainn saw himself as the most important king in Ireland. But the tradition that the Uí Néill were the premier dynasty, the paramount dynasty, and the title king of Tara had such a high honor and such a long history that the kings of Munster really don't make it for being dominant in Ireland until the tenth century." Nevertheless it is obvious from the career of Feidlimid that the idea of a powerful overlordship of Ireland was beginning to take hold in the minds of some of the more influential families. He died in 847 without achieving his ambition of the undisputed high-kingship, but his exploits serve to show us that Ireland was changing politically. Provincial kings were no longer willing to accept the status quo, and kingship in Ireland was beginning to develop along a more European-style model. The idea of a central kingship was taking root.

Ireland was about to undergo great social change as well. The Vikings from the northern European region had begun to plunder and attack the wealthy Irish monasteries. They came in their long-ships along the Irish coast but soon had penetrated the land by their voyages up the rivers. They would eventually settle and form the basis of the first Irish towns, and their legacy would play a significant and enduring role in Irish history and politics.

[9]

Raiders from the Sea

THE VIKINGS seemed to appear out of nowhere, slaughtering their way into history in A.D. 793 when they attacked the monastery at Lindisfarne on the northeast coast of Britain. They had first raided Britain several years earlier, but it was the destruction of a church at the religious heart of the kingdom of Northumbria that caught people's attention. Two years later these Norsemen (men from the North) swept down the west coast of Scotland to terrorize the lands around the Irish Sea. It was part of a much larger Viking movement out of homelands in Denmark, Norway, and Sweden that would—over the next two centuries—overrun much of Scotland, England, and France, create the first kingdoms of Russia, settle Iceland and Greenland, and reach as far as North America. But in 795 this was all in the future. The first Vikings to attack Ireland were just hit-and-run raiders who came from Norway, perhaps by way of the Scottish Isles. They attacked Colmcille's monastery island of Iona off Scotland's west coast before crossing the Irish Sea to come ashore on Rathlin Island, off County Antrim in the north. Then they continued around the northwest tip of Donegal and sailed south to the island of Inishmurray, four miles off the Sligo coast. Those first attacks had a shattering effect on Irish coastal communities.

THE RAID ON INISHMURRAY

The monastery island of Inishmurray is shaped like a leaf, less than a mile in length and half a mile at its widest point. It has been deserted since 1948, when the last forty-six islanders left for the mainland. Ruined houses still line the island's only road, an overgrown path that hugs the shoreline facing the mainland. Today gulls are the island's principal inhabitants—quarrelsome around people, especially during early summer breeding season when they do not hesitate to attack. They screech in so close their beaks can draw blood as they drive visitors back to the shore. Only then do the gulls circle back to land on the encircling cashel wall of the monastery, screaming defiance at all who dare invade their territory. Monks who lived here twelve hundred years ago were not so lucky.

Historian Charlie Doherty arrived on Inishmurray to visit one of those places where the Viking story in Ireland really started, little changed from how the island looked in A.D. 795. There is no harbor, so visitors must jump ashore from a small fishing boat onto sea-slimed rocks, just as early monks did, crossing in skin-covered currachs from the mainland only when the sea was calm enough for landing. Even today visitors cannot land in bad weather while only the foolhardy come in winter when sea swells against the rocks can rise and fall as much as six feet. There was a monastery on Inishmurray from the sixth century, abandoned in the twelfth century.

Charlie walked across treacherous seaweed-covered rocks and up past the ruins of the abandoned twentieth-century village, turning inland along the cobbled path leading to a fortresslike circular wall enclosing the religious settlement. The cashel wall is still fifteen feet high in places and ten feet wide, with only a narrow tunnel entrance leading through into the monastery enclosure. Guides from the mainland tell visitors the wall was built by monks as a defense against Vikings, but Charlie believes it pre-dates the monastery. If so, the monastery was built inside an earlier pre-Christian ring fort.

When Viking raids began at the end of the eighth century, offshore and coastal monasteries around Ireland were wide open to attack from the sea. "This was a peaceful, comfortable, and self-contained world for the monks," Charlie explained as he walked along the top of the cashel wall that circled the monastery. Inish-murray is unspoiled by tourism because it is so hard to reach. Stone beehive huts and other monastic buildings have hardly changed since Viking times, except that roofs were thatched then and much of the stonework painted. Outside the cashel wall, small dry-stone fenced fields worked by twentieth-century islanders are now over-grown with bracken and thorn. In the summer of 795 similar fields would have been full of ripening wheat and barley. In the haunted solitude of Inishmurray today, the ghosts of the past feel close—monks with their wives and children, slaves working the fields, monastery cattle grazing on whatever land was not either set aside for growing crops or useless bog; only a quarter of Inishmurray's land is free from bog today. A choir could have been chanting psalms in the church, tenant farmers singing more frivolous secular songs in the fields. Even if a sharp-eyed watcher had seen sails in the northeast, there would be no cause for alarm; island communi-ties were used to seeing traders sailing up and down the west coast of Ireland. But then the Viking longships swept ashore on the nar-row sand beach near the landing rocks and the killing would have begun.

"The attack must have been horrendous," Charlie said. "The people would have had no warning, no chance to defend them-selves. Some would have been slaughtered immediately, most dragged off into captivity as slaves." If people inside had time to barricade the entrance, brawny Viking warriors could have boosted each other over the cashel wall to leap down inside, axes swinging as they hit the ground. In those first Viking attacks, surprise was a fearful weapon.

Standing on the same cashel wall more than twelve centuries later, it is not difficult to picture the scene: the monastery filled with smoke as thatched roofs are set on fire, dogs barking, pigs squealing, people screaming in fear and agony, the whole mona-stery swarming like an ant hill stirred with a stick. Once they real-ized what was happening, people out in the fields might have run back to defend their homes, their courage buying them only slavery or death. Most would have run away, hiding in the cave at the far end of the island where fishermen say monks always took refuge during Viking raids. The terrified survivors would have huddled to-gether in the cramped hiding place, hushing the children to stop

A round tower dating from the mid-twelfth century at Devenish, the monastery island in Lough Erne, framed by an arch from the later medieval monastery. Round towers were once thought to have been built for defense against Viking raids but were in fact constructed when the Vikings were already established. (*Leo Eaton*)

them from giving away their position, hearts pounding as they waited for the sounds of battle to fade and the raiders to leave. Only then would they dare creep back to tend the wounded and bury the dead.

THE ATTACK ON SKELLIGMICHAEL

By 823 Viking raiders had sailed all around Ireland. Many places on Ireland's south coast have Viking names, like the Blasket Islands in County Kerry and the Saltee Islands in County Wexford. Not even the jagged rocky crag of Skelligmichael—eight miles out into the Atlantic off the coast of Kerry—was safe, attacked in 824. It is hard not to admire the determination of Viking warriors who fought their way five hundred feet up hundreds of precipitous steps cut into the mountain to where the monks built their monastic village. Any monk with a stout quarterstaff would have had a good chance of knocking an attacker into the sea. Viking invaders were probably winded and angry by the time they reached the top. The annals record: "Etgal, abbot of Skellig, was carried off by the heathens and died soon after of hunger and thirst."

Coastal monasteries learned to dread the sight of sails on the horizon. Marginal comments scribbled on manuscripts offer momentary glimpses into these monk's states of mind as they waited fearfully in their coastal monasteries, praying for bad weather to keep shipborn raiders away from the coast. One monk, grateful for a howling Atlantic storm, wrote a poem in the Latin gospel he was copying:

> The wind is fierce tonight
> It tosses the sea's white hair
> So I fear no wild Vikings
> Sailing the quiet main.

WHERE DID THE VIKINGS COME FROM?

Who were these Vikings? Why did they appear like a swarm of locusts at the end of the eighth century to plunder the coastlines of northwestern Europe? There is no simple answer, just a combination of economic and political factors that put the Norsemen in the right place at the right time. People in Denmark, Norway, and Sweden shared a similar culture, language, and religion during the eighth century, but there was no sense of unity between the various peoples of Scandinavia. The *Svear* kingdom (from which Sweden gets its name) was more interested in Russia and the rich markets of the Black Sea and the Eastern Roman Empire of Byzantium. Denmark, controlling lands in northern Germany, was preoccupied with the possible expansion of Germanic tribes into its territories. So it was the Norwegians, fragmented into more than a dozen petty chiefdoms and geographically isolated by mountains and impenetrable forests, who first seized the opportunity to trade and plunder across the North Sea in Britain and Ireland at the end of the eighth century.

The people of Norway were farmers and fishermen, traders and explorers, ruled by local warlords hungry for wealth and plunder but with scarcely enough men and resources to outfit even a single longship. Even the wealthiest warlords at the start of the Viking Age would have owned no more than three or four such ships. Yet it was the longships that gave the Norse their great strategic advantage during the Viking Age. Based on earlier Germanic boats, Norse seamen had perfected the design through centuries of sailing in the treacherous fjords and storm-tossed seas around the Scandinavian coasts until they had developed into Europe's finest warships.

Viking dragon ships—so called because of their carved prows—probably only reached their final form in the mid-eighth century, a case of the right tool being ready at the exact moment conditions were right for its use. They were the foundation of Viking power and the most treasured possession of any Viking warlord. Kings and chiefs were often buried in them, which is why so many boats have survived. The best known was excavated in 1880 at *Gokstad* in Norway and is still on display in a museum in Oslo; seventy-seven feet long and almost eighteen feet wide, its keel is carved from a single tree. Viking ships had planking that was tied—rather than nailed—to the ribs so the entire boat could flex and bend in heavy seas. The *Gokstad* boat was built for thirty-two oarsmen—sixteen on each side—but was fitted with thirty-two shields on each side, suggesting it might have carried a double crew to allow rowing in shifts. It shipped a forty-foot-high mast, holding a square sail that would have given it a top speed of more than nine knots in a good wind.

The chieftain who owned this mighty machine of war was buried on a bed at the stern, surrounded by everything he would need in the next life including weapons, clothes, tools, twelve horses, and six dogs. This was a ship for fighting and trading, possibly able to carry as many as sixty-five warriors all the way to Ireland and beyond. Other trading ships were wider and deeper, capable of carrying more cargo but less effective for hit-and-run attacks on a hostile shore.

The first raids would have been tentative. The Norse would not have known what to expect in Ireland, but word would quickly have spread that Ireland was ripe for the plucking. Vikings from Norway continued to be the chief threat to Ireland through the middle of the ninth century. Denmark was more interested in Britain and did not become involved in Ireland until later. Fleets grew larger as more powerful and ruthless Norwegian warlords brought lesser chiefs under their control. Monastic raiding was a growth industry, a gold rush for Norwegian nobles with households of quarrelsome and warlike sons. The Vikings were a vigorous and fast-breeding warrior race in a harsh land where plenty of strong sons were proof of a man's virility. The eldest son inherited the family land; younger sons were expected to find their own. Since so much of the country was mountainous, there was a severe shortage of good farming land, and fights over inheritance must have been common. Many a frustrated local chief may have outfitted a longship, packing his sons and followers off with instructions to "Raid west, my sons," just to get a bit of peace and quiet at home. More likely, being a good Viking, he would have led the raid himself, crewing his longship with sons, family, and retainers, and taking his "spring" or "summer" cruise when several months of good weather could be expected before approaching winter brought the Viking chief and his sons back home. There he would spend the winter surrounded by his family and slaves, drinking and feasting and boasting of all the battles he had fought and the treasure he had seized in the lands around the Irish Sea. And every spring as the weather improved, Irish monasteries braced themselves for raiding season.

THE EIGHTH CENTURY IN EUROPE—NEW POWERS AND NEW OPPORTUNITIES

For much of the century prior to the first Viking raids, Europe was getting itself organized after the barbarian invasions that caused Rome's fall. New nations were forming, new dynasties consolidating power. The people of Scandinavia had been traders for more than a thousand years, shipping furs, amber, slaves, and ivory—from the tusks of walruses—south to the Mediterranean since before the Roman Empire. But the Dark Age was not good for business. Trade routes had been disrupted as Germanic tribes spilled out of the east in the fifth and sixth centuries to establish new homelands in Italy, France, Spain, and even North Africa. Ancient Roman cities were either destroyed or in decline.

By the eighth century, a new stability was being imposed on Northern Europe by a Germanic tribe known as the Franks. Further south, Muslim armies from North Africa had conquered Spain, moving deep into France and seizing Sicily to dominate the south of Italy. For a thousand years Europe's heart had been the Mediterranean world of Greece and Rome, but now the Eastern Roman Empire of Byzantium was a shadow of its former self and the Mediterranean was a Muslim lake. In the north the Franks were ruled by the Carolingian dynasty that was building a new Christian civilization. When the pope crowned Charlemagne, king of the Franks, as head of a new Holy Roman Empire in 800, it was confirmation that the Frankish kingdom of Northern Europe—today's France, Germany, and a whole lot more—was the new center of European power. Trade routes were open again, and business was booming. Viking traders returning home to Scandinavia from lands in the south must have brought back plenty of stories about the wealth of Christian monasteries and the opportunities for plunder and settlement they had seen along the way.

GOING A' VIKING

Piracy, trade, and land-grabbing were inseparable to Vikings. They were pragmatists, trading with people stronger than themselves, carrying off anything that was not nailed down where coastal populations were weak. Slaves were the richest prize of all. Like other warrior cultures, including the Irish, Norse society was divided into three classes and life was defined by the class into which you were born. At the top of the heap were the ruling military aristocrats, called *jarls*—from which we get the English "earl." These were kings and nobles, warlords with sufficient resources to outfit and crew longships. Next came the freemen, called *karls*—warriors, farmers, and tradesmen, equivalent to our middle class, the backbone of society. Last and absolutely least were slaves and serfs, called *thralls*, who had no rights whatsoever and did all the hard and dirty work.

Vikings were the greatest slave traders of their age. Herds of human cattle were rounded up and brought back to slave markets scattered throughout the Viking world, then sold on south into Byzantium, Persia, and the new Muslim Empire. The slave trade was the cornerstone of all Viking commerce, and no Viking household could survive without slaves. Slaves worked the fields, harvested the grain, and if young and attractive warmed the warrior's bed at night. When Vikings settled Iceland at the end of the ninth century, thousands of Irish slaves were brought over to do the hard labor.

Monasteries were the major centers of population in ninth-century Ireland. They must have seemed like supermarkets of opportunity for Viking warriors out to make their fortune. Here were hundreds of potential slaves gathered conveniently in one place, with monastic treasure as an added bonus—silver and jeweled chalices and reliquaries that held the bones of saints. Chalices and shrines were melted down for raw silver or taken home as family souvenirs while books and manuscripts were burned or tossed aside in the mud, worth nothing to illiterate pagan raiders. A British monk at the court of Charlemagne in Germany declared the Vikings an instrument of God's anger, punishing the people of Europe for their sinful ways.

SAILING THE VIKING SEA LANES

Longships ruled the Irish Sea and Vikings were the greatest sailors of their age, but it is easy to forget how desperately vulnerable they were to being blown off course or sunk by storms and heavy seas.

Sailing the Viking sea lanes today in a modern warship, with position fixed by satellite navigation, computers tracking course and speed while charts and sonar identify unseen rocks, is a far cry from Viking sailors who navigated by the feel of the sea and the sky, an instinctive understanding of currents and tides, the smell of the wind, and the position of coastal landmarks and the stars. How many ships were lost? How many more Viking warriors were drowned than were ever killed in battle?

The *Roisin* is the Irish Navy's newest ship, a high-tech warship for the twenty-first century just as longships were for the ninth century. At 258 feet she is more than three times longer than the *Gokstad* boat but carries a smaller crew. Tom O'Doyle, *Roisin*'s captain, had invited Donnchadh Ó Corráin and Pat Wallace aboard to follow a Viking trade route up the east coast of Ireland from Cork to Dublin. Pat is one of Ireland's most respected archaeologists. In the 1970s and 1980s he spent seven years directing the excavations of Viking Dublin.

On a blustery wet summer day—typical Irish weather—with the sea high and the waves white with foam, Pat and Donnchadh stood on the *Roisin*'s bridge, hanging on grimly as the warship rode each crest only to slam down into the next trough, and spoke of the Viking ships and sailors who sailed the same seas twelve-hundred years earlier. "The ships were flexible and had a very shallow draft, useful for running up beaches or traveling up-river, but they wouldn't get a good bite of the sea," Pat explained. "They'd be pretty unstable with such a big sail and very top heavy, so if they went over, it would be almost impossible to get them right side up again. A terrible number of Viking ships must have been lost."

How easily Viking longships capsize was proved in recent years while a British television crew was making a program about Vikings in the North Sea. The reconstructed longship swung crosswise into the wind and flipped over in just a few seconds, too fast for anyone to do anything except swim for their lives. No one was hurt, although a lot of expensive TV equipment ended up at the bottom of the sea. Vikings were not so lucky. As Pat said: "Some ship archaeologists believe at least half the Vikings were lost at sea, even though they were by far the best navigators of their day."

Captain O'Doyle took a pragmatic seaman's view. "Safety and comfort wouldn't have been a consideration. The ships were designed to transport warriors to a particular location quickly and effectively." It was a strange conversation to have on the high-tech bridge of a modern warship. The shore was less than a mile away, a rocky headland looming out of the drizzle and framed by white-capped waves. In the distance white breakers crashed against the base of a gray cliff, yet the two scholars aboard the *Roisin* sailed into the rising storm inside a warm protected bubble.

"The cold would be deadly," Pat said. "You'd be wrapped up in furs, but you'd be soaked to the skin half the time. And the smells! The sail was dipped in boiled horse fat—can you imagine the stink of that on a sunny day when you're trying to pick up a breeze in the North Atlantic?"

THE BOOK OF KELLS AND THE VIKINGS

Colmcille's monastery island of Iona was particularly vulnerable to attack from these sea-raiders since it was off the west coast of Scotland, directly in the path of any Viking longship heading south to Ireland. By the ninth century it had become the center of a great federation of Columban churches spread out from Ireland to Scotland and northern Britain. Lindisfarne in Northumbria, site of the first Viking raid in 793, was part of this federation. Raided in 795, Iona was burned in 802 and again in 806, when sixty-eight of the community were killed by "the heathens" and many more taken into slavery. Quite obviously something had to be done. In 807 the annals record "building a new monastery of Colmcille at Kells." Kells had been a prehistoric Irish kingship site and was now a royal hill fort belonging to the Southern Uí Néill. It had the great advantage of being twenty miles inland, safe from marauding Vikings who in the early years never went too far from their ships. Seven years later the new monastery was complete, and Iona's abbot resigned and left the island, presumably to head the new monastery at Kells. For the next fifteen years Kells and Iona continued to be governed as a single community.

The *Book of Kells* is the greatest and most famous medieval illuminated gospel manuscript in the world, named for the monastery at Kells where it remained for so long, but scholars still argue about where it was made. Most think it was likely created on Iona, perhaps commissioned for the two-hundredth anniversary of Colmcille's death in 597. It would have been one of the most precious treasures of the monastery. And as Viking attacks grew more frequent, it must have been brought to Kells soon after the refuge was completed in 814.

It is tempting to think of Iona's abbot, saying goodbye to his fellow monks and walking down the beach below the abbey to where a hide-covered currach would be waiting to carry him back to Ireland, clutching the precious manuscript wrapped in animal skins to protect it from the salt water. Rowing out into the narrow channel between Iona and the larger island of Mull, the abbot and his crew would have pointed their bow south and raised the sail, making a run for the Derry coast of northern Ireland more than seventy miles away, no doubt praying that they would not run into Viking raiders along the way. There is no way of knowing if the *Book of Kells* was on Iona in 814, but the fact that the manuscript is unfinished supports this image of a great work of art being bundled up and carried out of reach of Viking raiders to the sanctuary prepared for the monks and precious relics of Iona.

Iona was not abandoned. The Vikings hit it again in 825 and murdered a monk called Blathmac and many of his companions because they refused to reveal the location of a valuable shrine said to contain the bones of the founding saint. As a later abbot brought Colmcille's bones back to Iona from Ireland in 829, there may have been different sets of saintly relics. As for Blathmac, it is said he came to Iona in 818, hoping for martyrdom at the hands of the Vikings. If so, it must have been frustrating to wait seven years before he got his wish.

THE ANNAL RECORDS

History is usually written by the winners, but in Ireland it was victims who kept the records, which is why Vikings always got such bad press. Irish kings had been raiding each other's monasteries for centuries. Even in the middle of Viking raids in 833, Feidlimid—the bishop king of Munster—killed monks at Clonmacnoise and burned their lands "up to the doors of the church" because the monastery was allied with the Uí Néill, his rival for the largely symbolic high-kingship of Ireland. Vikings were not doing anything new, but they were foreign and pagan, which meant that everyone hated them, the "sea vomitings from the north" as they are described in the monastery annals. Terror may also have been a deliberate tactic, convincing victims to surrender quickly rather than resist. Outfitting a Viking raiding party was expensive; healthy slaves get a better return on investment than dead bodies.

Annals offer a detailed if one-sided view of the Vikings in Ireland. Mostly they call them heathens, sometimes Norsemen or foreigners, and they make a clear distinction between "white foreigners" from Norway and the "dark foreigners" who arrived later from Denmark, which probably relates to a difference in dress between Norwegians and Danes. From 795, when the annals record the first attacks on Ireland, through the late 820s, the records show an increasing pattern of attacks around the coast, sometimes going a short distance inland but never so far that the raiders could not return quickly to their boats if they ran into heavy opposition. Sometimes the invaders were beaten off, as in 825 when they were routed by the Ulaid—the men of Ulster—but usually the story was a litany of monasteries burned, abbots, kings, and local leaders killed, and men and women taken into slavery.

The annals were not concerned only with Viking raids. They also provide a record of everything else going on at the time, from the succession of abbots and the dynastic wars between Irish kings to occasional glimpses of everyday life at the beginning of the ninth century. The winter of 822 was apparently so cold that "seas, lakes, and rivers" froze hard enough for wagons, cattle, and horses to travel across the ice. The following year the abbot of Armagh's house was struck by lightning—"fire from heaven"—and burned to the ground. Travelers moving from monastery to monastery brought news of what was happening around the country. Local and regional kings were probably well informed about Viking raids but initially saw them more as a nuisance than a serious threat, getting involved only when raiding occurred in their own backyards. Irish kings probably hired Viking warriors for their internal wars quite early, and the Vikings themselves had no sense of common purpose at this time. They were in it for the money. As Pat Wallace said, "Even though they shared a common language and culture, they were all different, warring with each other, just hit men, raiders, and traders, making alliances with certain small Irish kings against other small Irish kings, capitalizing on weaknesses all the time."

By the 830s this first casual raiding phase was over. Viking attacks on Ireland became much more serious once they started moving inland.

THE MOVE INLAND

Raiding coastal monasteries had reached a point of diminishing returns; populations were growing wary, hiding themselves and their valuables at the first sight of a sail. Vikings knew much more about Ireland by this time. They had spent thirty years exploring the Irish coast, long enough to learn some Irish while many of the locals would have picked up enough Norse for communication. The Vikings had learned that the real wealth of the country was in great inland monasteries like Durrow, Cork, Armagh, and Clonmacnoise. They certainly knew that many of Ireland's rulers were preoccupied with a dynastic dispute between the Uí Néill and the Eóganacht kings of Munster over the high-kingship.

These were the years when the Vikings made serious gains in Ireland and came close to overrunning the whole country, as they would in Britain, Scotland, and northern France. Between the 830s and the 850s, fleets were bigger and better organized, sailing up the rivers and lakes to strike deep into the heart of Ireland. Vikings were no better or worse warriors than the Irish, but their mobility— and initial lack of fixed bases vulnerable to counterattack—gave them an edge. Along with shallow-drafted longships carrying them far inland, the Vikings were also great horsemen. Back home in Scandinavia a warrior's horse was often buried with him. Raiding parties would have commandeered horses as soon as they landed and covered great distances as mounted infantry. Counting on surprise and speed, they would often be gone with their slaves and treasure before local troops could be organized against them. But there must have been plenty of times when it became a race back to the boats, Vikings hurrying their terrified captives at sword-point, killing any who slowed them down, while Irish warriors panted at their heels like hounds chasing a fox. When Vikings did face another army, their usual tactic was to lock their shields together into an almost impenetrable barrier called a shield wall. Since Irish warriors used similar tactics, battles could become stuck in a stalemate of shield wall against shield wall, each shoving and straining to break the other's line. Elsewhere in Europe there are descriptions of this going on for hours until finally, like water breaking through a dam, one side would either break or run and the slaughter could begin.

In 832 Armagh was attacked three times in a single month. "They'd found out about Armagh when they plundered some dependent churches on the coast the year before," Donnchadh Ó Corráin said. "Armagh sent a military force which was defeated. No doubt they had a little chat with their prisoners and learned how things worked. It wouldn't be difficult to figure that Armagh would be packed with pilgrims on March 17, the great feast of St. Patrick. They'd know it was the best time to attack." Armagh was always a popular Viking target, and the annals tell of one thousand prisoners taken in a single raid. The fact that Armagh continued to survive indicates just how large a population it could support.

The five years between 836 and 841 were particularly bad for the people of Ireland. Feidlimid, the Eóganacht king of Munster, and his Uí Néill rival were at each other's throats, and the Vikings chose this time to launch their deadliest assaults—hardly a coincidence. In 836 they struck inland from present-day Galway to devastate the lands of Connaught, and sailed up the River Shannon into the heart of Ireland. Unlike most Irish rivers, which are fast flowing and difficult to navigate, the Shannon is a long, lazy waterway that opens out into great lakes—Lough Derg and Lough Ree—ringed by rich and powerful monasteries like Killaloe, Holy Island, Terryglass, Clonfert, and Clonmacnoise. Once Viking ships were on the lakes, the fox was loose in the henhouse.

"Clonmacnoise was the greatest of the monasteries on the Shannon, a center of European learning," Pat Wallace said. "But there were no buildings on the site taller than a Viking ship. So when a fleet of dozens of ships came up-river, each one of them towered like a jumbo jet over that whole town. It put the fear of God, literally, into these men of God."

In 837 a raiding party came from Donegal Bay in the northwest to penetrate into Lough Erne, raping, and looting the monastery of Devenish along the way. But the most important development occurred that same year when two fleets—with 60 ships each—appeared on the Boyne and Liffey rivers in the east, putting the rich Uí Néill heartlands of Meath—and Tara itself—within reach. If each ship carried a minimum of 30 warriors, two fleets together could have landed more than 4,000 men, a considerable force by the standards of time. Fighting was heavy all through the following year. Annals record that 120 Norsemen died in one battle but that in another the Uí Néill army was defeated and an uncounted number were slaughtered, though the principal kings escaped.

If the two fleets on the Boyne and the Liffey arrived together, as seems likely, such a sophisticated joint action would have required time and planning to assemble the necessary ships and men. Donnchadh Ó Corráin believes that a powerful Viking dynasty from Norway had already established an independent kingdom in Scotland by the 830s, comprising parts of the mainland as well as the Northern and Western Isles. Their intelligence about conditions in Ireland was probably excellent. In 839 another fleet attacked Ulster, following the river Bann into Lough Neagh and then continuing south to Armagh. Later legends suggest a Norwegian warlord called Tuirgeis led the raid. He supposedly arrived in the north with a large fleet in 839, made himself "king of all the foreigners of Ireland," attacked Armagh where he "celebrated pagan religious rites on Patrick's altar," settled Dublin the following year, and was finally captured and drowned in Lough Owel in 845 by the king of Meath. Unfortunately there is no evidence to support the idea of an overall Viking leader in Ireland at this time.

Tuirgeis was turned into a bogeyman in later times, a name to frighten small children and a favorite target of Christian propaganda against the "vicious Vikings." Undoubtedly actions of different Viking leaders were attributed to him, just as stories accumulated around famous Christian saints, yet he was clearly an important leader. Only two Vikings are mentioned by name in the annals from this period. The first is Saxolb—described as "chief of the foreigners"—who was killed by the men of Connaught in 837, the year after Viking raiders plundered the province. Second is Tuirgeis, whose death is reported in 845, confirming his importance. In 845 annals note that there was "a great encampment of foreigners on Lough Ree," who plundered west into Connaught and east into Meath. Since Máel Sechnaill—the king of Meath—took Tuirgeis prisoner that same year and drowned him in a lake less than twenty-five miles away from Lough Ree, it is logical to assume he was one of the leaders—if not the leader—of this invading army. By the 840s, raiding had become full-scale invasion. Ireland's future would turn on the actions of the man who drowned Tuirgeis. In 846 the king of Meath—Máel Sechnaill—became rule of the Uí Néill and so high-king of Ireland.

SETTLEMENT AND THE FOUNDING OF DUBLIN

During the first decades the Vikings were in Ireland, they sailed away each year as winter approached, returning either home to Norway or to settlements in the Scottish Isles. There is no telling exactly when they started wintering in Ireland, although as early as 828 annals describe "a great slaughter of porpoises by the foreigners" that might indicate laying in food for a winter stay. Charlie Doherty thinks it likely the fleets on the Liffey and Boyne in 837 remained through the winter, but the first real evidence of Viking settlement in Ireland comes four years later. In 841 the *Annals of Ulster* report that two naval camps were established by the Vikings at Duiblinn (Dublin) and Linn Duachaill.

Each of these camps was situated on the borders of warring Irish kingdoms, strategically placed to dominate Ireland's agricultural heartland and several major routeways across the country as well as Tara itself, the symbolic heart of Ireland situated halfway between the two camps. Linn Duachaill is about 60 miles north of Dublin at the village of Annagassan on Dundalk Bay. These were not accidental choices, so it is likely the campaign was again planned and coordinated from the Viking kingdom in Scotland. Leaders of the colonizing fleets would have been expected to swear allegiance to the king. When a much bigger fleet of 140 ships was sent eight years later by "the king of the foreigners to exact obedience from the foreigners who were in Ireland before them," it is clear Irish Viking leaders had forgotten who was supposed to be running the show.

The naval camps at Dublin and Linn Duachaill were called *longphorts*, fortified camps where the longships could safely be hauled up on dry land for repair over the winter. Earth banks and wooden palisades, much like Irish forts of the period, would have protected houses and a landing place for the fleet. Archaeologists have not yet found the exact location of the first two Viking settlements in Ireland, but there is no shortage of theories. Historian

Howard Clarke suggests that Vikings first settled at or near Irish monasteries where existing infrastructure and possible Irish allies would have made things much easier for the newcomers. The abbot of the monastery at Linns (Linn Duachaill) on Dundalk Bay was killed by "heathens and Irish" in 842, perhaps because he objected to what was going on, so the monastery was clearly still in operation. The monastery of Dublin had been built on the banks of a tributary of the Liffey called the Poddle. Just before it emptied into the mouth of the Liffey, the Poddle widened into a natural harbor known as the Black Pool—in Irish *Dubh Linn*. Such an existing monastery with a good anchorage was probably useful at the start but not necessarily ideal for a more permanent *longphort* settlement. Annals in 842 record "the heathens still at Duiblinn" but by 845 there is mention of an encampment of foreigners at Ath Cliath—the Ford of the Hurdles—probably a couple of miles upstream on the Liffey where an island in the river—later called Usher's Island—might have been easier to defend. Ath Cliath was the main Dublin settlement on the Liffey for the next eighty years, a sprawling trading camp whose main business was slaves captured in raids up and down the country. The Vikings had come to Ireland to stay, but settlements such as Dublin and Linn Duachaill also made them vulnerable. Irish kings had awakened to the fact that their own power was now threatened. The next dozen years would decide who controlled Ireland—the Irish or the Vikings.

[10]

Viking Kings in Dublin

THE VIKING LONGSHIP came slowly up the main channel into Dublin. The great red-and-white-striped sail had been furled out in the bay and the oars were run out as they passed the red lighthouse on the end of the harbor mole. A crew member stood at the carved dragon prow, blowing a blast on a great cow's horn, its plaintive bellow reverberating back from spiderlike cranes and stacks of containers that lined the north side of the River Liffey. Except for the horn-blower and a man at the steering oar in the stern, the rest of the crew strained at wooden oars big as telephone poles, twelve feet long and thicker than the spread of a man's hand. "Eight . . . nine . . . ten! Come on, lads, put your backs into it." The skipper's voice called the rhythm of the stroke. "Once again, everybody together. One . . . two . . . three . . ." The *Dyflin* was coming home, and a ragged cheer rose from a watching group of Polish sailors who lined the rail of a rust-streaked freighter moored on the south side of the river. The rowers barely noticed, sweat streaming down their faces, ten men struggling to row a ship designed for more than thirty.

The *Dyflin*—old norse for "Dublin"—was built for Dublin's official 1988 millennial celebrations, copied from the *Gokstad* boat in Norway, seventy-seven feet long and eighteen feet wide, and built in the traditional Viking style with planking tied rather than nailed to the ribs. Over the past quarter-century the *Dyflin* has sailed several times to Britain, once as far as Norway, but now it spends much of its life tied up and forgotten at the Dublin Port Authority dock on Custom House Quay. On a winter Sunday with a heatless sun hanging low in the sky, a group of sailing enthusiasts had taken the ship out into Dublin Bay to put it through its paces. It sailed well, driven by a southerly breeze, before the wind dropped and everyone waited, chilled to the bone and tossed around in the wake of ferries coming and going from the Port of Dublin before a turning tide helped them pull back up-river with just a third of the rowers required for such a ship. Billy King, *Dyflin*'s skipper, said it was hard to get enough crew to maintain and sail the ship properly. "People are too busy, they don't have the time anymore," he explained. "This boat's not getting the attention and repair it needs. It's been in the water almost twenty-five years, a unique part of Dublin's past, but most people don't even know it exists." The same could be said for the remains of Viking Dublin, covered up by layers of concrete roadway and high-rise office buildings in the heart of today's city.

DUBLIN AND THE FIRST SETTLEMENTS

Only in the past generation has Ireland come to understand how important the Vikings were to their country. But even today old stereotypes survive—how Vikings were bloodthirsty plundering pagans finally kicked out of Ireland in 1014 by High-King Brian Boru at the Battle of Clontarf. But Brian could not have become high-king without their support, and Ireland would be a very different place today if they had never existed. They built the first towns—Dublin, Limerick, Cork, Waterford, and Wexford—and turned Dublin into a great European trading center that became the economic heart of the Irish Sea. For several decades in the tenth century, Dublin's kings also ruled the north of Britain from York, challenging Anglo-Saxon England for supremacy across all the lands of Britain. Viking fleets provided naval support for Ireland's kings in their dynastic wars for the high-kingship. They brought the first money into Ireland, established the first royal mints. Over the centuries the Norse gene pool merged with the general population to such an extent that few Irish today are without some Viking blood. "One of the things the Vikings lacked in Ireland was women," Pat Wallace explained. "And women are a fairly vital ingredient if you want to stay in business for another generation. So they married Irish women right from the start." Some Norse women came over from Scotland and Norway, wives and daughters of important men, but never enough. So the first settlers in Dublin and the other *longphorts* looked to Irishwomen to warm their beds on cold winter nights.

Standing beside the Liffey and watching the *Dyflin* row upstream, Pat Wallace explained how different things looked twelve hundred years ago. "The whole story of Dublin is the story of the Liffey," he said. "It's tamed today, flowing sluggishly between river walls. You've got to imagine huge fleets of ships coming and going on a fast flowing tidal river that was shallow and subject to flash floods. Their ships had a draft of only three feet, and you could probably have walked across the river anytime. It wasn't the best anchorage, but it was politically ideal, a no-man's-land between two rival Irish kingdoms. The town of Dublin grew up at the junction of the Liffey and the Poddle. There's high ground here: a good defensive place protected by two rivers with easy access to a big tidal estuary to float off the ships."

Viking Dublin did not become a proper town—the first in Ireland—until the tenth century. Prior to that the *longphort* at Ath Cliath, upstream from modern Dublin, was the center of Norse operations, a fortified camp and market that traded in slaves from around the Irish Sea. Ath Cliath was not the only Viking settlement in the Dublin area. Pat Wallace has dated the earliest Viking occupation around Fishamble Street—in downtown Dublin—to approximately 880, and the original monastery site on the Black Pool—Duiblinn—was still being used in 849, after the move to Ath Cliath. Mid-ninth-century Viking graves at Kilmainham, another nearby monastery, suggest it was occupied at the same time. The *Annals of Ulster* recognized the area around Dublin as a kingdom in the 850s, so there were clearly a number of Viking sites spread out along the Liffey and its tributaries. Since the monastery at Kilmainham continued to exist, along with other monasteries within easy walking distance of Dublin, the invaders must have quickly reached an accommodation with local abbots.

"Viking raiding on monasteries really belongs to the earlier period," historian Donnchadh Ó Corráin said. "After they set up in Dublin and got to know how Irish society worked, they came up with a more effective way of collecting wealth. They levied a tax on

A reconstructed Viking longship takes part in annual longship races in Peel Harbor on the Isle of Man. The Viking colony of Man was at the strategic center of the Irish Sea, often under the control of Viking kings in Dublin less than forty miles away. (*Leo Eaton*)

the monasteries; in other words, the monasteries paid protection money. When you get raids after the second half of the ninth century, it's usually a case of the arrangement breaking down, rather like a modern inner-city gang torching a store that won't pay up."

COEXISTENCE

Dublin and Annagassan were not the only *longphorts* established in the 840s. There were bases on the Shannon, at Cork and Limerick in the south, Wicklow in the east, and a number in the north on Lough Neagh and Strangford Lough. This part of Ulster, conveniently close to the Viking lands of Scotland and the Western Isles, was as thickly settled as the area around Dublin. Had the Northern Uí Néill not been so efficient about getting rid of Vikings in their territory in the late ninth and early tenth centuries, a major Viking town might have grown up close to where Belfast is today, challenging Dublin for control of the Irish Sea and perhaps altering Irish history down to the present. As with Dublin, other *longphorts* were often established on the borders of rival kingdoms. Monasteries in most of the areas occupied by Vikings held onto their lands and continued to function normally, just like the ones around Dublin. Richard Warner, keeper of antiquities at the Ulster Museum in Belfast, explained why.

"Once they'd settled a particular area," he said, "they needed to trade locally. They couldn't survive if they antagonized the Irish living around them, so they did their raiding in other parts of the country. You had Waterford Vikings being a nuisance in the north while northern Vikings with fleets on Lough Neagh pillaged further south. Vikings who lived for years on Strangford Lough were probably on excellent terms with the monasteries around them because they needed food, cattle, someone to sharpen their knives—all those good neighborly things that murder and mayhem tend to discourage. In fact when they did start being a nuisance locally they didn't last very long—the local king destroyed them. So the Vikings were very good at not messing in their own backyard."

Dublin and other *longphorts* may have been set up with the agreement of local Irish kings. Certainly the Irish were quick to see the advantage of Viking allies in their own dynastic wars. When in

850 the *Annals of Ulster* record that the king of Connaught's son rebelled against the Uí Néill high-king "with the support of the foreigners and plundered Uí Néill lands from the Shannon to the sea, both churches and states," Norse and Irish alliances were already accepted practice. "There was intermarriage at the very top levels of Norse and Irish society from the middle of the ninth century," Donnchadh Ó Corráin said. "The king of the Northern Uí Néill married his daughter to the Viking King of Dublin. And the Irish aristocracy seems to have been even happier to marry Viking women. The literature of the time makes it clear they found them very attractive." The Vikings had settled in but were becoming too successful. Ireland's kings—especially the Uí Néill—felt increasingly threatened. It was time to show who ruled in Ireland.

THE BATTLE FOR IRELAND (PART ONE)

In 847 Máel Sechnaill, the Uí Néill king of Meath who had drowned the Viking leader Tuirgeis in a lake two years earlier, became king of Tara and so high-king of Ireland. For centuries Uí Néill propaganda had built up the symbolism of the kingship of Tara—a sacred site with origins going back to Neolithic times—until everyone accepted Tara's ruler as having a special status in Ireland, even though the high-king was only "first among equals." The squabbling family of dynasties called the Uí Néill had held the high-kingship so long that they were the ones to beat for any ambitious king who wanted a chance at the title. Feidlimid—bishop king of Munster—tried to take over the high-kingship between 820 and 847, waging the war that allowed Viking invaders to get settled in Ireland when Irish kings were too preoccupied to pay them much attention.

There were Viking *longphorts* in Feidlimid's Munster, but it was Uí Néill lands in the midlands and the north that were most at risk. The Northern Uí Néill, ruling from Donegal to the Irish Sea, had problems with the Vikings on Lough Neagh while the Southern Uí Néill, with their rich agricultural heartland between the Boyne and the Liffey, were threatened by the settlements at Dublin and Annagassan. Throughout the ninth century the high-kingship alternated between the Northern and Southern Uí Néill, who fought each other as vigorously as they fought everyone else. But after 845, with the future of the country in the balance, Ireland's kings started getting serious about the Viking menace.

"The Irish put up a ferocious resistance," Donnchadh Ó Corráin said. "More Irish kings were killed fighting the Vikings than anywhere else in Europe. Few Anglo-Saxon kings in England were killed, although the Vikings conquered three-quarters of the country. They ruled all Scotland as over-kings and took a huge bite out of France—the future duchy of Normandy—yet they were unable to destroy a single Irish kingdom. Clearly the Irish had no intention of being overrun."

Máel Sechnaill, the new high-king, was from the Southern Uí Néill. At a battle in 848, the annals record he killed seven hundred "heathens." This was clearly a bad year for the invaders. The kings of Munster and Leinster won a major victory further south, killing two hundred Vikings including the heir to the Viking kingdom of Lochlann. The king of Cashel dispatched a further five hundred "heathens" while another twelve hundred were slaughtered in an oak forest up north. If the figures are accurate—and there is no reason to doubt them—the Vikings lost at least twenty-five hundred warriors in a single year, a huge number by the standards of the time. An Irish mission to Europe's Holy Roman Emperor Charles the Bald—Charlemagne's grandson—boasted that their Viking problem was under control. The emperor, who was having less success with his own Viking problem, was probably extremely envious. Yet Norse settlements in Ireland continued to expand, suggesting that large numbers of new Viking settlers were pouring in from Norway and the Scottish Isles.

THE VIKINGS HAVE THEIR OWN INTERNAL PROBLEMS

From 849 Viking leaders in Ireland had more to worry about than newly energized Irish kings. The king of Lochlann—either part of Norway or a Norwegian kingdom already established in Scotland— sent a fleet of 140 ships to enforce his authority over the Vikings in Ireland. Slaves and monastic treasures must have been generating huge profits for the new *longphorts*, and he probably was not getting his cut. Norwegian warlords in Ireland clearly resented his attempt at a hostile takeover since the annals record "there was confusion in the whole country."

Soon the Norwegians in Ireland faced a different threat when in 851 the Danes attacked the *longphorts* at Ath Cliath (Dublin) and Linn Duachaill (Annagassan). Ireland was clearly getting the reputation as a land of opportunity, luring the Norse with a golden potential of plentiful slaves and fertile farmlands. A year after the Danes seized Dublin—they were initially driven off at Annagassan—160 ships arrived with Norwegian reinforcements, more than 5,000 "white foreigners to do battle with the dark foreigners." The battle must have been epic; the *Annals of Ulster* say it lasted "three days and three nights" before the Norwegians were finally beaten off, survivors abandoning their ships to flee inland where no doubt they caused even more trouble for the Irish.

Irish kings found the dark foreigners preferable to the Norwegians, and the Danes held Dublin and Annagassan until they were dislodged in 853 by Amlaib—in Norse *Olaf*—son of the king of Lochlann, who arrived with such overwhelming force that Danes, Norwegians, and local Irish kings in the area promptly acknowledged his authority. The *Annals of Ulster* state that "the foreigners of Ireland submitted to him, and he took tribute from the Irish." For the next twenty years Amlaib and his brother Imar—in Norse *Ivar*—ruled Dublin, but their focus was split between Ireland and increasing their power in northwest Scotland. How many other Viking settlements around Ireland accepted their authority is debatable since there was as much war between Vikings as there was between Irish kings. Vikings were as likely to use Irish allies in their own wars as the Irish were to have Viking allies. These were confused times.

THE ENEMY OF MY ENEMY IS MY FRIEND

Throughout his sixteen-year reign, the Uí Néill high-king—Máel Sechnaill—always needed to keep one eye on Viking invaders and the other on Irish kings who would not accept his authority, especially his Uí Néill cousins in the north. In 851 he had taken revenge on the son of the king of Connaught—who had joined the Vikings in plundering his lands the previous year—by drowning him "most cruelly" in a pool. This may have been a form of ritual execution involving no shedding of royal blood, since in 845 Máel Sechnaill had disposed of Viking leader Tuirgeis the same way. Or maybe he just liked drowning people. The high-king then marched on Munster and took hostages, the traditional way of ensuring a rival king's obedience, but was soon back in action against the Vikings. The Annals record "great warfare between the heathens and Máel Sechnaill" but the Vikings had plenty of Irish help. When Amlaib and Imar of Dublin attacked the high-king's heartland of Meath in 859, they were joined by Cerball, an Irish king whose lands centered on the Barrow River flowing into the Irish Sea at Waterford.

Máel knew that his rival Irish kings were just as great a threat as any Viking. Later that year he called a council of "the nobles of Ireland"—probably under the auspices of the bishop of Armagh who, as successor to St. Patrick, had great moral authority across Ireland—to make peace and amity between the men of Ireland. Since the king of the Northern Uí Néill was not present, the high-king's purpose seems to have been to make peace with Cerball and get enough support to bring his northern rival under control. In 860 a combined army from Munster, Connaught, Leinster, and the Southern Uí Néill marched north under Máel Sechnaill's command.

His chief rival and leader of the Northern Uí Néill was a warrior called Áed mac Néill, son of the previous high-king. By 860 he had already smashed a large Viking army in the north and married his daughter to Amlaib, the Viking king of Dublin. This was an astute political move since Dublin could strike at Máel's heartland whenever his back was turned. The high-king's "Army of the South" was camped at Armagh when Áed launched what seems to have been a preemptive night attack, only to be beaten off with heavy casualties. Máel Sechnaill had won the battle but the war continued, and Áed invaded Meath the following year, accompanied by his son-in-law's Viking army. In 862 Áed and Amlaib again plundered Meath. Máel Sechnaill died in November, and Áed was chosen as the new high-king of Ireland; the Northern Uí Néill had taken back the title.

For the next few years Áed focused his attention on bringing the Vikings in the north under his control, perhaps with the approval if not the active support of Dublin's Viking rulers. In 866 "he plundered all the strongholds of the foreigners in the north and took away their heads, their flocks and their herds." The annals record that he collected 240 heads in one particular battle. According to custom he would have displayed them on spears around his camp. Collecting and displaying the heads of conquered enemies had been a common practice throughout Celtic Europe and continued in Ireland and Britain. As late as the seventeenth century, the heads of executed traitors were still being displayed on London Bridge as a warning to any who would dare rise up against the rightful king.

CAMPAIGNS IN SCOTLAND

By the time Áed was high-king, the Vikings had already been settled in Ireland for twenty-one years, and the immediate threat was over. The Norse—especially the kings in Dublin—had simply become players in the complex dance of dynastic alliances across Ireland. Amlaib must have understood there would be no new Irish lands to conquer and hold; Irish kings were simply too determined. Leaving his brother Imar as king in Dublin, he went back to Scotland where in 866 "he plundered the entire Pictish country and took away hostages from them."

Scotland at the start of the ninth century was split into four different regions. Britons held the kingdom of Strathclyde in the west. These were the same Celtic people who—centuries earlier— had sent Ireland a number of early saints from their monastery at Whithorn in Galloway. East of Strathclyde and bordering the North Sea was the kingdom of Northumbria, established by earlier Germanic invaders known as Angles. Scotland's north was occupied by another Celtic people called the Picts, while the Dál Riada—Irish colonists who had settled the west coast of Scotland above Strathclyde—ruled a kingdom centered on present-day Argyll. This was Scotland at the time of the first Norse attacks. By the 830s the Picts were so weakened by Viking raids that a Dál Riada king—Kenneth MacAlpine—was able to make himself king of both Picts and Dál Riada. It was the birth of a united Scotland.

There is no agreement about the location of the Norwegian kingdom of Lochlann mentioned in the Irish annals. It used to be assumed it was somewhere on the west coast of Norway, but Donnchadh Ó Corráin is convinced Lochlann is the name of an independent Norwegian kingdom in Scotland established prior to 837, when its king sent Viking fleets up the Liffey and Boyne Rivers in Ireland. Such a kingdom would have encompassed the Western Isles and Orkney and could also have included Scotland's far north and the coastal parts of the Western Highlands.

After Amlaib plundered the Picts in 866, he sent his captives back to the Dublin slave market at Ath Cliath, which was already the most important trading center in the Irish Sea. He then turned his attention to the Strathclyde kingdom of the Britons, which he and his brother Imar ravaged in 870 after a four-month siege of its royal fortress. The following year "Amlaib and Imar returned to Ath Cliath from Alba with two hundred ships, bringing with them in captivity to Ireland a great prey of Angles and Britons and Picts." A conservative estimate has longships carrying twenty slaves per ship meaning as many as four thousand captives might have been brought back for re-export through the Dublin slave markets—a "great prey" indeed!

The annals describe the captives as Picts, Angles, and Britons (from Strathclyde), but there is no mention of Dál Riada Scots. The Dál Riada suffered as much as the Picts from earlier Viking attacks, but they may have been allied with Amlaib and his Norwegians during this campaign. Constantine, king of the "Scots," would certainly have favored a weaker Strathclyde on his southern border as he was already having trouble with the Danes who had invaded England five years earlier from the east and taken over most of Northumbria. Although the motives of kings and warlords from such confused and distant times are unknowable, there is an intriguing possible reason for why the Dál Riada might have sided with their Norwegian enemies. The Dál Riada had always maintained close links with the Northern Uí Néill back in Ireland. Constantine, the Scottish king, was probably even related to the High-King Áed mac Néill—marriage links were common between leading Irish tribes. Since Áed was also Amlaib's father-in-law, one reason for the absence of Scottish captives and a possible alliance between traditional enemies could have been a family arrangement. By the time Amlaib returned to Dublin with his captives in 871, Constantine and the British king of Strathclyde had almost certainly acknowledged him as over-king.

Ruling a land kingdom was not Amlaib's primary concern, even though he controlled Dublin and large parts of Scotland and the Isles. Richard Warner of the Ulster Museum explained that "Norwegian Vikings saw the Irish Sea as a large pond which they controlled. Their settlements and centers of power tended to be on islands and the coastline around the edges of this big pond. The Irish Sea was their kingdom, their country. If they were kicked out of a particular place, they just set up somewhere else. So long as they ruled the Irish Sea and controlled trade on both sides of it, especially trade in silver and slaves, they had what they wanted."

THE FORTY-YEAR REST

Amlaib disappears from history after dropping off his captives at Dublin, killed somewhere in Scotland, while his brother Imar ruled the kingdom of Dublin until his death in 873 when the *Annals of Ulster* called him the "king of the Norsemen of all Ireland and Britain." It was the beginning of the end for the first period of Viking colonization in Ireland. They were still active, allied with or attacking various Irish kingdoms, but the energy seems to have gone out of their efforts. Many left for Britain and France, where there were still opportunities for plunder and new Viking lands could be carved out of Anglo-Saxon England and Carolingian France. This period became known in Ireland as the Forty-year Rest. In 893 the kingdom of Dublin was divided in civil war. The *Annals of Ulster* report "a great dissension among the foreigners of Ath Cliath and they become dispersed, some following Imar's son, others Sigfrith the jarl." It led to the main period of Icelandic settlement by the Vikings, most of whom came from either Ireland or the Western Isles of Scotland. Irish slaves were an essential part of this settlement, but many free Irish went as well. Hundreds of years later, many of the leading Viking families of Iceland could trace their ancestry back to certain Irish kings, especially Cerball— king of Osraige—who in 859 had helped the Dublin Norse invade Meath.

Cerball's kingdom was strategically located between Leinster and Munster on the river Barrow—a favorite Viking waterway with Waterford at its mouth—so he had become deft at manipulating Viking and Irish interests to his own advantage. He had married his daughters to Viking nobles and, after becoming king of Leinster, acted as protector of Viking Dublin for a while. But in 902, aware of Dublin's weakness, he attacked the Viking kingdom in partnership with the king who ruled north of the Liffey. The annals report "the heathens were driven from Ireland. They abandoned a good number of their ships and escaped half-dead after they had been wounded and broken."

"The kingdoms on either side of the river finally got their act together," Pat Wallace said. "A few Vikings may have stayed on as merchants, but the majority abandoned the settlement with what was left of their fleet and went first to the Isle of Man (named for the pre-Christian Celtic sea god Mannon Mac Lir), then on to England where they got involved in the Viking wars around Chester and York. This crisis in Ireland precipitated the main period of Norwegian settlement in northwest Britain."

IRELAND'S GAIN, EUROPE'S LOSS

Most of the Danes forced out of Dublin by Amlaib in 863 had joined the Danish army that invaded Britain two years later. In 866 Northumberian York fell to the Viking invaders. By 873 they had conquered Mercia, the Anglo-Saxon kingdom in the British midlands. The Danes now divided up the country, half going north to establish the Viking kingdom of York while the other turned south to invade Anglo-Saxon Wessex. When his kingdom collapsed, a Wessex king called Alfred was first powerless to resist the Vikings and hid out in the Somerset marshes until he could gather a new army and restore his kingdom. Alfred—known as Alfred the Great and the Father of England—eventually forced a Danish withdrawal from Wessex and defeated all further attacks on his territory until his death in 899. England was partitioned along a line running from Chester, on the northwest coast above Wales, to London in the southeast. The kingdom of Wessex, south and west of this line of demarcation, was the foundation on which Anglo-Saxon England would develop. North and east of the line was the Danelaw, a Danish "colony" where language, law, and social customs were all Norse. Alfred's successors gradually whittled away the Danelaw and eventually brought it under their control, but it would retain a distinct Norse character for another five hundred years. The ancient Roman city of York became the capital of the Danelaw and was first ruled by Danish kings. But after the fall of Dublin in 902, when so many Norse-Irish settled in northwest Britain, the kingdom of York became the new battleground between "white and dark foreigners," the Norwegians and the Danes.

Further south, Alfred's victories encouraged the Danes to look for easier pickings in present-day Spain, France, and Germany. They had raided frequently since the 840s, but in 879 a massive Viking fleet left Britain's Thames estuary on a twelve-year rampage through northwest Europe. The Carolingian Empire, already breaking apart, was incapable of mounting a concerted defense, although the Norse often faced stiff resistance from individual Frankish leaders. For thirty more years Viking attacks along major rivers like the Rhine and the Seine were an ongoing calamity, contributing to the fragmentation of the Carolingian Empire, until in 911 the king of Western Francia—modern-day France—bought off a Viking leader called Rollo by offering him lands in northern France that became known as Normandy—the Land of the Norsemen. A century and a half later, in 1066, William, duke of Normandy, would return across the English Channel to finish the job his Danish ancestors had been unable to do, completely conquer England.

During the second decade of the tenth century, Norwegians who were settled in the northwest of England and Scotland resumed their attacks on Ireland. Control of the Irish Sea trade may have been hampered by the loss of Irish bases. In 913 the Norse destroyed what annals called "a new fleet of the Ulaid" (Ulstermen) off the English coast. Ulster was probably trying to carve out part of the profitable Irish Sea trade for itself and the Vikings did not like it. Then the annals of 914 report the presence of "a great new fleet of the heathens" at Waterford. The Forty-year Rest was over and Ireland was again under siege.

THE BATTLE FOR IRELAND (PART TWO)

Over the next two years, large numbers of Viking ships arrived at Waterford where they either reoccupied an old *longphort* or built a new base from which to plunder the lands of Munster and Leinster. In 917 a terrible sense of doom hung over Ireland. The winter was abnormally cold with rivers and lakes hard-frozen and cattle, fish, and birds dying across the country. The *Annals of Ulster* report;

"horrible portents too, the heavens seemed to glow with comets and a mass of fire appeared with thunder in the west, and it went eastward over the sea." People must have imagined their worst fears realized when two enormous new Viking fleets appeared off the south coast of Ireland, commanded by Sitriuc and Ragnall, grandsons of Imar—the king who had ruled Dublin until 873.

Ragnall is described as "king of the white and dark foreigners," and probably had Danish as well as Norwegian ancestry, so the attack must have been a joint operation. Sitriuc landed farther north while Ragnall sailed into Waterford to attack the Vikings who had arrived earlier. Clearly they had muscled into territory he wanted for himself, so he lost no time slaughtering them. The Irish finished off most of those who got away.

Niall Glundub, the new Irish high-king, knew he had serious trouble on his hands. Niall was son of the same Áed mac Néill who, as high-king, had married his daughter to the Viking ruler in Dublin more than fifty years earlier. Through the complex web of intermarriage that now linked Norse and Irish aristocracy, Niall was related to both Viking leaders. Now he led an army of the Northern and Southern Uí Néill against Ragnall in Munster while his Leinster allies attacked Sitriuc at his camp. It was the first of two tragic disasters for the Irish. Although Niall's campaign was inconclusive, the king of Leinster and many Irish "leaders and nobles" were killed and a victorious Sitriuc reoccupied Dublin.

While the war in Ireland continued, Ragnall returned to Britain, defeating the Scots and the Northumbrians to make himself king of York. In 919 Niall gathered an army from across Ireland and attacked Ath Cliath, hoping to push Sitriuc and his people out of Ireland once and for all. The result was the single worst disaster the Irish suffered in all the Viking wars. The high-king of Ireland was killed, along with many senior Irish kings and nobles. A poem in the *Annals of Ulster* describes the horror and despair felt across the country:

> Mournful today is virginal Ireland
> Without a mighty king in command of hostages;
> It is to view the heaven and not to see the sun
> To behold Niall's plain without Niall
> Where now are the princes of the western world,

Where now the horror at every clang of arms
Since valiant Niall of Cnucha
Has brought desolation to his great province?

The balance of power between the Irish and the Norse was shattered. Had Sitriuc wanted to conquer more of Ireland, it is unlikely any Irish king could have stopped him. The country was in shock. But the king of Dublin was more interested in his trading empire around the Irish Sea than in acquiring new territory in Ireland. The following year Sitriuc left Ath Cliath with most of his army to replace Ragnall as king of York, leaving his brother Gothfrith as king of Dublin. Gothfrith stayed in Ireland until his death in 934, except for a brief adventure in 927 when he too went chasing off to rule York as regent for Sitriuc's young son. During his reign in Dublin he plundered and raided, sometimes winning and sometimes losing against his Irish enemies, but spent much of his energy trying to bring Limerick and the other Viking settlements in the south under Dublin's control. Dublin was beginning to be more than just a fortified camp, developing into a recognizable town on the high ground between the Liffey and Poddle rivers.

In the south, Limerick, Cork, Waterford, and Wexford were still little more than fortified camps, although they too would develop into towns before the end of the tenth century. In the north the Uí Néill were strong enough to make sure no Viking settlements survived, scouring the land of all invaders. In the long run this hurt the north of Ireland, turning it into an economic backwater once the Viking towns—especially Dublin—became engines of economic growth for the rest of the country.

By 930 the Viking passion for further conquest in Ireland was coming to an end. Sitriuc and his family's preoccupation with York meant their energies were spent outside Ireland. Areas around the towns were Norse but the country was Irish, and as intermarriage continued and Vikings began converting to Christianity, the difference between the races would narrow still further.

KINGS IN DUBLIN AND YORK

"Here they came, these kings from Ireland, calling themselves kings of Dublin and York, kings of Ireland, and the pagans of

Britain, looking to build their empire." Michael Wood is a British historian, well known for his documentary films on subjects like the conquistadors, the Trojan War, and Alexander the Great but with a passion for Anglo-Saxon England, especially the tenth century. He had come to York for the 2001 opening of the new Yorvik (Viking York) Center. Now he and its director, archaeologist Richard Kemp, were taking a route Sitriuc might have walked in 921.

York was the ancient Roman city built on the Ouse River that flows into the Humber estuary, one of the two best natural harbors on England's east coast (the other is the Thames). York was connected to similar estuaries on the east coast by a Roman road running through the only northern pass across the Pennine Mountains. It was the strategic heart of northern Britain, center of a kingdom that bordered both the Irish and North Seas. From its west coast kings of York and Dublin had complete mastery of the Irish Sea. From its east coast they were connected to highly developed Viking trade routes that ran across the North Sea and into the Baltic.

"The Roman walls were still standing very high indeed in the ninth century," Richard Kemp said, "so your impression entering York would be this great frontage of decaying walls and towers with the Viking town in front of them." Richard and Michael Wood climbed a ramp from the river—still called the Dublin Steps, where longships from Ireland once docked—and crossed the Ouse Bridge into Viking York, now covered by the later medieval city.

"There's a great description from the tenth century of the city teeming with people from different nations and crammed with the goods of far-off countries," Michael said, "with maybe tens of thousands of people. They're talking about a great mercantile city."

Richard agreed. "It was a tightly crammed mass of buildings, one on top of another. They're building cellars so they can create even more space. There are craftsmen working in their backyards, churning out goods. Yorvik was the place to be, all right." He and Michael went on to discuss the range of goods found during excavation—walrus ivory, silks from the Middle East, jewelry, pottery, amber, cowry shells from the Red Sea, silver coins minted in York, even a coin from Samarkand on the borders of China—it gave an incredible sense of the scale of Viking trade.

The historian and the archaeologist walked together along Coppergate, still following the course of the original Viking street. Richard had worked on the excavation of Yorvik and he pointed to where modern property lines still followed those established by Norse urban planners. A Burger King so narrow its customers must eat on two floors was built on an eleven-hundred-year-old ground plan. "It seems buildings and streets were laid out all at the same time in 910 on top of a ramshackle arrangement of earlier houses," Richard explained. York's Viking rulers built a new oak bridge, a new commercial district, and new streets where privately held house plots ran back from shop fronts and market stalls. These were the urban ideas carried back across the Irish Sea to create a true Norse-Irish capital in Dublin.

No wonder the kings of Dublin and York exchanged Ath Cliath—still little more than an overgrown fortified camp—for the wealth and comfort of a bustling and wealthy city. Even the Roman heating system of what was then a five-hundred-year-old citadel may still have worked. Sitriuc died in 927 when his son Amlaib—in Norse *Olaf Sitriucsson*—was only a child, so Gothfrith came over from Dublin as regent. He lasted less than a year. After the death of Alfred the Great in 899, his heirs had continued to expand Anglo-Saxon England into the Danelaw. In 927 a Saxon king called Athelstan took York and expelled Gothfrith and the young Amlaib. Gothfrith returned to Dublin where he died in 934, described as "a most cruel king of the Norsemen." Amlaib went back to Scotland where history loses sight of him for a while, so it was another Amlaib—Amlaib Gothfrithsson—Gothfrith's son and the new king of Dublin, who next claimed York and came close to stopping Anglo-Saxon England's expansion in its tracks.

THE BATTLE OF BRUNANBURH

The great Norse and Celtic alliance that Amlaib Gothfrithsson put together to win back the Viking north of Britain from the Anglo-Saxons may have been years in the making. When in 936 the *Annals of Ulster* report that "Clonmacnoise was plundered by the foreigners of Ath Cliath and they remained two nights at it, something unheard of from ancient times," it is safe to say Amlaib was building up his war chest. Sometime in the summer of 937 he sailed with his fleet from Dublin, traveling north around the top of Scotland and down into the North Sea, gathering reinforcements along the way.

Standing in the shadow of York's fortress walls, Michael Wood explained the sense of destiny that gripped the allies. "There's a great Welsh poem that describes the buildup to the invasion," he said. "We'll all join together, it says, the Celts, the Welsh, the Cornish, the Irish of Ireland, the Vikings of Ireland, the men of Dublin, the Picts and the Scots, we'll all come together and we're going to drive the English out where they first landed 400 years ago."

In spite of the rhetoric, Vikings and their allies just wanted the Anglo-Saxons south of the demarcation line that had been agreed to by Alfred the Great fifty years earlier. Amlaib was a pragmatic Viking. So long as Athelstan held York and Northumbria, he was losing profits. And Amlaib's allies saw how easily Athelstan picked off Northumbria. What was to prevent him doing the same to Strathclyde and Dál Riada? Athelstan was already calling himself *Rex Totius Orbis Britanniae*—king of the whole world of Britain. He had to be stopped.

"It's pretty certain a huge fleet of 615 ships sailed into the Humber," Michael Wood said. "That's Amlaib Gothfrithsson and Amlaib Sitriucsson, like a sort of family mafia, come back to claim their property. We don't know whether the Scots, Cumbrians, and Strathclyde Celts sailed with them in the boats or marched to join them somewhere along the way. But there's no doubt the Northumbrians of York joined with the invaders. Imagine the scene: it's late in 937—maybe November—and the weather's bad. Northumbria's fallen to the invaders, and Athelstan suddenly finds his whole house of cards is collapsing. What's he going to do, leave the North to Sitriuc and his allies, or attack immediately? Towards the end of 937 he brings a great army out of Southern England, drawn from Wessex and Mercia."

According to the Anglo-Saxon chronicle, the armies met at a place called Brunanburh, probably somewhere along the old Roman Road leading south from York into Saxon-held Mercia. Generations later the battle was still being called "the Great War." One of the best-known Icelandic sagas, *Egil's Saga*, written around 1230, makes Brunanburh a centerpiece of the story, although the hero—a Viking—fought on Athelstan's side.

"It was a catastrophic defeat for the invaders," Michael said.

"The *Annals of Ulster* report 'a great, lamentable and horrible battle was cruelly fought between the Saxons and the Norsemen in which several thousand of Norsemen, who are uncounted, fell but their king, Amlaib, escaped with a few followers. A large number of Saxons fell on the other side but Athelstan, the king of the Saxons, enjoyed a great victory.' An Irish source gives a list of famous dead—five Irish kings, the king of Strathclyde, the prince of Scotland, and the king of the Western Isles. You get the list of the great leaders that died like some kind of heroic poem."

The following year Amlaib returned to Dublin and immediately went off plundering monasteries to recoup his finances. What would have happened if he had won at Brunanburh? Like all Vikings, he was more interested in wealth and trade than lands. But York in the 930s was still the trading capital of Britain, and Dublin's king would have held great economic power over the south, which would have increased his influence back in Ireland. Also a reinvigorated king of the Scots after Brunanburh would certainly have extended his kingdom south into Northumbria, resulting in Britain being shared more equally between England and Scotland, with a Viking king of Dublin and York holding the levers of economic power. It is one of the great "what ifs" of history. The subsequent history of Britain, and therefore the world, could have been very different. But it was not to be, although Amlaib did end up with a victory of sorts. When Athelstan died two years later in 939, Dublin's king fought his way back into power at York.

Amlaib, followed by the other Amlaib—Sitriuc's son—ruled York on and off for the next ten years, but the tide of history had begun to flow against them. The Anglo-Saxon drive to unify all England under Alfred's successors continued. But when Almaib Sitriucsson was finally thrown out of York and returned to Dublin, he had learned the value of a major urban center. By the middle of the tenth century, Sitriuc's dynasty was creating an economic environment in Ireland heavily influenced by what they had already experienced in York.

THE CAPITAL OF THE IRISH SEA

On a wintry morning in modern Dublin, Pat Wallace took a taxi ride along the streets that still follow the lines of the Viking streets he had excavated between 1974 and 1981. "Dublin was the capital town," he said, "the big shopping center of Scandinavians in the west. There were no towns on Orkney, the Shetlands, the Faeroes, Iceland, Scotland, or the Isle of Man. Dublin was 'The Town,' the capital of the Irish Sea."

Dublin was cold and damp as only a northern European city can be in winter, rain coursing off buildings and running in torrents down the streets, buses and cars splashing unwary pedestrians who dodged from doorway to doorway hunched under black umbrellas. Viking Dubliners would have found such weather equally unpleasant. As Pat's taxi drove south over the Liffey at O'Connell Street Bridge and turned west along the river towards Wood Quay, he scrubbed at the misted window with his sleeve to point out the Liffey flowing sullenly between stone-lined banks. "All of this was underwater during the Viking period," he explained. "This was a broad tidal channel with fringing salt marshes, and maybe a subsidiary pool somewhere around here where boats could be moored. At high tide the water would be lapping at the walls of the town."

Halfway up Fishamble Street, Pat Wallace and his colleagues had excavated a huge earthen bank with a wooden palisade on top, the first of a number of different structures built before 1300 to push the Liffey back and defend the town from an attack from the river. They went on to find nine different stages where, between around 900 and 1300, the Liffey had been pushed back.

The taxi driver turned away from the Liffey into Fishamble Street, the steeply curving road that still follows the line of the earlier Viking lane. The taxi stopped halfway up while Pat explained the layout of the town. "This was where the river came to, the limit of the Viking town. Everything below here was reclaimed by the Normans in the thirteen century."

The National Museum of Ireland began excavations on Viking Dublin in the early 1960s, but it was not until 1969 that the main excavations at Fishamble Street and Wood Quay began. Derelict areas of Dublin were being cleared away to make room for extensive new municipal offices, and archaeologists like Pat Wallace had only a limited time until new construction covered the site. There was nationwide outrage. By 1979 thousands of Dubliners were taking to the streets to try to save the best-preserved urban Viking remains anywhere in Europe for posterity. But the saying "you can't fight City Hall" proved true when in 1982 the ancient Viking town of Dublin was covered up again with high-rise offices. But in the interim archaeologists had an opportunity to explore the lanes and visit the houses of Ireland's first town.

"We found all the evidence of town layout, the development of the dockside, ship timbers, environmental remains," Pat said. "We can reconstruct this town perfectly. It's different from Roman towns that are laid out in straight lines on a grid system. Here the accent was on defense, making use of the high ground. Dublin developed from the dockside up the hill in this direction. Up here we found twelve neighboring plots, all side-by-side with their houses, outhouses, backyards, laneways—the whole works."

Pat Wallace believes the waterfront settlement downstream from Ath Cliath started expanding soon after Sitriuc reoccupied the *longphort* in 917. By the mid 950s proper streets were being laid out, influenced by what was known in England. Sitting in a Dublin taxi waiting for the rain to stop, he drew a map of Fishamble Street with his finger on the fogged window. "The plots of ground faced onto the street. You bought your own plot, fenced it off from your neighbor, then built your house. This was your house, your property." Pat's finger traced out the Viking property lines on the window. "That's the essence of a Viking town, a neighborhood of individually owned plots and properties controlled by the king."

With the rain stopped, Pat Wallace left the taxi and tapped the pavement with his foot. "Eight feet under this roadway the Viking levels start," he said. This was the town of Amlaib Sitriucsson. For more than a generation, from 956 to 980, Irish kings left him mostly alone, and the growing town enjoyed political and military stability. During excavations in Fishamble Street, archaeologists discovered that the majority of houses from this period share a single design, rectangular with curved corners, thatched roof held up by interior posts to provide three distinct aisles—side aisles for sleeping and a central area for living. The size of a Fishamble Street house was—on average—twenty-five feet long by eighteen feet wide, which allowed room for manufacture as well as living. These houses were probably designed and built by local Irish carpenters and craftsmen who had come in from the surrounding area, using construction techniques employed in the local monasteries. They would need re-building about every fifteen years as supporting roof posts rotted away in the damp ground.

Wattle was the most common building material, hazel rods in-terwoven with springy tree-branches and saplings to make screens for walls, floor-surfaces and even to line the stinking cesspits that were dug in the fenced-off yards behind every house. "The smells must have been atrocious," Pat Wallace said. "I believe they insu-lated their wattle walls with cow dung. Can you imagine the stink of that: some fellow reaching inside a big basket to smear it all over the outside walls?" Dublin in the tenth and eleventh centuries was, as Pat Wallace described it, "a yellow, brown, organic, thatch, straw, and wattle hazel-rod world."

Interior floors were sometimes lined with gravel and paving stone but more often had a wattle mat laid directly on the ground. With no windows, light came in through doors at each end of the house, one opening into a backyard where animals shared the space with the cesspit and a small vegetable garden, the other onto the street where market stalls were set up and goods offered for sale. Houses were dark, smoky, and damp with a single cooking hearth in the center; no chimneys, just a smoke hole in the thatch. Houses were pressed so close together that a single out-of-control fire would endanger the whole town. And with cesspits leaking into the wells, epidemic disease was a constant reality. In 951 the *Annals of Ulster* record "a great outbreak of leprosy among the foreigners of Ath Cliath, and dysentery."

Walking up Fishamble Street to where it joins Christ Church Place, the modern name for Skinner's Row where cattle were brought into town for butchering, Pat Wallace explained the pas-sion that grips all archaeologists. "It's not about verifying history," he said, "it's about discovering humanity. We found a jeweler bring-ing in raw lumps of amber from the Baltic Sea to make earrings, necklaces—all sorts of amber things. Not only did we find his house but we could see where he'd walked in and out of his neigh-bor's plot, tracking chips of amber on his shoes. I once found a clay mold broken where the craftsmen had thrown it away. Imagine all the good Old Norse swear words he must have let loose when he broke it! Things like this bring people from a thousand years ago back to vivid life; the whole town becomes real. It would be full of noise, dogs barking, people shouting, a mass of different accents and languages—Old Norse, Old English, and Middle English because there's an awful lot of English influence from Chester and the western ports, Gaelic and the beginnings of Scottish Gaelic, exotic languages from the Mediterranean, along with traders from even farther afield."

The town developed westward in the late Viking Age, along present-day High Street. Property owners were important men with a voice in running Dublin. "There was a parliament called 'the Thing,'" Pat explained. "It wasn't democratic; you were there because you were important enough to own a block of land and were in favor with the king." Kings of Dublin—like Amlaib—had their royal halls at the top of the town, where Dublin Castle is today. They ruled over the first real townsmen in Ireland, already a mixture of Irish and Norse.

By the middle of the tenth century Christianity was beginning to take root in the Viking towns. Amlaib Sitriucsson was Christian, and the first Viking church in Dublin may have been built during his reign. Late in life he married Gormlaith, daughter of the king of Leinster. The integration of Norse and Irish was well under way, although Amlaib still wanted to control the rich agricultural heartland between the Boyne and the Liffey Rivers, as his predecessors had tried unsuccessfully to do for a hundred years. Amlaib's hopes were dashed by another Irish king with the name Máel Sechnaill—the future high-king of Ireland—who defeated the Dublin Vikings at the Battle of Tara in 980, killing Amlaib's son. It was the beginning of the end for Dublin's Viking kings; the end of their hopes for a wider political role within Ireland. After the battle Amlaib Sitriucsson gave up the kingship of Dublin to another son—Sitric Silkenbeard—and retired to the monastery island of Iona where he died "a Christian penitent" the following year. His wife Gormlaith lived on for another fifty years, next marrying Brian Boru and then—after Brian's death—Máel Sechnaill, her first husband's conqueror. But it was Gormalith's second husband, Brian Boru, who would become the most famous king in Irish history, nearly succeeding in uniting Ireland into a single European-style monarchy.

[11]

Brian Boru—
Emperor of the Irish

THE STORY OF the rise of Brian Boru is one of the most remarkable in early Irish medieval history. His emergence from a minor
dynasty to become the most important leader that Ireland had ever
known was a sign that the country was changing. Until the time of
Brian, Ireland had been made up of a number of small kingdoms
and lordships which were more or less independent of each other. A
high-kingship existed, but it was a ceremonial position which carried no real power. The title "high-king" was the customary title of
the king of Tara, but he did not have the power of the European
kings who ruled over entire countries. Each *Túath* in Ireland was
responsible for itself and did not have to pay taxes to a central overlord. The high-king merely claimed jurisdiction over the area of
Tara, the principal ceremonial site since ancient times, but he did
not rule Ireland as a monarch in any real sense. Brian Boru would
change all that and herald in a new era in Irish history.

For centuries before Brian the title high-king had been held by
the Uí Néill dynasty. They were the most prominent family in Ireland and lived on their traditional lands in Ulster and Meath. They
had acquired Tara and the area surrounding it in the eastern part of
Ireland hundreds of years before Brian Boru's time and had held it
ever since. They were a strong and respected dynasty and would
have had little use for a small unknown *Túath* from an obscure

area. The very idea of such a family producing even a moderate leader must have seemed absurd to them. They were in for a surprise.

THE DÁL CAIS

Brian was born in about 941 to a relatively unimportant dynasty in Thomond, in what is now County Clare, close to the Viking city of Limerick. The family name was Dál Cais, but after Brian's success his descendants would take the name of Ua Briain, or O'Brien, in honor of him. Their homeland of Thomond was part of the ancient province of Munster. There were many small dynasties like this throughout the country, living in comparative obscurity and just getting on with the business of their own local communities. Usually these small dynasties would have little or no contact with the larger royal houses. The most prominent royal family in Munster was the Eóganacht. For centuries they had called themselves the kings of Munster and had claimed Cashel as their seat. Next to the Northern Uí Néill they were the most prominent family in the country and guarded their prestige by alliances and marriages into the right families. They had, however, submitted to the Uí Néill in the 850s and accepted them as overlords, so the likelihood of one of the Eóganacht becoming a powerful leader of all Ireland was remote. But this probably made them even more determined to hold onto their traditional position in Munster and not tolerate any competition there.

BRIAN IN BÉAL BORU

Brian Boru, who became the leading figure in Ireland in the tenth century, grew up in a place called Béal Boru, near the mouth of the River Shannon in County Clare. It was from this place that Brian probably took his name. It is situated very close to Mag Adair, the prehistoric inauguration site of the Dál Cais which dates to times long before that of Brian. Today Mag Adair is an obscure, isolated place and somewhat difficult to find. We traveled there by car with Donnchadh Ó Corráin, and even he had trouble locating it. The journey took us through a maze of small rural roads. But it was fun driving through the winding roads of County Clare trying hard to see if we could catch a glimpse over the hedges of the ancient site's mound and stone.

Eventually we came to a gate, and Donnchadh informed us that this was the entrance—confirmation from a farmer on a tractor was the signal for us to don our boots and start trekking through the wet grass and mud of an Irish field. A climb over a hedge at the end of the field and suddenly, we were there: the ancient inauguration site of the Dál Cais, the family of Brian Boru. A small official government notice, somewhat overgrown by white thorn bushes, is all that distinguishes it. Donnchadh remarked that, for an inauguration place, it was "modest in proportions and truly well neglected." But one of the charms about Ireland is that so many of these ancient sites are still untouched and not vulgarized by commercialism.

Walking over the now-deserted area, we could almost hear the ghosts of the past whistling by and wondering why we were bothering to come. Not too many people visit here these days. But it was here that Brian was inaugurated king of Thomond after he was elected king on the death of his brother. It was a pagan site long before the time of the Dál Cais inaugurations, so its importance and spiritual significance went back a long time before Brian. This gave the site an added dimension.

In the small town of Killaloe we enjoyed a pub lunch of fresh Irish salmon, speculated on the feasts that the Dál Cais would have enjoyed nearby, and then drove down the road to search out Béal Boru, the birthplace of Brian Boru. We hiked through more fields and then came upon the spot where once a thriving community made its home. A large, high, grassy mound, thickly covered with trees, is all that remains today. Sitting right next to the River Shannon it is still a beautiful and secluded site. In Brian's day Béal Boru would have been equally obscure to outsiders but thronged with the family that he grew up around. Excavations of the site showed that it was once a high ring fort with internal stone walls. It was also, according to the archaeological evidence, once surrounded by a ditch or a moat. It was an excellent fortification for the Dál Cais family.

Being so close to the largest river in Ireland, the Shannon, gave the young Brian a lasting appreciation of waterways and the importance of controlling the rivers and seas. Pointing to the Shan-

Grianan of Aileach in County Donegal was the center of Uí Néill royal power and their family home for generations. (*Carmel McCaffrey*)

non from the top of the mound, Donnchadh explained, "For many years before his birth the Vikings had gone up and down the river and had shown the Irish what could be done with warships and also with commerce." The Vikings would have been sailing up and down the river with their commercial enterprises. Even before the Vikings there had been river activity as Irish ships brought wine to the monastery of Clonmacnoise up-river. But in Brian's youth the Vikings controlled the Shannon. Rivers and seas were the super-highways of their day. From their vantage point in Béal Boru, Brian's family would have had a perfect view of all the River Shannon activity, or as Donnchadh said, "Nothing, not even a swan could pass on that river without them knowing about it." It left Brian with a keen knowledge and understanding of the importance of controlling the waterways.

THE YOUNG PRINCE BRIAN

Brian was born a prince as his father was the king of Thomond, but he was not expected to become king after his father's death. There were many cousins and brothers who were more likely to be elected to that position. So, as a child, Brian would have been free of the burden of knowing that he must someday be king. This would have allowed him to pursue whatever activities he chose. There are historical references to his love of music, poetry, and storytelling. It was also said of him that he was skilled in the use of the spear and the Irish wooden sling.

Nothing has been left that would indicate to us where Brian went to school or indeed what type of schooling he might have had. At the time there were a number of monastic schools close by his home that he might have attended, but we have no way of knowing whether he went to any one of them. When at home he would have been instructed by court scholars in music and poetry. He would also have heard extraordinary stories, invented by his father's storytellers, that the Dál Cais dynasty was descended from the great Celtic hero Fionn Mac Cumhaill. It was quite common at the time for the court *file* or poet of every royal house to invent noble ancestors for their patrons.

Much of Brian's youth would also have been spent at the nearby family royal seat of Kincora, which is said to have been close to the modern town of Killaloe. It is thought to have been uphill from the present town in the area of Thomond and probably close to Béal Boru. But wherever it was, we know that as a child Brian would grow to love Kincora and indeed the whole area of Thomond. It was from Kincora that Brian actually ruled and held his great feasts. He never chose to live anywhere else. As an adult he is said to have rebuilt the palace at Kincora as a great fortification for the Dál Cais and it became the home he would always return to, even in old age.

THE VIKINGS

One thing that Brian would have been aware of as a child was the Viking presence in the nearby city of Limerick. The Vikings had settled there and developed the city as a trading center many years before he was born. They had originally used the River Shannon, Ireland's largest river, to travel inland and plunder monasteries along the riverbank. In later years they developed trade routes on the river. During Brian's childhood the Vikings had managed to gain control of a large area around Limerick and had brought many smaller Irish *Túatha* under their control. Brian's family, the Dál Cais, did not surrender to the Vikings but did lose some traditional land to them as they were pushed further back into County Clare. But the Dál Cais were building a powerful base, and the Viking success against the other Irish kings meant that the field was open for newcomers. When Brian's father, Cennétig, died in 951, the annals referred to him as king of Thomond and a claimant to the kingship of Munster. Clearly he had been a successful leader of the Dál Cais and had laid a foundation on which his dynasty could build.

HIS BROTHER'S KINGSHIP

On the death of his father, Brian's older brother, Mathgamain, was elected king of Thomond. From about the age of seventeen Brian would have been among the young men of Thomond who would have fought against the Viking intruders. His later biographer, of unknown name, would write of the young Brian going out to battle with his brother. Controlling the Viking colonizing advance would have been an important part of life then for the smaller Irish kingdoms, especially those near the coasts or rivers where the Viking presence was most felt. Within ten years Mathgamain was considered to be as powerful as the Eóganacht king. The two were bitter rivals.

Brian's awareness of Viking power was growing, and by the age of twenty-one it is said that he led a campaign against them. Whether this is a fanciful story we do not know, but it may be something remembered by the family and told later to scribes. The story goes that even when his brother, the king, grew tired of the length of the campaign, Brian kept going. His chief strategy, as it was always to be, was surprise. He persisted in pushing the Vikings back across the River Shannon and off the lands of his ancestors. After eighteen months of bloody struggle Brian succeeded. When the moment of victory came it is said that the Vikings fled "to the ditches and the valleys and to the solitude of the great sweet flowery plain."

But more was to come. A few years later, bolstered with this success and concerned that the Vikings were teaming up with other Irish kings against them, Brian and his brother attacked the city of Limerick and plundered it. It was a rich jewel. Records tell of the bounty they seized: "beautiful foreign saddles, jewels, silver and gold and silks." It was a bold strike for the Dál Cais against what was considered to be one of the strongest Viking strongholds in the country. It did not go unnoticed by the other Munster kings who in time would seek to curtail the ambitions of this upstart tribe.

THE DEATH OF BRIAN'S BROTHER

For a while things were peaceful with the Dál Cais. Brian had likely married at seventeen (the normal marriage age at the time) and had three sons and a daughter. He was close to all of them but especially to his eldest son, Murchadh, who would remain loyal and faithful to his father until their deaths. The annals of the time tell of a great closeness between the two. But storm clouds were gathering. This somewhat obscure family was now drawing the attention of other Irish kings who were not so sure they wanted this unknown dynasty from the backwoods of Clare rising in importance. Following their victory over the Vikings, the Dál Cais found they had new enemies—the other Munster kings who considered themselves to be of more aristocratic blood and who resented the rise of this family to a prominent position.

Most significantly the Eóganacht, who had been kings of Munster for generations, felt threatened by the success of the Dál Cais. There were many disputes over the years until finally in 976, according to the annals, a rival Eóganacht-allied king, Donnabhán, invited Mathgamain to a banquet with the man who considered himself the most powerful king in Munster, Máelmhuadh. He was one of the Eóganacht, and he was determined to see that his family, with its perceived ancient claims, remained the prominent force in Munster. Máelmhuadh did not at all like the rise of this previously insignificant dynasty and its humble origins. The purpose of the meeting was supposedly to settle past disputes and form a friendship for the future. It was a trap. With the help of the Limerick Vikings, Brian's brother, Mathgamain, was taken prisoner and killed shortly after. Brian was devastated. He is said to have cried out when the news was brought to him of his brother's death, "My heart shall burst within my breast unless I avenge this great king." Brian would do more than that. He would go on to raise his dynasty to a level never before achieved for a small kingdom, and in the process he would become the greatest king Ireland would ever have.

BRIAN, KING OF THOMOND

In the *dáil* or assembly following his brother's death, Brian was elected king. He was thirty-four years old. There was apparently no opposition to him. Brian was inaugurated king of Thomond at Mag Adair. Donnchadh described the inauguration ceremony: "You would have had the clergy, the bishops, the abbots in their robes, the gentry, the nobility. There would have been feasting and drinking with the poets there to celebrate in verse the achievements of the ancestors [of Brian Boru]." He had proved himself worthy of this honor years before when he had fought the Vikings alongside his brother and shown himself to be a clever tactician. In the minds of the lords of the dynasty who elected him, no one else could fill the role of king of the Dál Cais. This in itself was an enormous tribute to Brian. His brother had been well loved and much respected. In later years a scribe was to write of Brian's succession to his brother's throne that he "was not a stone in place of an egg, nor a shred in place of a club, but he was a hero in place of a hero, and he was valor after valor." This was the kind of emotive reaction that Brian was to inspire in people until his death and beyond.

REVENGE

Brian, as he had promised, wasted no time in setting about to gain revenge for his brother's death. But he was more of a thinking king than his brother had been. He saw the strategic importance of the River Shannon and of controlling the Viking cities of Limerick and Waterford and of then using their troops to overcome the major dynasty, the Uí Néill, in the north of Ireland. So when Brian took action against the Vikings it was with a further plan in mind.

In 977 he marched into Limerick and plundered the city in revenge for its part in his brother's death. Ivar, king of the Vikings, fled from Brian and eventually took shelter in a church sanctuary in the monastery on Scattery Island. By this time the Vikings were becoming Christianized and were allies of some of the monasteries. Brian followed Ivar into the sanctuary and slew him and both of his sons there. No Christian Viking or Irish monk would stand in the way of what Brian felt compelled to do. Brian was no fool, however, and realizing the need for a good commercial stronghold, he permitted the Vikings to remain in Limerick in return for an annual payment of the best European wine. In later years these very Vikings were to play an important role in financing Brian's expeditions. Their Shannon fleet would also be an invaluable source of support.

Shortly after this, in 978, Brian assembled his army and challenged the Munster king, Máelmhuadh. He was determined to avenge his brother's death. The two armies met at the borders of their territories at Thomond and Desmond. The battle lasted a day and seems to have been ferocious. At the end of the day Brian's army was victorious. Legend has it that Brian sent his oldest son, Murchadh, who was seventeen at the time, to hunt down and kill his uncle's murderer. This is probably not true, but we do know that Máelmhuadh was killed. With the head of the Eóganacht dynasty dead, Brian now declared himself king of Munster. He had no opposition.

Legends concerning Brian grew in number over the years, very few of which have any authenticity. His biographer, whose identity is unknown but was one of his O'Brien descendants and who wrote

A seventeenth-century rendition of the legendary Brian Boru. (*Hugh Weir*)

nearly a hundred years after Brian's death, embellished and invented many anecdotes about his life. But legends did not need to be invented about Brian Boru. The truth, which comes to us from historical sources in the annals, is a great story in itself. And the truth is, this was the biggest turning point in Brian's career. It was also a major turning point in the history of Ireland.

GAINING ALLIES AND HEADING FOR THE HIGH-KINGSHIP

Having gained the allegiance of the Vikings of Limerick and having assured himself of the services of their Shannon fleet, Brian proceeded to broaden his horizons and look further afield for conquests. His mind was already forming along the lines of a powerful high-kingship in which he as high-king of Ireland would play a central role in running the country. In other words, Brian was now attempting to bring a European-style monarchy to Ireland. He would be the central ruler of the whole island, including the Viking towns. With a large fleet of ships he sailed up the River Shannon and attacked parts of Connaught, winning the allegiance of large sections of that province. He seemed to fear no one. Dublin, with its independent wealth and trade, was still the strongest threat to a unified Ireland. The Irish kings of Leinster also posed a problem. Brian knew that to govern the entire country he had to gain control of Leinster and the Dublin Vikings. With that in mind, in 984 Brian entered into a close alliance with the Vikings of the town of Waterford on the south coast.

UÍ NÉILL DYNASTY REACTS

In the north, in modern Tyrone the Uí Néill were watching the success of Brian with growing uncertainty and a great deal of unease. They began to attack Brian's army in order to prevent him from encroaching on their territory. To the Uí Néill the idea of this upstart even coming close to the high-kingship was unthinkable. Again and again the king of the Uí Néill, Máel Sechnaill, tried to force Brian to curtail his ambition. He marched into Munster a number of times with a large army, causing devastation wherever he went. He even cut down the sacred inauguration tree of the Dál Cais at Mag Adair. But he could not halt Brian's march forward. With superior tactics Brian always managed to defeat the attempts of the Uí Néill to stop his progress. So in 997 Brian and Máel Sechnaill, king of the Uí Néill, met at Clonfert near Galway and agreed to divide Ireland between them. The Uí Néill would keep their northern territories. This agreement made Brian overlord of Dublin and Leinster, but neither Dublin nor Leinster was happy with the agreement. Two years later they both revolted against him, but Brian eventually forced the Viking king of Dublin, Sitric Silkenbeard, into submission. Brian was unstoppable. Ireland had never seen a king like him before.

THE HIGH-KING—EMPEROR OF THE IRISH

This victory against the Vikings made Brian believe he was strong enough to break his agreement with the Uí Néill in the division of Ireland. He assembled an army made up of Munster, Connaught, Leinster, and the Dublin Vikings and marched on Tara, the ancient "capital" of Ireland and symbolic seat of Uí Néill power. This was a bold step, and even though his plan did not immediately work, within a year Máel Sechnaill, king of the Uí Néill, submitted to Brian by giving him his allegiance. In 1002 Brian Boru, who had grown up in an unknown family in what many considered to be the wilds of Thomond, was now the high-king of Ireland. He was not only high-king, he also held the position in a way no one else before him ever had. He had the allegiance of most of the country including the ancient claimants to the title, the Uí Néill. This was an extraordinary moment in the history of Ireland. Brian Boru had broken the centuries-old monopoly of the Uí Néill. The high-kingship had passed to a man who was attempting to unify the country politically under one king. The high-kingship was no longer simply the ceremonial prerogative of the king of Tara but a kingship based on allegiances and tribute.

Shortly afterward Brian visited Armagh, now the ecclesiastical center of Ireland, as a way of securing the support of the church. In his presence a scribe at Armagh wrote of him that he was "Brian, *Imperator Scottorum,*" or Emperor of the Irish. The annals also record that Brian placed a gift of twenty ounces of gold on the altar of the church. This was a very large sum at the time and much needed by the church as a recent fire had damaged the building and restoration work was slow and money scarce. Some time after this Brian confirmed Armagh as the primacy of Ireland. Armagh had claimed the primacy for hundreds of years, but the welcome confirmation from this new and powerful ruler cemented relations between the two.

That he did not try to give Cashel the primacy says much for Brian's political astuteness. Cashel had long been the southern rival of Armagh, and Brian might have been expected to champion a Munster claim for primacy; but he was far too clever a ruler to try a move like this and make such a powerful enemy as Armagh. He knew the value of keeping the church on his side and under his control. A year later he made a royal circuit in the north of Ireland accompanied by royalty from Connaught, Leinster, and his Viking allies. A display of power and prestige of this type was important in letting the smaller kings know that he really was the "Emperor of the Irish." Brian was probably also aware of how fragile the unity was.

CLOUDS OF DISCONTENT

Within the ranks of his ostensible allies, opposition to Brian's rule was growing. Leinster was not happy with him. In their desire for their own independence, they were prepared to break up the unity that Brian had built. Leinster had never willingly submitted to the Uí Néill, and in spite of what they agreed to they were now not about to accept this king from Munster as their overlord. Also, according to later annals, a quarrel broke out between Brian's son Murchadh and the king of Leinster, Máel Morda. As a result of this, Máel Morda sent envoys to the north of Ireland asking them to join in a revolt against Brian. In 1013, in a show of strength, Brian's son Murchadh attacked Leinster and carried off booty and hostages. In early winter of 1013 Murchadh withdrew, but Leinster and the Dublin Vikings knew that Brian and his son would return early in 1014, so they prepared for the attack.

The Vikings in Dublin had already grown restless with Brian. The city was rich, and the Vikings within it had not yet been absorbed into the Irish political system. The Dublin Vikings had always looked eastward, across the Irish Sea, and considered their wealth and their overseas possessions to be of vital importance to them and their economic well-being. They were not about to surrender this to an Irish high-king. Even though they had supposedly submitted to Brian, they believed he was too strong a king to serve their purposes well. Outside of Ireland the Vikings were still dominant on the seas. If Brian were defeated, the prospect of an independent Viking kingdom in Ireland was politically realistic. So the Dublin Vikings decided that if they could get help from other Vikings outside of Ireland, they could confront Brian and defeat his army, putting an end to his power and, most important, what they saw as his threat to their way of life.

DUBLIN VIKINGS CALL FOR HELP

Aware of the strength of Brian's support, the Dublin Vikings and the Leinster kings called for help from overseas to take on this high-king of Ireland. They got it. The Vikings in the Orkney Islands off the north coast of Scotland and the Isle of Man, an island in the middle of the Irish Sea, responded that they would mount fleets and sail to Ireland. Sigurd, the earl of Orkney, promised to come and Brodar, who ruled the Isle of Man, agreed to participate. They both planned to invade Ireland and help the Leinster Irish kings and the Dublin Vikings defeat the forces of Brian Boru. They must have felt that the conflict with Brian was of major importance to the future of the Viking sea empire. The landing was to be near Dublin on the coastline about a mile north of the city. The place, which is now a Dublin suburb, is called Clontarf. The battle fought there would go down as one of the most important battles in Viking and Irish history.

THE BATTLE OF CLONTARF

It was on Good Friday, April 23, 1014, that the first major Irish battle was fought. The annals record that Brian's army was smaller than the one he faced. It is estimated that there were twenty thousand troops on the invasion side; Brian had something less than this. He had to march all the way from his home at Kincora in Thomond to command the battle. Brian was seventy-three years old and a tired man. He had been fighting for most of his life, but he knew that for Ireland and the high-kingship that he had established, this was to be a decisive moment. His son Murchadh and his grandson came with him.

THE BRIAN BORU PUB

There is a story in Dublin that says that the Brian Boru Pub in modern-day Glasnevin stands on the exact site of Brian's tent at the Battle of Clontarf. He is said to have commanded the battle from this position. The location of the pub is probably close to where his tent might have been. Anyway, what better way to commemorate a battle then to pitch a pub on the site. To talk about the battle we went to the pub with historian Donnchadh Ó Corráin and Commandant Eamonn Kiely of the Irish Army. They chatted about the battle and the various positions taken by both armies in their attempts at victory. Spreading maps out in front of us as we drank coffee and looking back a thousand years to the morning of the battle, Commandant Kiely explained how the battle was probably fought. Although technology has changed dramatically since that time, he said, some things in battle remain the same. He remarked on how important troop positioning is in a battle. Brian Boru's army took the high ground close to the sea, just outside Dublin on the north beach near Dollymount. The Dublin Vikings with the Leinster kings came out of Dublin and marched about a mile north of the city towards the coast of Dublin Bay. But as the commandant explained, "The person who took the key terrain as Brian Boru did would have made a major move and a winning move usually in a battle. For if you end up in a hole or in low ground, your enemy has the commanding ground and you are at a great disadvantage."

THE VIKINGS LAND

The overseas Viking fleet, under the command of Brodar of the Isle of Man, came into Dublin Bay and arrived at Sutton, which lies just north of Clontarf. They then sailed slowly southward down the coast about a mile or so to meet up with their allies. Another Viking fleet, under the command of the earl of Orkney, sailed in more directly to the beach and formed the middle ground of the attack. The Irish kings of Leinster commanded the forces to the earl's left. The center of the battle was fought at Clontarf.

The Vikings were well equipped and had superior armor and weaponry. They are described as coming ashore carrying shields, and their weapons were a mixture of axes, swords, spears, and bows. They were renowned swordsmen and were known for their straight broad-bladed, ornamented swords. Brian's army had swords and spears and carried shields with metal studs. The Irish apparently wore no armor; according to the descriptions they wore only cloth. The main Irish weapon at this time for close combat was a casting spear or dart that had a long silken string attached to it. The purpose of the string was to retrieve the spear after it had done its job and presumably use it over and over again. Both the Viking and Irish records mention the many banners that were carried into battle. Brian is said to have had seventy banners of many different colors.

According to the annals, Brian Boru's men fought with valor and kept pushing the enemy back, allowing no advance. They fought from high tide to high tide, all day long and far into the evening. It was, by all accounts, an exhausting fight. The problem for the invading fleet and their Dublin allies was that they had their backs to the sea and to the Tolka River. It seems that a main problem for the invaders was their failure to get enough beachhead and thereby gain a commanding position. The scribes described their confusion in retreat as Brian Boru's forces marched forward on them. They were pushed back into the sea and into the Tolka River which was in full tide. Donnchadh mused, "Many of them [Vikings] were drowned in the sea and in the Tolka."

VICTORY FOR BRIAN

By the end of that very long day the forces of Brian Boru were victorious. Summing it all up the Inisfallen annalist wrote that "the foreigners of the western world were slaughtered." By dint of sheer strength, Boru's forces had pushed the invaders and the Dublin Vikings back into the sea. The Viking invasion was stopped and their forces badly defeated, but it was a bloody and costly battle. Exact figures are uncertain, but some reports say that about seven thousand troops lay dead, among them Brodar from the Isle of Man and the earl of Orkney. The king of Leinster was also killed. Brian's eldest son Murchadh was killed as was his grandson. Then the Irish suffered a shocking and devastating blow. Shortly after victory was achieved, Brian himself was killed. According to the story, "Brodar, chief of the Danes of Denmark, was the person who slew Brian." Brodar was killed shortly after this. Brian's death and that of his son were to have far-reaching effects on the future course of Irish history.

The battle was so extraordinary and on such a grand scale that even the normally eloquent and loquacious Irish scribes seem to become more highly emotional and graphic in describing it. One characterized the scene of battle as "wounding, noisy, bloody, terrible, crimsoned, fierce, quarrelsome"—before the age of the camera he seems determined to describe in the best detail possible the agony of the battle. Ireland had never seen anything like it. Until this time such large-scale warfare had not been a part of the Irish experience. In fact a battle lasting a whole day was highly unusual. Being outside of the Roman Empire, the Irish had not been exposed to the violence of European wars. It must therefore have been a tremendously bloody and tragic sight to those witnessing the scene. The mopping up must have gone on for some time, and there was much to lament in the loss of life.

It is difficult to place this vast slaughter and carnage in the context of today's Dublin suburb of Clontarf and the sandy beaches that lie on the north coast of Dublin. In the summer months Dubliners crowd to this popular area, parking cars on the beach to picnic on the dunes and swim in the sea. Bull Island now sits in the Dublin Bay area just off the coast where the battle was fought. The island slowly evolved in the 1600s through natural silting and is now a part of the shoreline where the Viking ships once docked. The island is now an official bird sanctuary. It is an ironically suitable memorial to the bloody battle of long ago: some of the birds who nest there come from the northern regions of Europe to winter, just as the Vikings once did in establishing Dublin. Brant geese, redshanks, sandpipers, knots, godwits, curlews, and pintail ducks all now make their homes on the small island that lies just off the coast of Clontarf.

MYTHS OF THE BATTLE

The Battle of Clontarf was a significant event in Irish history because it ensured that the central high-kingship established by Brian would remain the dominant political position in Ireland. It also ensured that the Vikings were a spent force on the Irish Sea. As time went on, however, the battle and Brian's life would enter mythology. Great myths would grow up around this battle and why it was fought. Donnchadh was quick to point out the fallacy of one of the more enduring myths: "Well, there is an old view of Clontarf that it was a conflict between Irish Christianity and Scandinavian paganism. This just doesn't hold up because the [Viking] people who ruled Dublin were Christians. Olaf, the father of Sitric Silken-beard, had actually died in religious retirement in Iona. Sitric Silkenbeard himself was a great patron of the church in Dublin." That Irish kings fought on the side of the Vikings is also very often forgotten, as is the fact that Brian himself had many Viking allies. The Viking cities of Waterford and Limerick had been on his side. But that Brian fought a valiant battle and died a hero is no myth. It is also no myth that he changed the status and power of the high-kingship, consequently impacting in no small way the future of Irish history.

THE PURPOSE OF THE BATTLE

The Battle of Clontarf was primarily a battle for the unity of Ireland and was not a struggle between the Irish and the Vikings for the sovereignty of the country. That the side of Brian Boru won and the invading Vikings were defeated confuses the issue of what the outcome actually achieved. True, there were no more Viking invasions after the battle, but Brian's death was a tragedy for Ireland. Had he lived and been a younger man he would probably have rounded up the Leinster kings and brought them under his high-kingship. Ireland would probably have been unified under a strong king whose intelligence and insight could have benefited the future of the country. For Brian was no tyrant. He was attempting to bring about a better federation of Irish kingdoms without doing away with anyone's boundaries or thrones. He gained the high-kingship by winning allegiances. Throughout his campaigns he had respected Brehon Law and the ancient rules of succession. His rise to power broke with tradition, but he never broke the law.

LEGACY OF THE NEW HIGH-KINGSHIP

Brian's victory at Clontarf essentially gave Ireland a stronger high-kingship than it ever had and curtailed Viking expansion and ambitions. Yet what Brian had done with the high-kingship would have far-reaching political repercussions within Ireland. Because of his death at the battle the dynasty, which he had essentially founded, could not hold onto the high-kingship. Brian's power essentially died with him. He never established a network, like a civil service, which might have upheld the central control of the high-kingship. Historians wonder about what might have happened had Brian not been killed. But he was old and could not have continued to face opposition to his kingship. Had his son Murchadh not been killed at the battle, he would probably have rallied his fellow Dál Cais after the shock of Brian's death. He was a much respected leader and seen as Brian's successor. As it turned out, the Ua Briain, or O'Brien, as they now called themselves, were unable to command the support of all of the kings of Ireland, which is what they needed in order to remain unchallenged as high-kings. It fell immediately to the Uí Néill, Máel Schnell, to assume the high-kingship left vacant by Brian. This was not to be a stable solution. The high-kingship, now a position of power, was something to which every ambitious regional king believed he could aspire. For the next 150 years a political struggle emerged that would eventually, in the twelfth century, shake the country to its foundation.

[12]

How the English Came to Ireland

POLITICALLY, Ireland would never be the same after the Battle of Clontarf. Before Brian Boru's time the country had been made up of various kingdoms with little or no political relationship to each other. These kingdoms might vary in size, but there was no central authority to which they all owed fealty. King Brian had effectively established a high-kingship that was closer to the European model of kingship than anything Ireland had seen before. He had been a strong and powerful ruler and had gained the support of a majority of the Irish kingships, but he did not have the allegiance of the whole island. The Leinster Irish had fought alongside the Vikings against him at the battle. He nevertheless made the high-kingship potentially so powerful that now other dynasties and royal families would fight to gain control of it. This new kingship became something to be sought after by anyone with ambition, and there was plenty of that around in Ireland at the time. But in the ensuing struggle for the high-kingship an event, unprecedented in Irish history, would eventually bring about an invasion from the neighboring island of Britain. This invasion would forever leave its mark on Irish history.

DUBLIN—CAPITAL OF IRELAND

Although the Viking invasion and expansion had been stopped in its tracks, the Viking influence did not die out. Those who had settled in Ireland remained. While the Viking population might have been small in overall numbers, the towns and cities they had founded would forevermore be a feature of the Irish landscape and lifestyle. Because few women had traveled with them, the Viking men intermarried with Irish women and soon became a part of the general Irish population. Familiar Irish names such as Doyle, MacAuliffe, Reynolds, and MacIvor are of Viking origin. Many of the native Irish were also now living in urban areas drawn in by the wealth of the new towns. Dublin, on the east coast, was the largest and most important of the Viking towns, and it grew and prospered.

Dublin now became essentially the capital of this new Ireland. From now on economic and political control of Ireland would always start with control of Dublin and its wealth. Control of Dublin initially went to Brian's descendants. Donnchadh Ó Corráin explains, "I think that what victory at Clontarf did was put Dublin under the control of Brian's descendants. That was of strategic importance for Irish history for the following years. And then you find that everybody who wants to be king of Ireland, one of his first cares is to get control of Dublin—Dublin and its resources." Workshops, making and selling a variety of goods, became the focus of this new Irish economy. Fine cloths like silks and satins and elaborate jewelry were being produced, very often for export and trade.

The Dublin Viking fleet was not destroyed at the battle and became a merchant fleet, lending itself out for hire to anyone who would pay for it. For instance, at the Battle of Hastings in England in 1066, the Dublin fleet fought on the side of the Anglo-Saxons against the invading Normans. They actually brought the family of the English King Harold back to Dublin for safety after the Anglo-Saxon defeat. Ireland entered another age of prosperity. Pat Wallace of the National Museum of Ireland said that "Money flowed into Dublin. So by about 1050 or so, Dublin became very, very rich. 'Filled with the wealth of barbarians,' is the phrase of the [Danish] historian Saxo Grammaticus. That's how he describes Dublin and that's exactly what it was and that's how we find all these buildings, all these manufacturers, and by 1052 the king of Leinster occupies Dublin. Before that a king would have burned Dublin down to the ground. Dublin has been the capital of Ireland in effect from 1052."

Dublin, now the main economic center of Ireland, nevertheless looked outward towards the rest of the then-known world. Trading was an important part of this economy. Dublin streets would have been filled with the hustle and bustle of people from many foreign countries, all speaking different languages. Ships coming in and out of the Dublin harbor would have been trading in leather, textiles, silk, satin, and wine. The ultimate proclamation of Dublin's importance can probably be seen in the high-kingship when in 1166 the O'Connor high-king entered Dublin and had himself inaugurated king there. He was the first Irish high-king to do so. This was the absolute sign that if Tara belonged to ancient times, Dublin belonged to the future.

VIKING INFLUENCE ON ARTS AND CRAFTS

Viking craftsmen now also brought their influence to Irish arts and crafts. As they settled and lived in Ireland the Vikings became Christianized, and crafts from cities like Dublin began to reflect this new fusion. Chalices, crosses, personal curios, and jewelry made at this time show a remarkable Viking influence. Pat Wallace explained that the Viking art style "was brought in here to Ireland by the Scandinavians about the year 1020, digested by Irish craftsmen, mainly in Dublin, and regurgitated." The Viking style known as *Ringerike,* called after a district in Norway, was to be found throughout Europe in the second half of the eleventh century, but it is in Ireland that it had its major development. Pat explained that the *Ringerike* style "finds its greatest expression in the town of Dublin, in the artifacts produced here." The well-known Norse design known as the "gripping beast" can also be distinguished on some Dublin Viking artifacts, most especially on the Clonmacnoise crosier that was produced at this time. Aesthetically the blending of these Viking designs with the native Irish Celtic tradition was a success. The twelfth-century Cross of Cong is a magnificent example of Viking and Irish artistic fusion.

VIKING HOARD

In the National Museum of Ireland at Collins Barracks in Dublin, Raghnall Ó Floinn, an archaeologist who works at the museum, has investigated a collection of Irish Viking artifacts found in County Kilkenny's Dunmore Caves. This hoard is remarkable for many reasons: it contains many expensive items like silver hair decorations, brooches, and coinage; it was obviously hidden by someone who might have been in danger of having it stolen, and the decorations on these items show a Viking-style design and yet do not seem to have been made by Vikings. As Raghnall explained, "There is a local flavor to the material. It is quite possible that this hoard, like many of the hoards of mixed silver, were in the hands of the Irish. So it was an Irish man or woman who, this being their personal wealth, [hid] it in a time of great danger." But of course what exactly that danger might have been is only guesswork. That the Irish of the time were rich enough to own such luxury items gives us some idea of what the society must have been like. Wealthy Irish merchants and traders were prospering in the new towns and cities. Even regional Irish kings recognized the importance of the towns, and many of them built new residences there.

Irish money also owes its origins to the Vikings. In the year 997 the first Irish coinage was struck by the Viking King Sitric of Dublin. The coinage was designed with the head of the monarch on one side and on the other the signature of the coin maker. Hard currency was a necessary ingredient to the growing economy. The older barter economy based on cattle was giving way to this new world of money and commerce. Pat Wallace explained that the Vikings also "brought better techniques of shipbuilding. All the words in our Irish language for ships and boats come from the Scandinavian influence, from Old Norse, the language of the Vikings in Dublin. Another thing the Vikings introduced was much better blacksmithing, much better ironworking, better edges on swords and weapons and hatches. Even the stirrup of the horse, and the spur—all of that comes in to Ireland with the Scandinavian influence."

While they were once regarded as savage heathens from the north, the Viking influence on Ireland is now acknowledged as being of primary importance in the physical development of the towns and cities and in the development of the commercial economy of the country. Their contribution to establishing Dublin as the wealthy capital of Ireland in the eleventh century is without dispute.

POLITICAL CHAOS

Yet, in spite of the growing economy, Brian's death at the Battle of Clontarf left the country in political chaos. There was no clear succession to Brian's high-kingship. In spite of the Irish tradition of election for succession, Brian had groomed his eldest son—now also dead—for kingship and probably had hoped that, European style, he would succeed him as high-king. His younger son, Donnchadh, lacked the charisma and political astuteness to hold the fragile union together. He did, however, become king of Munster and held the title for many years until his death in 1064. But the power that Brian Boru had generated around his high-kingship had died with him. The Irish had not introduced primogeniture, so allegiance to the son of the high-king was not guaranteed. From ancient times a new leader had usually been "elected" by senior community members after the death of a king or chieftain. The fact that a leader had no real power made the system work quite well. Now that system would break down as the high-kingship meant power over the whole country and not just the local community. The election system was not designed to cover a situation like this. It had worked on a local level, but the high-kingship established by Brian now meant control could pass from a local level to a national level. The *Annals of Ulster* reflect the confusion after Clontarf and all that it would mean in the future. "Numerous indeed are the events of this year" wrote the scribe in 1014 with a note of wonder. Worse "events" were to come.

The absence of any ordered way of succession meant that the high-kingship would be up for grabs to anyone who could win the allegiance of the other lesser kings. Few regional kings could resist the possibility of becoming high-king. It became a perennial struggle within Ireland without easy resolution. Because there was no universal consensus on the question, very often those who took the title high-king were referred to in the annals as "high-king with op-

position." Even a seemingly strong king had difficulty being univer-
sally accepted. One of Brian Boru's great grandsons, Muirchertach
O'Brien, did become high-king and held the title from 1086 to 1119,
yet the annals referred to him throughout his long career as being
"high-king with opposition." There never developed an established
line of succession by which the title king of Ireland would pass
from father to son. Because of this, regional kings continued to feel
that the title should or could be theirs for the taking.

It would be a mistake, however, given the many historical references to these struggles, to suppose that the entire population of
the country was caught up in these battles. Most of this political
juggling did not impinge much on the ordinary life of the individuals living and farming on their own piece of land. The plundering
and attacking that went on for kingship was not without its lighter
side. One of the main purposes seems to have been to at least ag-
gravate your opponent, even if you could not defeat or subject him.
The *Annals of Clonmacnoise* describe Hugh O'Connor, king of
Connaught, going to Thomond in 1061 where he "broke down the
palace built by Brian Boru in Kincora and also did eat the two
salmons that were in the [O'Brien] king's fountain or fishpond
there." It must have been a dismal scene for the O'Briens to come
home to—house wrecked and dinner eaten by the vandals.

IRISH CHRISTIANITY UNDER FIRE

Into the arena of this political chaos came also the conflict between
European Christianity and the Irish church. In the eleventh and
twelfth centuries the Irish church was considered very insular and
out of touch with the Gregorian reforms sweeping the rest of Europe. Rome was developing a stronger papacy and now wanted to
bring the whole of Christianity within its orb. A formerly independent Irish church would have to learn to toe the line. In this atmosphere a campaign of propaganda was conducted in Europe against
the Irish church, which was depicted as barbarous and pagan in its
practices. Much of the propaganda was not true, but the stories of
barbarism became so widespread that the Irish began to be referred
to as *insula barbarorum*—the island of barbarians. The clerics were
charged with corruption and with being lax in their Christian
teaching. The morals of ordinary people also came under fire from

outside reformers who accused the Irish of immorality as regards marriage. At this time the church in Rome was now making new rules and laws regarding marriage. The Irish were still following their own customs in Brehon Law on this subject, so divorce was quite common in Ireland. One source said the Irish "exchanged wives as fast as they exchanged horses." The church in Rome did allow for annulment, but this had to be done under church, not civil, control. Annulment also tended to be reserved for royalty and high-ranking people who could afford the process. The Irish Brehon Law would have applied to all levels of society.

Behind the propaganda lay the real issue that the Irish church and monastic system could not continue to be as independent as it had been. It was not only the papacy that wanted to bring the Irish church under its control but also the archbishop of Canterbury in England. For, despite Armagh's claim to primacy and its acceptance throughout Ireland, there is no evidence that it actually meant very much. Individual churches and monasteries enjoyed a great measure of independence without any reference to a primary church. Because of this lack of centralized structure, the English church had ambitions of bringing the Irish church under its jurisdiction. Both forces, papal and English, would combine against the Irish to attempt to bring about serious reform and eventually invasion.

THE LATER MONASTIC SCHOOLS

The monastic schools were still conducting a lively intellectual life and were in touch with the new European learning in the French and German schools. But one of the problems for the papacy was that the Irish monasteries had too much power and controlled the wealth of the church. That wealth was staying within these monastic families and was not going to the church itself. The abbots were now almost all laymen who were passing the monasteries and their assets on to one of their sons or close relatives. Conversely the bishops in the church had practically no power at all. It is true that the bishops were the ones who controlled ordination and fitness to minister, but the wealth of the church remained within the family-owned monasteries. Outside of the towns founded by the Vikings, the church was not organized in a way that we would recognize today. For instance, there were no parishes. So "clerical laymen" essentially held the power and, most important, the income of the church.

REFORMING SYNODS

Reform of the old system came from a number of synods held in the early to mid-twelfth century and by the introduction into Ireland of European religious orders. Many Irish pilgrims had found their way to Rome and were aware of how the church was developing outside Ireland. Some of these brought back information on the organizational church reforms that were sweeping Europe at the time, as power within the church was becoming concentrated under a stronger Rome. More important, the newly Christianized Viking cities in Ireland were not under the influence of the Irish church but looked abroad for spiritual direction. From the early eleventh century the bishops of these Irish Viking towns were being consecrated by Canterbury in England. These bishops disapproved of how the Irish church was structured and did not much like the power of the abbots or abbesses. Reform of the old Irish system was inevitable.

Attempts at change actually started from within Ireland. In Armagh in 1105 Cellach Ua Sinaig inherited the position of abbot. He was the seventh member of his family to inherit the position without having being ordained. But Cellach had himself consecrated bishop and became the primate of Ireland. Armagh's position as the ecclesiastic center was not to change, but Cellach was determined to see changes in the Irish church. Some years later he oversaw a synod at Ráth Breasail near Cashel when Ireland was officially divided into twenty-four diocesan sections in an attempt to replace the old monastic system. But it would be almost forty years before this new structure could successfully be implemented. The family-owned monastery system was too strong to be simply put aside so easily.

When Cellach died in 1129 he left instructions that the position of bishop of Armagh should be given to his younger friend Malachy, later known as St. Malachy. Nevertheless it would be five years before he could actually take up the title because of opposition from the family-owned monastery. Seven generations of Ua Sinaig had previously held the title, and they were not happy about having to give it up to an outsider. Malachy did eventually win out over their objections and some years later decided to travel to Rome to seek help in reforming the Irish church. Malachy was convinced that much of the church's problems in Ireland stemmed from its lack of organizational structure.

On his way to Rome he met with Bernard of Clairvaux, who impressed Malachy with the new monastic rules he had developed for his own religious community, the Cistercians. They became close friends, and Malachy did not hesitate to tell him of his frustration with what he saw as the poor organization of the Irish church. From this time on, Bernard would become one of the most arrogant propagandists against the Irish church. He was, however, enamored of Malachy and would later write his biography. In Bernard's *Life of Malachy* he is somewhat patronizing of his friend whom he describes as being of "a barbarous tribe," who surprisingly did not betray a "mite of his rude origin." Bernard oversaw the introduction of a continental monastery system to Ireland. In 1142 the first Cistercians arrived and built a house in Mellifont in County Meath. They would be the first of many continental orders to arrive over the next half-century and eventually totally replace the older native Irish monasteries.

The most important synod in changing the Irish church was held in Kells in 1152 when Ireland was divided into thirty-six sees with four archbishops overseeing them. They would reside at Armagh, Cashel, Dublin, and Tuam. The historian Elva Johnston points out another change that came into force at this synod: "Significantly the abbess of Kildare was no longer to hold the status of bishop, as this was revoked." The position of women in the Irish church was thereby considerably reduced. Hereditary succession in monasteries was formally abolished and clerical celibacy was insisted upon. Celibacy for ordained men had recently been introduced into the European church as an absolute requirement. The papal legate who attended the synod reported to Rome that Ireland was now successfully organized along a Roman model. Nevertheless propaganda against the Irish was enormous, and the momentum for further outside interference was too strong to be stopped. More reforms would follow until the Irish church, which had survived for centuries as a beacon of light in European learning, would lose all trace of its former status. The reforms eventually killed the spirit of learning and artistic expression that had been the hall-marks of Irish Christianity.

THE DEATH OF THE IRISH MONASTERIES

We visited Clonmacnoise with the purpose of trying to get a sense of that ancient monastic Irish church and its contribution to European learning. Clonmacnoise had been one of the greatest of these establishments and had produced scholars of the highest caliber. The twelfth-century reforms diminished the status of the monasteries, which were reduced to the rank of parish churches. They were no longer able to collect taxes on their own behalf. Walking through the ruins of the once noble and powerful monastery, Donnchadh Ó Corráin explained that "The reform was a triumph for the administrators and a disaster for Irish literature and general culture. The reformers destroyed the social, economic, and cultural base of Irish learning. Nothing replaced the greater monasteries with their schools and learned cadres, which were now robbed of their resources and their status." Reform spelled the end of the native Irish monastery system and its contribution to European civilization. The continental orders, which arrived in Ireland after this period, would never achieve the level of scholarship or mastery of ornamental art of the once great early Irish church.

Meanwhile an English pope, Adrian IV, had come to the papacy. Given the perceived state of the Irish church and the political unrest over the issue of the high-kingship, he would play a major role in changing the course of Irish history. But within Ireland the struggle of the kings was about to come to a boil.

KINGSHIP IN IRELAND—WHO RULES?

For the hundred or so years after Brian's death his descendants held on to the kingship of Munster, but it was the high-kingship that had become the great prize. This period in Irish history is probably the most confusing of all as many powerful families vied with one another in their desire for the status of high-king. It seemed that every provincial king in Ireland sought to attain it. Eventually the jostling for it became a central issue in Irish politics, and by the twelfth century the fight for the high-kingship was center stage.

Turlough O'Connor was the greatest Irish king of the early twelfth century. He was the king of Connaught in the west of Ireland, maintained a large army and navy, and built a number of fortresses or castles throughout his province. He also built a number of bridges across the River Shannon which were heavily guarded by his own army. He had ambitions to be high-king, and to achieve it he knew he had to break the power of the O'Briens of Munster. Between 1115 and 1131 he waged a long war against Munster and finally brought the province under his control. Turlough O'Connor died in 1156 without having achieved the supreme position he wanted, but he paved the way for one of his descendants to do so. It was this king, Rory O'Connor, who would have the distinction of being the last high-king of Ireland.

The struggle of the kings of Ireland for the high-kingship is complex because there were so many contenders for the title. Gaining allies was an important part of the process. After the death of Turlough O'Connor, the Uí Néill king, Muirchertach Mac Lochlainn, allied himself with the king of Leinster, Dermot Mac-Murrough, and they sought to destroy the power of the O'Connors and the newest claimant to the high-kingship, Rory O'Connor. Dermot MacMurrough had strong ambitions himself. He was king of Leinster, and his family had controlled the area of south Leinster for generations. In spite of the fact that their lands were not large, they were no upstart dynasty. For generations they ruled the small kingdom of Uí Chennselaig with its center at Ferns. It lay in what is now north County Wexford. They had claimed to be kings of Leinster and with that went control over the Vikings of Dublin with their small but wealthy city-state.

The Battle of Clontarf had weakened Dublin's independence but enhanced its economic importance. As the city's autonomous political power declined, its economic importance increased, and it became obvious that any king with pretensions to the high-kingship had to control Dublin. Control of Dublin became a bloody struggle for generations with power changing hands many times. Dermot was known as "Dermot of the Foreigners" because of his lordship over the *Gaill* or foreigners of Dublin. He must have felt that he was in a powerful position. It was this very familiarity with the city of Dublin and its trading partners across the Irish Sea that would bring about an event unparalleled in Irish history.

DERMOT MAC MURROUGH AND HIS IDEAS

Dermot MacMurrough wanted to be high-king. If the one time obscure Dál Cais could produce Brian Boru and the Ua Briain/O'Brien high-kings of Ireland then the Uí Chennselaig could rival them with Dermot. At the time in Ireland he was probably the most likely candidate for greatness. Dermot was only sixteen years old in 1126 when he assumed leadership of his kingdom. From the start he had to fight members of his own family to establish his position, and eventually he succeeded. Descriptions of him are full of grand accolades with some reservations about his personality. Giraldus Cambrensis, the twelfth-century Norman chronicler, says of Dermot that he was "tall and well-built, a brave and warlike man among his people, whose voice was hoarse as a result of constantly having been in the din of battle. He preferred to be feared by all rather than loved. He treated his nobles harshly and brought to prominence men of humble rank."

From his kingdom of Uí Chennselaig, Dermot MacMurrough dreamed of controlling the whole of Ireland. He also knew that in order to realize his ambition he would have to do some careful planning. He knew he had to challenge the power of O'Connor. In order to succeed he needed the help and support of other small kingdoms. Consequently Dermot went on campaigns throughout the country and gained allies for himself. When Muirchertach Mac Lochlainn, who was one of the Uí Néill of Ulster, became his ally he must have felt that he had a powerful ally indeed.

DERMOT AND DERVORGILLA

But by this time Rory O'Connor had strong allies too, and one of them was Ua Ruairc (later O'Rourke) of Bréfne, a small kingdom in the northwest of Ireland. In the struggle for the high-kingship the battles were small but numerous. Both sides fought each other frequently in their attempts at supremacy. It was in an attack on Bréfne that Dermot did something which is much recorded in the Irish annals. The facts surrounding this event are numerous and quite detailed, and it is probably one of the best stories to come out of medieval Ireland. MacMurrough invaded Bréfne territory,

Jermuci' uix
tcorpore paplo.
ex I gente sua.
oq; belli cla
ra. Timeri a
malens. Nobi
imliu erectoi.
lheins. Man'
m. I ipe ceri'
aut missis ad
tus. donaris
missis qin pro
I quis nullu
tar: cu pate I
uuis suasir uer
inci tio ad q̃i
ur in exteras

This twelfth-century manuscript drawing of Dermot MacMurrough is by Giraldus Cambrensis. MacMurrough, who was partly responsible for initiating the English invasion, is depicted carrying the long axe of original Viking design. (*National Library of Ireland*) burned Ua Ruairc's fortress, and then carried off his wife Dervorgilla on the back of his horse. The amount of documentation that describes this act tells us how important a factor this must have been in how future events unfolded. The annals contain numerous references to this abduction. Some describe Dervorgilla climbing willingly onto the back of the horse and then crying out in mock anguish as she was taken away. Dermot is described as being in love with her and having planned the event for some time. Her relationship with her husband does not fare too well in the reports. The *Annals of Clonmacnoise* blame her brother for persuading her to flee with Dermot in order to get back at her husband for his harsh treatment of her.

Dervorgilla may in fact have been an abused wife who was looking for a way out of her marriage. She may even have colluded with Dermot in her escape. The Norman writer Giraldus, shortly after the events, says tartly, "No doubt she was abducted because she wanted to be." Significantly, annalists also say that with her went her own wealth, her cattle, and her furniture. Under Brehon Law a wife's possessions always remained her own. To make matters worse for Ua Ruairc, she was "rescued" the following year by one of the O'Connors and was allowed to leave without opposition from MacMurrough. Her wealth and her cattle, we are told, again left with her. Dervorgilla did not travel lightly. She did not return to Ua Ruairc but chose instead to live her life out in a convent. She apparently distributed her wealth to the building up of women's religious houses. She was the benefactress of the Nuns' Church at Clonmacnoise and died in 1193 in religious retirement in Drogheda at the age of eighty-five.

Things did not go so peacefully with Dermot. When his chief ally, Mac Lochlainn, was killed in a small battle in 1166, Dermot's support system fell apart. At this point Rory O'Connor declared himself high-king. Ua Ruairc immediately set about in revenge for what must have been a huge embarrassment for him. The whole of Ireland knew of the abduction of his wife and her refusal to go back to him when she was "released." If the extensive reports in the annals are accurate, it was the talk of the country. Burning with anger, he marched into Uí Chennselaig and captured and burned the capital of Ferns. There he demolished MacMurrough's stone residence and within days put MacMurrough to flight. If he had killed MacMurrough, Irish history would have been very different. But MacMurrough lived to cause more havoc than even he could have imagined.

Being an enterprising and informed man who knew well the world beyond Ireland, Dermot immediately thought of getting help to regain his kingdom. He therefore crossed the Irish Sea and went to the English port of Bristol, which had long been a trading partner of Dublin. Dermot, always thinking of allies, was looking for Henry II of England. He felt secure in his relationship with Henry. In 1165 Henry II had actually hired the Dublin fleet in an attempt to conquer Wales. So perhaps in Dermot's mind Henry owed him. Dermot traveled to France to find him and talk with him. At the time Henry was engaged in a war with France over French territory claimed by the English monarchy. When he reached Henry in France, Dermot asked for help in regaining his lost throne. By this one simple act Dermot MacMurrough unwittingly and unintentionally changed the direction of Irish history forever. The invitation for help did not end there. What Dermot had sought was an ally for his immediate problem. What Ireland ultimately got was an invasion.

THE ANGLO-NORMANS

The eleventh century in Europe had witnessed the emergence of a new and important power. The Normans had taken over England after they defeated the Anglo-Saxons in 1066 at the Battle of Hastings. Normans were originally descendants of Vikings who had settled in Normandy. In the eleventh century they had crossed over to England, defeated the Anglo-Saxon King Harold of England, and taken control of England and the English throne. A hundred years later these Anglo-Normans were setting their sights on Ireland. Even before Dermot's request for help there had been some indication that the Normans planned to invade. The pope, Adrian IV, the only Englishman ever to hold the chair of Peter, was approached by the English hierarchy in 1155 concerning reform of the Irish church. The archdiocese of Canterbury was ambitious to take over Irish diocesan affairs and thereby expand its own territory. The Gregorian reforms of the Christian church throughout Europe made many dioceses ambitious to expand their territories and play greater roles in the management of this new-style Christianity with its absolute center in Rome.

So within this climate John of Salisbury, secretary to the archbishop of Canterbury, approached the pope, possibly at the request of the archbishop, and asked for permission to enter Ireland and "reform" the Irish church, which was described as barbarous. John of Salisbury was an Englishman who traveled widely and had strong connections in Rome. This claim of Canterbury was not without some expectation of success. For some years Canterbury had been ordaining a number of Irish bishops, those serving the Viking towns, and saw this as a natural stepping-stone to taking over the entire Irish church system. As early as 1121 the burghers and clergy of Dublin had written to Canterbury that "the bishops of Ireland are very jealous of us, especially that bishop who lives in Armagh, because we are unwilling to be subject to their rule but wish always to be under your authority."

Given the propaganda also circulating throughout Europe on the condition of the Irish church, the climate was right for such a move. But the synod of Kells had angered Canterbury by establishing Irish bishoprics, especially one in Dublin, which were answerable to Armagh. Here was a possible attempt at redressing the situation. So in 1155 Pope Adrian IV issued a papal bull, usually referred to as *Laudabiliter,* in which he granted permission to the king of England, Henry II, to invade Ireland and bring the Irish within Roman jurisdiction. Henry had been too busy with other disputes within his own kingdom to pay much attention to the document. So no action had been taken on the decree—that is, until a rather distraught but determined Dermot MacMurrough turned up at Henry's court some ten years later and asked for help in regaining his Leinster kingship.

HENRY II'S "HELP"—AN ENGLISH INVASION

Henry II saw his opportunity and agreed to help Dermot. Too busy with his war with the French, he could not personally oversee the campaign. He gave MacMurrough a letter to his lords in England, asking them to travel to Ireland to help Dermot win back his kingdom. Dermot returned to Ireland in 1167 with a small band of Norman mercenaries and was able to reestablish himself in Uí

Here is Giraldus Cambrensis's depiction of Henry II. The king's involvement in Irish politics resulted in the English invasion. (*National Library of Ireland*)

Chennselaig. The *Annals of Inisfallen* simply record the moment in 1167 as: "Dermot MacMurrough returned from overseas, and Uí Chennselaig was taken by him." Little attention was paid to this at first, but when he tried to renew his claim to his lost title king of Leinster, the high-king, Rory O'Connor moved against him. Dermot was defeated and forced to recognize O'Connor as high-king and abandon his plans for recovery of his Leinster kingship. He was also, interestingly enough, forced to pay one hundred ounces of gold to Tigernan Ua Ruairc as reparation for abducting his wife fifteen years earlier. In exchange for all of this Dermot was allowed to retain the small area of Uí Chennselaig.

But MacMurrough was only biding his time for another, greater force to arrive. It came on May 1, 1169. The Anglo-Normans landed at Bannow Bay in Wexford with three shiploads of soldiers and quickly took over the town. The town of Wexford was granted by Dermot to the invading Norman leader Robert FitzStephen and his half-brother Maurice FitzGerald. Norman names had arrived in Ireland. A year later it was the earl of Pembroke, Richard FitzGilbert, commonly known as Strongbow, who was willing to assemble yet another force to go to Ireland. To sweeten the request Dermot had also offered him the hand of his daughter Aoife in marriage and the right of succession to the kingdom of Leinster on Dermot's death, in violation of Irish succession law. Dermot also held out the possibility of the high-kingship itself to FitzGilbert. Dermot knew how to get allies. Strongbow, an ambitious man, liked the offer and took it. He arrived in August 1170 with a reported two hundred knights and a thousand troops. They easily took the town of Waterford and shortly afterwards Strongbow married Aoife. With their superior weaponry, including their notoriously deadly crossbows, and their armored knights on horseback, the Normans were well able to combat any Irish resistance to their presence. The Irish had never seen this type of organized European warfare before. They had nothing to compare with it in either weaponry or armor.

Within a short time Dublin, now the economic axis of Ireland, had fallen to the invaders. Dubliners had tried to resist them and had arranged for assistance from the high-king, but the Normans reached the city first and the town was taken by storm and buildings burned. The Normans were here to stay. The High-King Rory O'Connor failed in an armed attempt to regain Dublin for the Irish and was forced to surrender. When Dermot MacMurrough died in May 1171, Strongbow established himself as lord of Leinster. Henry II of England was somewhat disturbed at this turn of events and demanded that Strongbow recognize Henry's overlordship of the Irish acquisitions. The English king was afraid that his Norman lords were rather too successful and might attempt to establish Ireland as a separate and independent kingdom. Wisely, Henry II traveled to Ireland in the autumn of 1171 with a large army of five hundred knights and about four thousand archers to make sure that his Norman lords did not try to grab Ireland for themselves. Henry also had the blessing of the pope, now Alexander III, who wrote to Henry listing four grievances against the Irish. The first concerned lax marriage practices, the second the eating of meat during Lent, and the third accused the Irish of not paying tithes to the church. Fourthly they were showing insufficient respect for church property and for clerics. The suggestion was that Henry put an end to all of this irregularity and bring the Irish under papal control. In 1172 the synod of Cashel implemented this re-organization.

Rory O'Connor, the high-king, did not submit to Henry II when Henry came to Dublin in 1171 but reached an accommodation with him in 1175 in the Treaty of Windsor. This treaty recognized O'Connor's rule over the unconquered parts of Ireland not under the Normans. It was broken shortly afterwards by the Normans who kept up their incursions into Irish areas, and O'Connor's rule was gradually eroded. He died in 1198 in Cong and was buried, quite prophetically it would seem, at the monastery of Clonmacnoise. Both the high-kingship and the Irish monastery system would be supplanted as a result of this invading force. Rory O'Connor was the last high-king of Ireland.

NORMAN CASTLES

Large stone fortifications and castles were the landmarks of the new Norman presence in Ireland. Everywhere they went they built impressive, strong homes as if to indicate the permanence of their intentions. It must have been a bewildering and frightening experience for the native population. An Irish poet of the twelfth century wrote in bitterness and frustration:

> Numerous will be their powerful wiles
> Their shackles and their chains
> Numerous their lies and executions
> And their secure strong houses . . .

The largest and greatest of these castle fortifications was Trim Castle in County Meath, which lies about thirty miles west of Dublin. It was the first Norman castle to be built in Ireland. In its day it marked the outer boundary of English power emanating from

Dublin. It was once a huge rampart of gigantic proportions set on a picturesque site on the River Boyne. Nowadays it lies in ruins but a large-scale restoration is planned on the site, and work has been done to reinforce the structure. In 1993 it was handed over to the Irish government by its owners.

We walked through the ruins with historian Edel Bhreathnach to discuss the Normans and the effect on Irish society of this invasion. It was a major turning point in Irish affairs because, whether the Irish wanted it or not, they were not to remain outside European politics from this time on. Standing outside of this still-impressive fortification with its once-strong walls weathered by time, Edel talked with us about the Normans and Dermot MacMurrough: "Associated with the coming of the Normans to Ireland you have the idea, which is true, of new military strategies. They had archers and built great defenses like Trim Castle. They also made Ireland a part of a greater world which ultimately stretched from Ireland southwards into the south of Europe."

THE ANGLO-NORMAN LEGACY

Scholars debate whether it is correct to use the term invasion as regards the Norman arrival in Ireland, because the invitation to come had been proffered from an Irish king. But in the final analysis an invasion is what occurred. The invitation inevitably became an invasion. Dermot in fact had no official political standing in Ireland at the time of his "invitation," as he was a deposed king. But once they had gained a foothold on the country, the Normans were never to leave. Within a short time they had spread out all over the country in invasion style, forcibly removing many Irish families from their traditional homelands. For more than six thousand years the Irish had lived in Ireland and controlled their own destiny, however uneven that destiny might have been. Christianity had not significantly changed Irish society. It had arrived and taken on a uniquely Irish shape. But with the arrival of the Anglo-Normans major changes were coming to the country. Christianity would take on a more Roman, or diocesan, form. Most significant, political control of the island would pass to a new power outside of Ireland.

Yet in time Ireland would take to these newcomers just as these newcomers would take to Ireland. Names like Fitzgerald,

Burke, Joyce, Butler, and others would eventually become an integral part of the Irish tapestry of ethnicity. That these newcomers would become "more Irish than the Irish themselves," as later records indicate, would not, however, diminish the noxious role that the connection to the English crown would play in future Irish history. The political repercussions of this legacy and the bitterness of that struggle have not been resolved to the present day.

Chronology of Early Irish History

c8000 B.C.	Arrival of first hunter-gatherers in the northern part of Ireland, gradually spreading across the country.
c4000 B.C.	First Neolithic farmers arrive in Ireland by boat, bringing cattle, sheep, and crops. The beginnings of a settled agricultural economy.
c3500–2000 B.C.	Construction of Ireland's great Neolithic tombs. Larger tombs show knowledge of astronomy.
c2400 B.C.	Arrival of metalworking settlers and techniques. The start of the Bronze Age in Ireland.
1159 B.C.	Worldwide climate disaster. Rise of an Irish warrior aristocracy.
c800 B.C.	Gold archaeological evidence suggests Ireland has become one of the wealthiest places in Europe. The height of the Bronze Age.
c700–300 B.C.	Traditionally believed to be the period when the Iron Age Celtic warriors arrived from Europe, although there is no archaeological evidence for such an invasion.
A.D. 43	Roman conquest of Britain. Ireland never becomes part of the Roman Empire.
c150	Ptolemy's map shows Ireland to be a Celtic-speaking country. The Celtic culture and language came, but there remains no material evidence of a shift in population or a Celtic invasion of any kind.

c432	Christianity comes to Ireland around this time. The traditional date given for the arrival of Patrick. Writing comes to Ireland, and the first written history begins to be recorded.
c492	Patrick dies.
c550–650	The flowering of early monasticism in Ireland.
563	Monastery of Iona founded by the Irish saint, Colmcille, otherwise known as Columba.
c590	St. Columbanus begins his missionary work on the Continent, as do other Irish Christian missionaries.
c615	St. Columbanus dies in Bobbio, Italy.
600–750	The writing down of Irish laws and vernacular literature begins. The Great Irish epic *The Táin* is first written down. The history of Ireland and the Irish people is written, and the myth of Celtic invaders is invented at this time.
c700–c1150	The later Irish monasteries of this period become great centers of wealth and affluence.
c700	Armagh becomes the center of Irish Christianity. Propaganda for Patrick begins by Tirechan and Muirchu who write "lives" of Patrick.
c750	Armagh comes under the control of the Uí Néill.
795	First Viking attacks against the centers of wealth, the monasteries.
c800	The pinnacle of Irish scholarship. Over the next few centuries Irish scholars, like the philosopher Scottus, travel to the Continent to be courtiers and advisers.
820–847	Feidlimid Mac Crimthainn is king of Munster and also bishop of Cashel. He ultimately fails to gain the high-kingship from the Uí Néill.
841	Vikings "winter" in Dublin and eventually form a settlement there. The start of Dublin as a center of economic power.
c850	Viking raids continue inland as Viking ships now sail up rivers to attack inland monasteries. Dublin, Wa-

	terford, Wexford, and Limerick are developed out of Viking settlements.
941	Birth of Brian Boru, prince of Thomond.
976	Brian Boru becomes king of Munster and begins his attempt for the high-kingship.
1002	The Uí Néill submit to Brian, recognizing his claim to the high-kingship. He is proclaimed "Emperor of the Irish" at Armagh. Most of the country is united under his control.
1013	Support for Brian wanes. The combined forces of some Irish kings and Vikings begin to assemble an army as a threat to King Brian.
1014	The Battle of Clontarf, the first major conflict on Irish soil. Brian's forces are victorious, but Brian is killed at the end of the battle. Political chaos ensues within Ireland. Dublin becomes the economic center and capital of this new Ireland.
c1100	"Reform" of the Irish church begins.
c1100–1150	A number of synods attempt to bring the diocesan model to Irish Christianity.
1142	First Continental monastic order arrives in Ireland.
1152	Synod of Kells. The Irish church takes on a new diocesan form.
c1152	Dermot MacMurrough, king of Leinster, abducts the wife of Teirnan Ua Ruairc.
1155	Pope Adrian IV issues a papal bull giving Henry II of England permission to invade Ireland. Henry does not yet act.
1160s	When Rory O'Connor becomes high-king, his ally, Ua Ruairc, seeks revenge for his wife's abduction and has Dermot MacMurrough removed from his kingship in Leinster.
1167	Dermot MacMurrough goes to England to seek the help of King Henry II in regaining the Leinster kingship. The Anglo-Normans arrive and never leave.
1170	Richard FitzGilbert, also known as Strongbow, ar-

rives in Ireland with an army of Anglo-Norman knights to complete the invasion.

1171   Henry II of England arrives in Ireland. Submission of Irish bishops and most Irish kings. The pope, now Alexander III, backs this move. The ages-old conflict begins.

Pronunciation Guide

Following is a partial listing of Irish terms appearing in the book.

Áed: ē
Ailill: al-il
Amergin: av-ir-in
Ard Macha: ård ma-ha
Ath Cliath: å klee-ah
Banfile Éireann: ban-filå air-in
Béal Boru: bāl bå-rů
Beltine: be'al-tinna
Céli Dé: kael-ee day
Cellach Uí Sinaig: ka-lach u shin-å
Cennétig: k'in-ēd-ig'
Chennselaig: kin-sal-ach
Colmcille: koll-m-kill
Crunnóg: kran-ōg
Cú Chulainn: kū chul-in
Dáil: dawl
Dál Cais: dāl kos
Dál Ríada: dāl rē-da
Duiblinn: dů-vlin
Dún Aengus: doon en-gus
Dún Ailinne: doon all-ī
Emain Macha: ow-n moc-ha
Eóganacht: ōn-acht
Ériu: ēr-e
Feidlimid Mac Crimthainn: fē-l'im-ī mok k'ri-tawn
Fianna: fee-anah
Filí: fee-lah
Finnbennach: finn-bawn-ach
Fionn Mac Cumhaill: finn mok cool
Fir Bolg: fir bull-ug
Fulacht fiadh: full-ach fee'a

Gormlaith: gurm-la
Imbolg: im-vol'g
Lebhar Gabhála: lauer g'vola
Lia Fáil: lee-ah fall
Lugh: loo
Lúnasa: loo-nah-sah
Máel Morda: mēl-vor-a
Máel Sechnaill: mēl shach-lin
Máelmhuadh: mēl-vūa
Mag Adair: moy ad'r
Mathgamain: mo-g'-hūn
Medb: maeve
Míl: meal
Murchadh: mir-īch
Ollamh: oh-l-ive
Pangur Bán: pan-gur bawn
Ráth: raw
Samain: sow-n
Seanchaí: shan-ach-ee
Sliabh na Caillighe: slieve nah kal-ee
Táin Bó Cuailgne: toyn boe kool-ee
Taoiseach: tee-shoc
Túatha Dé Danann: too-āh dae donnan
Uí Néill: O'Neill
Ulaid: ul-ad

Bibliography

Geoffrey Barraclough, ed. *The Times Atlas of World History.* London, 1985.

Lisa Bitel. *Isle of the Saints: Monastic Settlement and Christian Community in Early Ireland.* Cork, Ireland, 1990.

———. *Land of Women.* Ithaca, N.Y. 1996.

Johannes Brondsted. *The Vikings.* Harmondsworth, England, 1965.

Jerome Burne, ed. *Chronicle of the World.* London, 1989.

Francis John Byrne. *Irish Kings and High-Kings.* London, 1987.

———. *The Rise of the Uí Néill and the High-Kingship of Ireland.* O'Donnell Lecture, National University of Ireland. Dublin, 1969.

Julius Caesar. *The Gallic War.* London, 1970.

Giraldus Cambrensis. *Expugnatio Hibernica: The Conquest of Ireland.* Edited and translated by A. B. Scott and F. X. Martin. Royal Irish Academy. Dublin, 1978.

H. B. Clarke, M. Ní Mhaonaigh, and R. Ó Floinn, eds. *Ireland and Scandinavia in the Early Viking Age.* Dublin, 1998.

Gabriel Cooney and Eoin Grogan. *Irish Prehistory: A Social Perspective.* Bray, Ireland, 1994.

William Dalrymple. *From the Holy Mountain.* London, 1997.

Liam de Paor, ed. *Milestones in Irish History.* Cork, Ireland, 1986.

———. *Saint Patrick's World.* Dublin, 1996.

Maire and Liam de Paor. *Early Christian Ireland.* London, 1978.

Seán Duffy. *Ireland in the Middle Ages.* London, 1997.

———, ed. *Atlas of Irish History.* Dublin, 1997.

R. F. Foster, ed. *The Oxford Illustrated History of Ireland.* Oxford, England, 1996.

Miranda Green. *The Gods of the Celts.* Godalming, England, 1986.

David Greene and Frank O'Connor, eds. *A Golden Treasury of Irish Poetry: A.D. 600 to 1200.* London, 1967.

Lady Gregory. *Cuchulain of Muirthemne*. London, 1902.

———. *Irish Myths and Legends*. London, 1998.

Peter Harbison. *Pilgrimage in Ireland*. London, 1992.

———. *Pre-Christian Ireland*. London, 1988.

G. A. Hayes-McCoy. *Irish Battles*. Belfast, 1990.

John Haywood. *The Penguin Historical Atlas of the Vikings*. London, 1995.

Marie Heaney. *Over Nine Waves: A Book of Irish Legends*. London, 1994.

Francoise Henry. *The Book of Kells: The Book and Its Decoration*. London, 1974.

Patrick Heraughty. *Inishmurray: Ancient Monastic Island*. Dublin, 1996.

Gwyn Jones. *A History of the Vikings*. Oxford, England, 1985.

Fergus Kelly. *A Guide to Early Irish Law*. Dublin, 1988.

David Keys. *Catastrophe*. London, 1999.

Declan Kiberd. *Inventing Ireland*. London, 1995.

Anne Korff and J. W. O'Connell, eds. *The Book of Aran*. Kinvarra, Ireland, 1996.

Brian Lacey. *Colum Cille and the Columban Tradition*. Dublin, 1997.

Sean MacAirt, trans. *The Annals of Inisfallen*. Dublin Institute for Advanced Studies. Dublin, 1988.

Sean MacAirt and Gearoid Mac Niocaill, trans. *The Annals of Ulster to A.D. 1131*. Dublin Institute of Advanced Studies. Dublin, 1983.

Margaret MacCurtain and Donnchadh Ó Corráin, eds. *Women in Irish Society: The Historical Dimension*. Dublin, 1978.

Conell Mageoghagan, trans. *The Annals of Clonmacnoise*. Dublin, 1627.

F. X. Martin. *No Hero in the House: Dermot MacMurchada*. O'Donnell Lecture, National University of Ireland. Dublin, 1975.

Joseph Falky Nagy. *Conversing with Angels and Ancients: Literary Myths of Medieval Ireland*. Ithaca, N.Y., 1997.

J. F. X. O'Brien. *Confession of Saint Patrick*. Dublin, 1924.

Donnchadh Ó Corráin. *Ireland Before the Normans*. Dublin, 1972.

Michael J. O'Kelly. *Early Ireland: An Introduction to Irish Prehistory*. Cambridge, England, 1989.

Barry Raftery. *Pagan Celtic Ireland: The Enigma of the Irish Iron Age*. London, 1994.

Pierre Riche. *The Carolingians: A Family Who Forged Europe.* Translated by Michael Idomir Allen. Philadelphia, 1993.

John Ryan, S. J. *Irish Monasticism: Origins and Early Development.* Dublin, 1992.

John Waddell. *The Prehistoric Archeology of Ireland.* Galway, Ireland, 1998.

Michael Wood. *In Search of England.* London, 1999.

Index

A NOTE ON THE AUTHORS

Carmel McCaffrey is a native of Dublin, Ireland, and currently lectures on Irish history, literature, culture, and language at Johns Hopkins University in Baltimore. Active in literary and historical societies in both Ireland and the United States, Ms. McCaffrey founded *Wild About Wilde,* the acclaimed literary review she published and edited between 1986 and 1996. Along with her popular university courses on early Irish history and Celtic studies, Ms. McCaffrey also lectures on major Irish writers. She is a Gaelic speaker and frequently travels back to Ireland. She lives in Mount Airy, Maryland.

Leo Eaton is a writer and filmmaker who has produced, written, and directed television and film in Europe and the United States for thirty years, and has been honored with many of television's major awards. Among his many credits are Michael Wood's *Conquistadors* (PBS and BBC-TV, 2001) and *In the Footsteps of Alexander the Great* (PBS and BBC-TV, 1998). He also co-created and executive-produced the Emmy Award–winning PBS children's series *Zoboomafoo* with Chris and Martin Kratt, as well as their earlier PBS school-age series *Kratt's Creatures.* London-born, Mr. Eaton currently lives in New Windsor, Maryland.